Populism, Authoritarianism and Necropolitics

Ihsan Yilmaz · Omer Erturk

Populism, Authoritarianism and Necropolitics

Instrumentalization of Martyrdom Narratives in AKP's Turkey

Ihsan Yilmaz
Alfred Deakin Institute
Deakin University
Burwood, VIC, Australia

Omer Erturk
Freie Universität Berlin
Berlin, Germany

ISBN 978-981-19-8291-0   ISBN 978-981-19-8292-7   (eBook)
https://doi.org/10.1007/978-981-19-8292-7

© The Editor(s) (if applicable) and The Author(s), under exclusive license to Springer Nature Singapore Pte Ltd. 2023
This work is subject to copyright. All rights are solely and exclusively licensed by the Publisher, whether the whole or part of the material is concerned, specifically the rights of translation, reprinting, reuse of illustrations, recitation, broadcasting, reproduction on microfilms or in any other physical way, and transmission or information storage and retrieval, electronic adaptation, computer software, or by similar or dissimilar methodology now known or hereafter developed.
The use of general descriptive names, registered names, trademarks, service marks, etc. in this publication does not imply, even in the absence of a specific statement, that such names are exempt from the relevant protective laws and regulations and therefore free for general use.
The publisher, the authors, and the editors are safe to assume that the advice and information in this book are believed to be true and accurate at the date of publication. Neither the publisher nor the authors or the editors give a warranty, expressed or implied, with respect to the material contained herein or for any errors or omissions that may have been made. The publisher remains neutral with regard to jurisdictional claims in published maps and institutional affiliations.

Cover illustration: © Alex Linch/shutterstock.com

This Palgrave Macmillan imprint is published by the registered company Springer Nature Singapore Pte Ltd.
The registered company address is: 152 Beach Road, #21-01/04 Gateway East, Singapore 189721, Singapore

CONTENTS

1 The AKP's Civilizational Populist Authoritarianism and Necropolitics   1
Introduction   1
Three Pillars of Authoritarian Stability   5
Civilizational Populism   6
Necropolitics   9
The Civilizational Populist Necropolitics in the AKP Authoritarianism   12
Structure of the Book   17
References   23

Part I Civilizational Populist Necropolitical Propaganda

2 Martyrdom and Martyr-Icons in Turkish Politics   31
Introduction   31
Kemalism and Martyrs   32
Kemalists' Martyr Hero Icon Kubilay   37
Conclusion   40
References   41

3 Martyrdom in the Erdoğanist AKP's Politics   49
Introduction   49
Erdoğanism and Martyrs   50
Erdoğanists' Martyr-Icons   58
Conclusion   63

vi   CONTENTS

	References	64
4	**Necropolitical Sermons**	69
	Introduction	69
	Militarism in the Friday Sermons from Kemalist to Erdoğanist Times	70
	Jihadism in Friday Sermons	74
	Martyrdom in Friday Sermons	79
	Conclusion	85
	References	87
5	**The Use of TV Series for Civilizational Populist Necropolitical Propaganda**	91
	Introduction	91
	The State's Use of TV Series from Kemalist to Erdoğanist Times	92
	The TV Series as a Means of Necropolitical Re-Production	94
	Glorifying Death, Beheading, Martyrdom, and Graves in a Jihadist Context	105
	Conclusion	109
	References	110
6	**Targeting Children via Education for Populist Necropolitical Propaganda**	113
	Introduction	113
	The Necropolitical National Curriculum from Kemalism to Erdoğanism	116
	Jihad and Martyrdom as Necropolitical Instruments in Texts	119
	Civilizational Populist Necropolitical Investment at the Schools	123
	Glorification of Martyrdom in Diyanet's Children's Magazines and Comics	128
	Conclusion	129
	References	131

Part II   Necropolitics in Authoritarian Action

7	**Necropolitics and AKP's Blame Avoidance**	141
	Introduction	141
	Blame Avoidance Tactics	142

Redefine, Reshape, Spin, and Manipulate the Blame	144
Impose Restrictions on Access to Opposing Voices and Media	147
Turn Blame into Credit	148
Bargaining via Rewards	150
Conclusion	158
References	160

**8 Necropolitics and Martyrdom in AKP's Authoritarian
Stability**   167
Introduction   167
Necropolitics and Repression   168
Necropolitics and Legitimation for Authoritarianism   171
Necropolitics and Co-optation   172
Conclusion   173
References   175

Part III Necropolitics and Turkish Society

9 Necropolitics and Turkish Society   181
Introduction   181
'Tell Us to Kill, We Will Kill; Tell Us to Die, We Will Die'   182
*Sacrificing Life for Erdoğan and His Religious Cause
(da'wa)*   184
Conclusion   191
References   191

**10 The Authoritarian Role of Necropolitics
and Martyrdom in Turkey Under AKP Rule**   195
References   207

Index   211

CHAPTER 1

The AKP's Civilizational Populist Authoritarianism and Necropolitics

INTRODUCTION

The literature on populists in power is evolving and expanding (Albertazzi and McDonnell 2007; Kriesi and Pappas 2015; Pappas 2014; Kyle and Gultchin 2018; Muno and Pfeiffer 2022; Yilmaz et al. 2022). This literature has shown the authoritarian tendencies of the populists in power (Grzymala-Busse et al. 2020). A confrontational cosmos, enmity, politics of victimhood, and siege mentality have been studied as some of the usual aspects of populism (Yilmaz and Morieson 2021). However, there is particularly a lack of engagement in the literature on the relationship between the populist movement narratives and violence. Even rarer are the analyses of the populists' use of necropolitics for authoritarian purposes (see for an exception Yilmaz and Erturk 2021). This book addresses this gap by investigating the empirically rich case of Turkey.

Turkey's Justice and Development Party (AKP), which has governed Turkey since 2002, has over the course of its rule evolved politically from a pro-European Muslim democratic party to an authoritarian Islamist civilizational populist party that represses opposition, dissidents, undesired minorities, journalists and human rights advocates. As the AKP evolved in this direction, it began to produce and employ civilizational populist necropolitical narratives to stabilize and perpetuate its control over Turkey. While necropolitics was originally a term used by Achille Mbembe to describe the right of the sovereign to determine who shall live

© The Author(s), under exclusive license to Springer Nature
Singapore Pte Ltd. 2023
I. Yilmaz and O. Erturk, *Populism, Authoritarianism and Necropolitics*,
https://doi.org/10.1007/978-981-19-8292-7_1

and who shall die, the term has since been expanded upon and complexified to encompass a discursive and representational necropolitics that fetishizes death for the nation, and is fascinated with and champions death on behalf of the nation (Mbembe 2003, 2019; Carney 2018, 94, 101; Yilmaz and Erturk 2021). It is this expanded understanding of necropolitics that we employ in this book, and through which we try to analyse the actions of the AKP government in Turkey. This book therefore argues that as the party transitioned from socially conservative 'Muslim democratic' (Yilmaz 2009) values to authoritarian Islamism (Erturk 2022), coupled with civilizational populism, it embraced a necropolitical narrative based on the promotion of martyrdom, and of killing and dying for the Turkish nation and Islam, as part of their authoritarian legitimation, co-optation, repression, political mobilization and blame avoidance. This narrative, the book shows, is used by the party to legitimize its actions and deflect its failures through the framing of the deaths of Turkish soldiers and civilians, which have occurred due to the AKP's political errors, as martyrdom events in which loyal servants of the Turkish Republic and God gave their lives to protect the nation, Islam and the Muslim World in a time of great crisis. This book also describes how, throughout its second decade in power, the AKP has asserted control over Turkey's education system and its Directorate of Religious Affairs (Diyanet) (Yilmaz 2005), media, and produced television series and used them to perpetuate its civilizational populist necropolitical martyrdom narrative.

Turkey is no stranger to necropolitics. Glorification of death for the religion and the homeland was modified and transferred from the Ottoman Empire into the Republican period by the founding fathers. Thus, the modern Turkey has been established through necropolitics. Throughout the history of the Turkish Republic, governments have encouraged citizens to perceive deaths in the service of the nation as normal, and praiseworthy, and when called upon to be willing to die for the homeland or to sacrifice their limbs (Yilmaz and Erturk 2022). This necropolitical martyrdom narrative is therefore not the invention of the AKP. Rather, it was part of the secular nationalist Kemalist regime's authoritarian toolkit from its earliest stages (Yilmaz and Erturk 2021). This narrative has been constantly propagated to the masses through the state ideology, public education, and everyday power structures. Besides, partly due to Turkish political culture and partly due to civil war in the 70s and the necropolitical practices of military junta in the 80s, almost all ideologies and worldviews in the Turkish context are imbued with a distinctive martyr narrative. This narrative has especially been an integral part of the Turkish nationalist (*Ülkücü*), Kurdish nationalist and far-left political ideologies (the last two were the main victims of necropolitics of the 1980 military junta). This social support has provided an opportunity for the Islamist civilizational populist Erdoğan regime to exploit necropolitics to their own advantage in advancing authoritarianism and repressing dissidents, minorities, journalists and human rights defenders.

When the AKP won government for the first time in 2002, the party first turned away from the authoritarianism and martyrdom narrative of its secular predecessors. Moreover, the AKP successfully faced the pressure of the fear mongering coalition of the left and the right nationalist (*Ulusalcıs* and *Ülkücüs*) opposition (Yilmaz et al. 2020). However, a series of political events in Turkey dramatically altered the AKP's political agenda and drew the party towards Islamism and authoritarianism. As a result of a process starting with the Gezi Park Protests and Egyptian coup and accelerating with the major setback in the 2015 June elections, and the failed mysterious 2016 coup, the AKP—fearful of losing power—further steered away from liberalism and democracy and became progressively more authoritarian with each major event. Firstly, PKK-Turkey peace process (known as solution process) ended. Then, the whole pro-EU narrative did a U-turn and AKP was headed towards radical nationalism and anti-Western populist Islamist authoritarianism to maintain the rule over Turkey. Eventually, circumstances pushed the AKP to form informal alliances with far right and far left nationalist parties (MHP and Vatan), which it was once an enemy of.

As part of this political transition to radical nationalism and Islamist populist authoritarianism, the AKP began to employ a civilizational populist (see Yilmaz and Morieson 2022) necropolitical narrative. The AKP's necropolitics are in certain respects similar to those employed by the Kemalist regime. Both took advantage of Turkish fears that Western powers were seeking to dismantle their Republic by using Turkey's internal enemies as pawns, just as the West dismember the Ottoman Empire at the end of the First World War by supporting its minorities, and portrayed Turkey as a nation threatened by outside and internal forces (Yilmaz 2021), and which therefore required brave souls willing to sacrifice themselves in its defence (Yilmaz and Erturk 2022). Yet while the Kemalist's necropolitical narratives were secular nationalist in nature and encouraged citizens to die on behalf of the nation, homeland and people of Turkey, the AKP's necropolitical discourse draws on Islamic ideas such as *jihad* and encourages Turkish citizens to become martyrs in defence of not only the nation, homeland and the Republic of Turkey but also for Allah, Islam, Ummah (the Muslim World) and Erdoğan. The otherization of dissident groups and minorities such as Kurds, Alevis, Gülenists, leftists, liberals, and non-Muslims is another common ground both Kemalist and Islamist authoritarianism share (see in detail in Yilmaz 2021). Their necropolitics targets these groups but is also strengthened by enmity towards these groups and extended much more intensely to journalists and human rights advocates.

This book therefore analyses the Islamized civilizational populist necropolitics of the AKP, how the party's necropolitical narrative is based on the Kemalist and Islamist necropolitical mindsets and is propagated throughout Turkish society—including in the education system, through the Directorate of Religious Affairs, television series—and its reception by AKP supporters. The necropolitical narrative of the AKP posits, we show, that Turkey and the broader Sunni Muslim world are threatened by non-Muslim external (primarily 'the Crusader West and Zionists') and internal forces (enemy citizens, i.e. dissidents and many of the minority groups), and that as the leading member of the Islamic world Turkey and its (Sunni Muslim pro-AKP) people have a duty to defend their homeland and Islam from their external and internal enemies. In the Turkish case, the political use of martyrdom is partly rooted in this Islamist messianic narrative that is based on Huntingtonian civilizational clash. Most importantly, the AKP's civilizational populist necropolitical narrative emphasizes that the Turkish people ought to be willing to die in the service of the regime, the Turkish homeland, and Islam. The AKP's necropolitical martyrdom narrative therefore portrays martyrdom as an act which will be rewarded by God in the next world, and as a sweet drink (*şerbet*) which all Turkish citizens should wish to enjoy.

The book argues that this narrative instrumentalizes Islam and nationalism, as well as the fears Turkish people have of further dismemberment of their 'homeland', to mobilize support for the ideology and agenda of the AKP government. Furthermore, the book argues that the AKP also uses this necropolitical martyrdom narrative to frame the deaths of Turkish civilians and soldiers—who may have died due to government failure or accidentally—as martyrdom events to avoid blame and accountability. We argue that by framing these deaths as martyrdom events the AKP turns potentially disastrous events, and which might therefore hurt the party electorally, into positive events which aim to legitimize the

AKP's rule and political decisions. Of course, the AKP would not have hoped to achieve this result if the AKP had not been the hegemonic party in right-wing politics, if the examples of Syria and Iraq had not triggered the desire for a strong state and a strong leader in the right-wing political base, and if the state of emergency conditions had not allowed the AKP to stigmatize all narratives contrary to its narrative as support for terrorism. To state succinctly, the book:

1. Contributes to the study of necropolitics and makes an inquiry of dynamics between authoritarianism, civilizational populism and necropolitics.
2. Systematically examines the Erdoğan regime's use of necropolitics in order to legitimize the authoritarian order of Erdoğan's 'New Turkey'.
3. Applies the idea of civilizational populist necropolitics to understand why the AKP regime in Turkey emphasizes the need for Turkish citizens to martyr themselves to defend their 'homeland' and religion against internal and external enemies of Turks, Turkey, Turkish State, Islam, Muslim World and Allah.
4. Describes how and with which instruments the AKP regime propagates its populist necropolitical martyrdom narrative throughout Turkish society.
5. Explains how the AKP uses a populist necropolitical martyrdom narrative to legitimize, stabilize and perpetuate its populist authoritarian rule and to co-opt and/or repress the dissidents.
6. Examines the manner in which the AKP's grassroots supporters have received and responded to the AKP's civilizational populist necropolitical narrative.

Three Pillars of Authoritarian Stability

Authoritarian regimes use multiple, non-exclusive survival strategies (Maerz 2020). The research on the new authoritarianism that emerged since the 1990s has identified repression, legitimacy and co-optation as the three major tools (or pillars) that authoritarian regimes use to secure their continuing rule (Gerschewski 2013; Schneider and Maerz 2017).

It is clear that there is a direct relation between authoritarian regimes and political repression (Sluka 1997, 2). Repression is 'commonly used by authoritarian and totalitarian governments against their own people, to spread fear and make political opposition impossible' (Walzer 2004, 130). However, relying on repression alone can be too costly as a means of sustaining authoritarian rule and cannot provide the necessary stability to autocracies since it can have destabilizing effects in the long run (Davenport 2007; Escribà-Folch 2013). Thus, as a second pillar of authoritarian stability, a regime's claim to legitimacy is important for explaining its means of rule and, in turn, ensuring its stability and resilience. Legitimation means 'the process of gaining support' and seeking 'to guarantee active consent, compliance with the rules, passive obedience, or mere toleration within the population' (Gerschewski 2013, 18). Regimes and citizens exchange political support for decreased repression. This exchange makes the regime less vulnerable to conspiracies, military coups, and violent rebellions and reduces the extent of repression of citizens (Gerschewski 2013, 21; von Soest and Grauvogel 2017, 288).

The third pillar of authoritarian stability is co-optation, which refers to the capacity to 'tie strategically-relevant actors (or a group of actors) to the regime elite' (Gerschewski 2013, 22). Co-optation usually involves neo-patrimonial arrangements between the ruling elite and the co-opted groups, such as those belonging to military, business, and political spheres, and aims to prevent the emergence of strong opposition actors. Co-optation thus becomes a more viable and cost-effective way to consolidate power, legitimate actions, and advance authoritarian reach (Holdo 2019; Maerz 2020). Patronage, clientelism, and corruption are the most commonly used instruments in co-optation (Maerz 2020, 67).

The AKP has used civilizational populist narrative for each of these three pillars (Yilmaz and Erturk 2021). Let's now discuss very briefly what we mean by civilizational populism.

CIVILIZATIONAL POPULISM

Populism has alternately been defined as set of ideas, a thin-centred populist ideology, a type of political strategy, a discourse, or a style (Gidron and Bonikowski 2013). The most accepted definition describes populism as a group of ideas that together argues that politics should be an expression of the volonté générale (general will) of the people and considers society to be ultimately separated into two homogenous and antagonistic groups, 'the pure people' versus 'the corrupt elite'

(Mudde 2004, 543). Since populism as a thin-centred ideology lacks the sophistication of other ideologies like socialism or liberalism, populism is usually combined with other beliefs and ideas of politics (la Torre 2019). Especially, right-wing populism usually focuses on internal and external dangerous others who are clear and present threats to the people but are favoured by the corrupt elite. In contrast, populists present themselves as the only true representatives and the saviours of the people against these corrupt elite and the dangerous others.

In right-wing populisms, the corrupt elite usually are framed to be collaborating with the dangerous others. This form of populism is essentially a cultural populism, which designates 'the people' as the authentic people of the nation, and therefore others ethnic and religious minorities and—above all—'cultural elites' (Kyle and Gultchin 2018). These populists emphasize religious traditionalism, law and order, sovereignty and portray immigrants as an enemy other. This populist rhetoric is a powerful tool of division and polarization, punching both up and towards political, cultural, and economic elites, but also across and down towards minority groups and immigrants (Kyle and Gultchin 2018, 33–34).

Right-wing populists—as cultural populists—construct 'the people' and their enemies along civilizational lines (Brubaker 2017), arguing that there is a crisis in which the people are faced with an existential threat to their culture, identity, way of life, religion, and civilization. In the West, right-wing populists have incorporated civilizationalism to define 'the people' of their respective nations as Christian or Judeo-Christian, and to exclude Muslims by claiming Islam represents a threat to Judeo-Christian values and culture (Brubaker 2017). It must be noted, however, that while the boundaries of belonging and the semantics of self and other are reconceptualized in civilizational terms, civilizational populism largely remains a hybrid form of nationalism rather than an anti-nationalist ideology (Brubaker 2017). Yilmaz and Morieson (2022, 19) 'define civilizational populism as a group of ideas that together considers that politics should be an expression of the volonté générale (general will) of the people, and society to be ultimately separated into two homogenous and antagonistic groups, 'the pure people' versus 'the corrupt elite' who collaborate with the dangerous others belonging to other civilizations that are hostile and present a clear and present danger to the civilization and way of life of the pure people.' In this book, we mean this definition when talking about civilizational populism.

Civilizational populism can be observed inside populist discourses across the democratic world. In India, Prime Minister Narendra Modi's BJP is beholden to the Hindutva ideology that asserts 'Hindu religious or cultural identity is the national and primary identity of Indians' (Saleem 2021). Turkish President Recep Tayyip Erdoğan and his AKP are attempting to build a 'New Turkey' (Yilmaz et al. 2020) for their supporters based on Islamist populism and Turkish neo-Ottomanism (Yilmaz 2018, 54–55). This civilizational populism is a conspicuous manifestation of a civilizational of populism within Muslim societies, and its survival and maintenance are highly dependent on continued antagonism between Islam and religious others that are usually framed as the Judeo-Christian West, Crusaders, Zionists, infidels, secularists, and their internal pawns. In other words, in this Islamist civilizational populism, the struggle between 'the people' and their enemies ('elites' and 'others') is constructed as part of a broader religious and civilizational struggle between righteous Muslims and those outside of/hostile towards Islam (Barton et al. 2021, 397).

Most of the literature available on the growing authoritarianism and populism deals with the supply and demand factors and how the socio-economic and socio-political crises play into the emergence of populist narrative. Yilmaz and Erturk (2021) raise a point by establishing a linkage between populism and violence. The violent imagery associated with populist slogans make it a populist strand of necro politics. This mixing of two streams is then used to consolidate the political grip of the ruling party over the corridors of power. What basically happens is that survival instinct of the people is turned on by presenting modern times as definitive and dark period that would determine the future course of nation's life. Once this image is constructed, real or imagined threats are then highlighted. Only two alternative futures are presented before the nation, either that of magnificent historical restoration or that of utter and complete destruction. It can be argued that primary conflict between tradition and modernity that gives rise to these issues is a primary feature of almost all the third world or non-European societies. Turkey, in this regard, is in a unique position when it comes to the dynamics of this conflict evident in Turkic society. Thus, when the AKP took an authoritarian turn after its general electoral victory, it has not only started employing civilizational populism to mobilize its supporters and to repress its critics, but it has also employed a necropolitical narrative.

Necropolitics

In its original meaning, and as conceptualized by Achille Mbembe, necropolitics is the right of the sovereign to determine who shall live and who shall die (Mbembe 2003, 2019). In a similar vein, necropower either decimates populations through massacres, or else commits populations to unliveable conditions in which they are continually exposed to violence and deprived of a proper human life, and in which they are destined to a death-in-life (Mbembe 2003, 21). To date, Mbembe's concept has been applied to several other contexts (for works on the Turkish context see, Ahmetbeyzade 2008; Bargu 2016, 2019; Zengin 2016; Akıncı 2018; Islekel 2017; Carney 2018). Necropolitics has now been expanded and complexified to include how the realm of the dead can be a site of violence, a surrogate for the government of the living, a means of delineating the boundaries of political community and a conduit for the production of collective memory (Bargu 2016, 2019, 17). In this usage, necropolitics is not the reduction of the living to 'the status of living dead', but 'the dishonouring, disciplining and punishment of the living through the utilization of the dead as post-mortem objects and sites of violence' (Bargu 2019, 9; Verdery 2000).

Further studies have complicated the concept and offered new dimensions of necropolitics, examining how it is operative in courts, prisons and political cemeteries, martyrdom, gender politics, collective memory, and reparation claims (Bargu 2019, 5–6). The meaning of necropolitics has also been expanded to include positive means of constituting community through the practice of caring for the dead, and positive interventions into dead bodies, burials, and grief (Akıncı 2018, 47).

Carney has also elaborated the concept and talked about a discursive and representational necropolitics that fetishizes death for the nation, and is fascinated with and champions death on behalf of the nation (Carney 2018, 94, 101). The term has also been applied to show how the authoritarian governments employ different politicizations of death: they control the narrative around the news of death to maintain discursive hegemony regulating death; depoliticize death to eliminate the risk of dissident mobilization after deadly incidents; normalize death as an inherent feature of some citizens' occupational, socio-economic, and—in some cases—gender position (Bakıner 2019, 26; Yilmaz and Erturk 2021).

For many centuries nationalistic and religious rhetoric from many countries and cultures have expressed encouragement of self-sacrifice for a greater cause. Before the emergence of nationalism, martyrdom appeared in the earliest human history. The religions of Egypt, Mesopotamia and ancient Greece included the notions of heroism and sacrifice in defence of good against evil (Szyska 2004). Until the age of democracy, from Pharaohs to Caesars, from kings to sultans, the sovereign had been possessing the right to kill and the power to declare the killed as martyrs. In ancient Greece, ritual ceremonies were dedicated to fallen heroes in patriotic wars, and in these ceremonies and orations, heroic death was skilfully presented as desirable. In the most famous of these, Pericles praises the sacrifices of the dead so that others will imitate them as Athens was so glorious that it was worth dying for (Bosworth 2000; Bowersock 1995). In repressed societies, such as the Jews during the Hellenistic period or the early Christians in the Roman era (York 2007), martyrdom played several roles at once: forging authority, escalating the struggle, reinforcing the ranks, legitimizing the alternative culture, and creating a sense of differentiation and animosity vis-à-vis the enemy (Hatina 2014, 233).

From the 'cult of the martyrs of liberty' during the French Revolution (Soboul 1989) to the 'cult of the fallen soldier' after WWI (Mosse 1990), there are uncountable examples of the use of martyrs for the sake of nationalist political goals. Nationalism's ability to mobilize people through the power of the dead has been described as 'the necromantic power' (Açıksöz 2012, 115). Among world religions, Islam, for a variety of reasons, is now the most well-known for its emphasis on the virtues of martyrdom (See Hatina 2014 and its bibliography for many works on Islam and martyrdom). Apart from jihadist interpretation of Sunni Islam, martyrdom is also a central part of the narrative of contemporary Shia and Alevi Islam (Soileau 2017; Rolston 2020).

Martyrdom is a significant paradigm in creating political myths and collective memory (Castelli 2004). The martyrdom narrative, be it secular or religious, is one of the most 'powerful tools of political action and potent weapons employed in political struggles' for 'creating and maintaining popular support' for nationalist as well as religious struggles (Sluka 1997, 49). The powerful receive benefit from the glorification of martyrdom, death, and blood narratives, which become a tool for building authoritarian tools that would extend the political life of the autocrats. Martyrdom narratives have 'functioned to forge a sense of solidarity, enhance mass mobilization, and preserve the sacred values of the community' (Dorraj 1997, 489). Here, martyrs play a dual role by delegitimizing the enemy outside while consolidating the status of the martyr's group in the community (Klausner 1987, 231–232; Rosoux 2004).

Governments have imposed cemeteries of martyrs or martyry monuments upon the daily lives of citizens whose daily routines and commutes traverse these spaces. These monuments and spaces have been called 'necropolitical spaces' (Yanık and Hisarlıoğlu 2019) as they condition the masses to die for the sovereign, in a process in which the sovereign's overt 'right to kill' is transformed into a covert 'encouragement to die' (Yanık and Hisarlıoğlu 2019, 48).

Glorification of martyrdom, death and blood narratives have been especially used by non-democratic regimes as a tool for building collective memory, rituals, symbols, myth-making, and mass mobilization (Anderson 1983; Dorraj 1997; Gruber 2013); It has been used for mobilization, myth-making, and building a collective memory of culture; the recent examples in the history for this 'successfully' blending, religious-cum-authoritarianism, can be seen in Sudanese and significantly in the Iranian revolution (Gruber 2013; Swenson 1985). On martyrdom and building collective memory of culture and myth-making, see Castelli 2004). Thus, in our study, we classify and name this use of necropolitics as 'authoritarian necropolitics', and we test this concept in our case study of the authoritarian civilizational populist AKP government in Turkey and argue that our case shows the concept's salience.

The AKP's necropolitics has been studied earlier (e.g. Değirmencioğlu 2014; Bargu 2016; Carney 2018; Yilmaz and Erturk 2021). For instance, Bakiner has shown 'the *expansion of martyrdom*, a concept hitherto used as a religious justification for military casualties, into the civilian sphere' (Bakıner 2019, 26) by Turkey's Justice and Development Party (*Adalet ve Kalkınma Partisi*, AKP) government. Yanik and Hisarlioglu also analysed the same issue by looking at the creation of necropolitical spaces (martyr cemeteries and monuments) in post-2016 coup attempt Turkey (Yanık and Hisarlıoğlu 2019). However, the literature on necropolitics has not so far analysed in detail in terms of authoritarian necropolitics dimension and necropolitical icon-heroes, ideal model citizens who sacrificed their life for their nation, homeland, state, regime, and rulers. What is more, this book not only looks at how the AKP has been propagating its civilizational populist authoritarian necropolitics but also how this narrative has been received and disseminated further by its grassroots supporters.

The Civilizational Populist Necropolitics in the AKP Authoritarianism

Although the legitimation arguments of the AKP's authoritarianism, such as its ideational narratives, have been studied (Yilmaz et al. 2020; Yilmaz 2021; Bayulgen et al. 2018), its necropolitical use of martyrdom for authoritarian legitimation has not been examined. There are few scholarly studies of Turkey that investigate the relationship between democracy, biopolitics and sovereign violence in light of the theoretical arsenal of the necropolitical problematic (For recent examples, see Ahmetbeyzade 2008; Akıncı 2018; Bargu 2019; Islekel 2017; Zengin 2016; Yilmaz and Erturk 2021).

Similar to many other historical and contemporary contexts, blood and death and martyrdom narratives have been used for political purposes in Turkey for myth-making, building a collective memory, inculcating the masses with the nationalistic emotions and fervour, militarism (Altinay 2006) and collective mobilization (Azak 2007). As we will demonstrate throughout the coming chapters, this outlook has been propagated and perpetuated through national curriculum, media, popular culture, law, and state-controlled religious institutions (Yilmaz 2021; Yanık and Hisarlıoğlu 2019, 55; Özkan 2012, 9–11).

Partly because of Turkey's militaristic culture and partly because of its political worldview, embedded in the rhetoric of 'fatherland first' (*önce vatan*) or 'so there can be fatherland' (*vatan sağolsun*), the 'Turkish fatherland' has been constructed as a place that supplants everything of political importance, including human life. The fatherland, therefore, is a concept used to perpetuate the notion that inhabitants of Turkey should sacrifice themselves without question. This rhetoric is coupled with Sevres Syndrome' (Jung 2003) and the siege mentality, which is the fear that Turkey is surrounded by external enemies that are collaborating with internal foes with the aim of destroying the Turkish state and sending the Turks back to Central Asia (Yilmaz 2021). This is one of the few commonalities in Turkish politics shared by both secularists and Islamists. In the Islamic sense, this notion is strengthened by a fabricated hadith *hubb al-watan min al-iman* (love for one's fatherland is part of faith)

1 THE AKP'S CIVILIZATIONAL POPULIST...   13

and the Islamist maxim that 'unbelief is one nation' (*küfür tek millettir*), which dictates a continuous sense of alertness against the outer world.

According to this mentality shared by both Kemalists and Islamists, Turkey's territory is a source of envy for other peoples (especially the West) who wish to take it from them and if not, divide and rule Turkey (Yilmaz 2021). As a result, this necessitates that Turkish subjects should be willing to die for the fatherland, the nation, and the state without question (Yanık and Hisarlıoğlu 2019, 57; See also Bircan 2014). As remarked in the Turkish national anthem, the Turkish fatherland is a 'paradise' (*cennet vatan*) that every citizen is required to sacrifice his or her life for it. This has been called the 'necrogeopoliticization of Turkey'. In combination with the Sèvres Syndrome, the concepts of the fatherland, martyrdom, and blood further intensify the necrogeopoliticization of Turkey (Değirmencioğlu 2014).

Since the 1980s, and even much more so during the AKP period, these themes of fatherland, martyrdom, and blood have not only become more frequently invoked by the ruling elite but have also become everyday themes for other strata of society as well (See for example Bircan 2014). Recently the AKP has actively started capitalizing on this aspect of Turkish political culture. Erdoğan and the AKP have consistently used this militarist, Islamo-nationalist, civilizational populist, and necrogeopolitical culture of Turkey to rally the people around the flag. For example, President Recep T. Erdoğan frequently refers in his speeches to two lines of a poem written by a nationalist poet Mithat Cemal Kuntay that say, 'what makes a flag a flag is the blood on it; the earth can only become a fatherland (*vatan*) when there are those willing to die for it'. In one astonishing necropolitical case, from a stage where Erdoğan was leading a rally, he spotted a 6-year-old girl in the crowd, dressed in military-style camouflage and wearing a maroon beret worn by the Turkish special military forces and he asked the girl to be lifted towards the stage to meet with him. However, she was shy and began crying. After kissing her on both cheeks, Erdoğan turned to the flag-waving crowd and said:

> Look what you see here! Girl, what are you doing here? We have our maroon beret here, but maroon berets never cry. God bless her. Her Turkish flag is in her pocket. If she becomes a martyr, God willing, she will be wrapped with it. She's ready for everything. Isn't she? (The New York Times 2018)

14   I. YILMAZ AND O. ERTURK

This is the 'new normal' in the 'New Turkey', a concept Erdoğan and his colleagues started talking about (Yilmaz et al. 2020) after the AKP established its domination of Turkish politics, especially after the Gezi Park protests in 2013. One commentator, however, suggested that even though 'they had a name for the era, they did not have a perfect day that marked it' and they have 'been searching for new commemorations to mark their rule'. They were also not happy with the fact that all Turkish national day celebrations 'were established by the single party regime of Atatürk and commemorate the establishment of the Turkish Republic' (Özyürek 2016). The coup attempt in July 2016 which was mysterious in many respects and was called a 'gift of God' by Erdoğan provided the AKP with the opportunity to rectify this.

In his live TV speech on the coup night of 15 July 2016, Erdoğan called civilians to occupy city squares and airports to protest the plotters. In response to Erdoğan's invitation, some members of the public tried to capture the Bosporus Bridge back from the soldiers, while others tried to occupy military bases in various cities. During these clashes, 251 anti-coup people died and about 30 soldiers were either lynched to death or shot by unknown civilians. The incident has been fixed by the AKP as one of the most important official memorial days of Turkey. In Erdoğan's words:

> July 15 has become one of the symbols of our national history just like the Victory of Manzikert, Conquest of Istanbul and August 30 Victory as well as the foundation of Seljuk and Ottoman states and our Republic. (Erdoğan 2017)

Thus, 15 July was declared the Day of Democracy and Martyrs (Özyürek 2016; Solomonovich 2021, 1), and this incident has become the new milestone, founding identity, and symbol of the Turkish Islamists after the battle of Manzikert in 1071, which is deemed as the conquest of Anatolia, and the conquest of Constantinople in 1453 .

Erdoğanists have used this new holiday to shape the Turkish collective national memory by introducing a national celebration that does not revolve around secularist and pro-Western Atatürk, 'but rather around the Justice and Development Party government and its more traditional and religious ideology' (Solomonovich 2021, 1). The July 15 coup attempt, combined with the AKP's allegation that it was a USA-led Western conspiracy against the leader of the Muslim World and Erdoğan's metaphor of the coup attempt being a 'Gift of God', has become a cornerstone for the AKP's anti-Western Islamist ideology and personality cult of Erdoğan who was constructed as the leader of the Ummah. Following the coup attempt, the AKP has invested heavily in producing and circulating its preferred narratives in a range of media while restricting and even punishing alternative narratives (Hammond 2020, 539). Digital and architectural commemorative projects have been created by the AKP 'to create a memorial public in which President Recep Tayyip Erdoğan's position is both naturalized and justified' (Hammond 2020, 536). In these projects, imaginaries, symbols, discourses, and media intersect with physical necropolitical sites in an attempt to create 'a memorial public that is ostensibly foundational (and thus prepolitical), agentive (because people can choose to participate), and that naturalizes a political arrangement focused on President Recep Tayyip Erdoğan' (Hammond 2020, 536).

Because the AKP has tried to construct New Turkey, Erdoğanists have seen 15 July as an opportunity for the 'invention of tradition' (Hobsbawm 2012), collective memory, and myth-making. The civil resistance against the coup attempt has 'been coded as 'the 15 July Epic' and rendered visible on every corner of urban public areas of the country through billboards, newspaper advertisements, television broadcasts, and street demonstrations' (Küçük and Türkmen 2020). This was the exact underlying message that propelled the spatial changes or the formation of necropolitical spaces that took place throughout Turkey in the wake of the 15 July 2016 coup attempt—with one difference, however: the everydayness embedded in the necropolitical spaces repeatedly produces necropolitical boundary markings and attempts to operate subconsciously to bring about the active participation of the subjects in the sovereign's message (Yanık and Hisarlıoğlu 2019, 57). In addition to the formation of necropolitical spaces around Turkey, the AKP has been engaged in a representational necropolitics that fetishizes death for the nation, and has shown a fascination with and championing of death on behalf of the nation, that has stark implications for everyday life and politics (Carney 2018, 94, 101).

Thus, the civilizational populist necropolitical narrative based on martyrdom has become a consistent and strong theme in the discourse of Erdoğan and the AKP following the 15 July 2016 coup attempt (Yanık and Hisarlıoğlu 2019, 57; Baykan et al. 2021). Of the 251 people who died, 182 were civilians. The AKP declared the fallen civilians martyrs (Bakıner 2019, 29). As quickly as possible, statues of those martyrs were erected, monuments depicting that 'bloody' night were built, and special prayer sessions were organized in memory of the martyrs. The names of the people—the martyrs—who were killed during the coup attempt were given to streets, parks and public transport stations, with a martyr (şehit) prefix before their names (Bişkin 2017). Naming those who died during the fighting as 'martyrs'—and not simply 'casualties' or 'victims'— elevates the role of the protestors to a sacred act (Hammond 2020, 539). *Şehitlik*, the parts which 'martyrs' are buried in the cemeteries, are redesigned, and the ones which possessed July 15 martyrs declared as pilgrimage sites. The first week of the school year has been officially dedicated to the subject of the 'epic' of July 15, and the martyrs who fell that night, and all teachers have been obliged to fulfil this task by the government (Yanık and Hisarlıoğlu 2019, 57–58). Commemorations have been held to honour the martyrs during the anniversaries of the coup attempt, and dissenting voices have fallen on deaf ears due to the atmosphere of commemorating and celebrating martyrdom (Bakıner 2019, 29).

By the means of such immortalization and visibility, Yanık and Hisarlıoğlu state 'one cannot escape being reminded of the coup attempt and the people who were killed because the monument and its surroundings are a part of the daily commutes' of Turkish people (Yanık and Hisarlıoğlu 2019, 60). The insights of Busra Erkara, a New-York-based writer, during her visit to Istanbul in March 2017 are quite significant. She equates the atmosphere in Istanbul to 'post-revolution …Iran' in terms of propaganda and social indoctrination of the 'cult of martyrdom' on every corner from subway stations, rooftops to billboards, many of which were decorated with martyr photographs and details of 'where and how the person was martyred', and slogans such as 'my martyr, I celebrate your martyrdom' (Erkara 2017).

'Martyrdom' was not the only adjective that accompanied the date of 15 July, a variety of other concepts were associated with the date of the coup attempt including 'democracy' and 'national will'. The message that was given by equating these concepts with 'martyrdom' was that martyrdom was the price that needed to be paid for democracy and national will. This message was possible because Turkish politicians and bureaucrats (re)narrativized the coup as not simply an attempt to topple the government, but, rather, as an 'invasion' of the fatherland by traitors (dissidents, journalists, human rights advocates and undesired minorities who are depicted as Western powers' puppets) trying to redesign the region and world politics in accordance with their civilizational onslaught against the Muslim World. Thus, the narrative about those who were killed resisting the coup attempt was reimagined as those 'martyred' while 'saving the fatherland', allowing one to 'feel both sorrow and pride' for them, to quote President Erdoğan on the second anniversary of the coup attempt (Yanık and Hisarlıoğlu 2019, 58).

STRUCTURE OF THE BOOK

In this book we delve into how a civilizational populist authoritarian regime produces and propagates necropolitical narratives, and how it instrumentalizes these narratives so as to prolong, deepen, and stabilize its existence. The book is structured in the following manner.

The book is composed of three parts. Part I is titled 'Civilizational Populist Necropolitical Propaganda' and it has 5 chapters: Chapter 2, Martyrdom and Martyr-Icons in Turkish Politics; Chapter 3, Martyrdom in the Erdoğanist AKP's Politics; Chapter 4, Necropolitical Sermons; Chapter 5, The Use of TV Series for Civilizational Populist Necropolitical Propaganda; and Chapter 6, Targeting Children via Education for Populist Necropolitical Propaganda. Part II's title is 'Necropolitics in Authoritarian Action', and it has two chapters: Chapter 7, Necropolitics and AKP's Blame Avoidance and Chapter 8, Necropolitics and Martyrdom in AKP's Authoritarian Stability. Part III is 'Necropolitics and Turkish Society' and it has one chapter: Chapter 9, Necropolitics and Turkish Society. The concluding chapter is Chapter 10, The Authoritarian Role of Necropolitics and Martyrdom in Turkey under AKP Rule.

The second chapter describes how necropolitics and martyrdom narratives have been used in Turkey since the foundation of the Republic. Since Erdoğan and his AKP have been using the religio-nationalist martyrdom understanding and concept inherited from the secularist Kemalists, it is important to discuss this background before moving on to the analysis of the Erdoğanist period. This chapter first looks at the fears and traumas of the Kemalists, their response to these, establishment of the Turkish Republic, the militarist political culture, and use of education and religion to propagate the Kemalist militarism and necropolitics with a focus on martyrdom. Then, we will analyse the Kemalist martyr-icon construction and its necropolitical use: Kubilay, the military officer beheaded by a fanatical pro-Caliphate crowd protesting against the secularist reforms in the town of Menemen, İzmir in 1930.

18   I. YILMAZ AND O. ERTURK

The third chapter shows how, like the Kemalists, the AKP has also been trying to create its alternative versions of martyr-icons, who provide an Islamist alternative to the secularist martyr-icons created by the secular Kemalist regime. The AKP tried to create the civilizational populist version of the Kemalists' Kubilay by making use of the deaths of Ömer Halisdemir, Muhammet Fatih Safitürk, Erol Olçok, and Abdullah Tayyip Olçok and a few others. It has aimed to create new legitimacy for its regime by framing its rule as the choice of the people who were ready to die for it and thus blessed by God. Simultaneously, this civilizational populist necropolitical narrative portrayed the coupists as murderous criminals hated by God in an excommunicative manner. Then, all opposition and dissidents in addition to journalists and human rights defenders were presented as the allies of the coupists who were the pawns of external conspiratorial powers that are enemies of Islam. In this narrative, Erdoğan is the national saviour and protector of the people (not only the Turkish people but the entire Ummah), further legitimizing his position as leader.

The fourth chapter examines the role played by Turkey's Directorate of Religious Affairs (Diyanet) in propagating the AKP's necropolitics and martyrdom narrative. The chapter provides content analysis on the Diyanet's Friday sermons delivered in the last decade, and examines how the necropolitical use of militarism, jihadism, and martyrdom, which existed during the secularist Kemalist Diyanet era, have been used by the Islamist AKP government. Diyanet is the official and state funded religious body which controls all mosques, and the content of their Friday sermons, in Turkey. More than half of the entire adult male population of Turkey attends regularly these prayers and listen to the sermons. In addition, its Quran schools are attended by hundreds and thousands of people every year and it has several media and publication outlets. Therefore, Diyanet has a great deal of power in Turkish society and can influence people's thoughts and behaviour. The Directorate has always been a tool of the state, but the relationship between the state and Diyanet has grown—alongside the body's budget—under the AKP rule. In this chapter we discuss how an expanded Diyanet has been captured by the AKP, and show how the AKP subsequently used the Diyanet to propagate the party's civilizational populist necropolitics and martyrdom narrative. In particular, the chapter demonstrates, the Diyanet has helped the party further Islamize and radicalize the martyrdom narrative, giving it especial power in the majority Muslim nation, by introducing the concept of *jihad* as warfare into the martyrdom discourse in addition to propagating that jihad is a duty of the once-secular Turkish military.

The fifth chapter investigates the AKP regime's instrumentalization of television series to propagate its civilizational populist necropolitics narrative. The chapter argues that the AKP produces and funds popular television shows to indoctrinate the Turkish people into their necropolitical cult of death and martyrdom. The party produces television programmes that show Turkish/Muslim heroes sacrificing themselves in defence of Islam and Turkey, and which therefore encourage Turkish people to perceive sacrifice and death in the service of the nation and the Ummah as normal and praiseworthy. Throughout the AKP produces television series Turkey is portrayed as a nation threatened by foreign forces and their local pawns such as the corrupt elite and the dissidents who wish to dismember the country. Through the heavy bombardment of post-truth elements, conspiracy theories, and the sense of siege mentality in the series, the viewers have been aimed to be shaped over the populist binary opposition, us, and them, 'them' including not only sinister foreign powers but their internal pawns such as journalists, human rights defenders, dissidents, and undesired minorities. The TV series are not only indoctrinating martyrdom/death, or the self-sacrifice for the nation, but also, they strongly incite the sense of lynch, assault or intolerance through hatred and bloody violence scenes with epic folk songs behind, against the external and internal enemies such as the opposition, dissident groups, and the 'corrupt' Kemalist/secular elite. The TV series are also important since almost all have scenes of beheading enemies or publicly violent scenes as a deterrent to others, in which viewers easily replace antagonist characters with the infidel Westerners, their extensions within the country (domestic traitors, opposition political parties, journalists, human rights advocates) while identifying the protagonists with themselves, the people who are the true members of the nation, Muslim World and Islam. The series are, therefore, the chapter contends, intended to provoke fear of and anger towards foreigners and internal Turkish 'traitors'. This chapter very briefly scrutinizes the self-sacrifice and martyrdom motives significantly in the AKP-sponsored TV series Diriliş Ertuğrul (Ertugrul Resurrection), İsimsizler (The Nameless), Payitaht Abdülhamit (the Capital Abdulhamid), and Mehmetçik Kut'ul Amare. These productions, the chapter concludes, serve two purposes: they create a sense of fear and hatred of the AKP's enemies, and also encourage Turkish citizens to believe that killing and dying for the regime while fighting its enemies is something glorious, and perhaps even a religious if not a national duty.

Chapter six examines the ways in which the AKP propagates its civilizational populist necropolitical narratives through the national curriculum, school textbooks, and children's magazines. In addition to the national curriculum, the chapter also briefly examines the necropolitical themes over the example of a religious magazine, Diyanet Çocuk, published by Diyanet for children. The chapter describes how the AKP merges nationalist and Islamic concepts such as jihad, martyrdom, nationalism, and patriotism in the education system to encourage Turkey's youth to become willing to die on behalf of the regime, and to perceive deaths caused by the regime as necessary and admirable human sacrifices. The chapter also examines how, particularly following the July 2016 failed coup, the AKP has attempted to re-educate the nation's children by reforming the national curriculum. It also describes a number of texts, including schoolbooks and comics, which are designed to indoctrinate children into the party's cult of martyrdom and encourage them to hate the AKP's internal and external enemies. This part contains some relevant political speeches and discourse of Mr. and Mrs. Erdoğan, which they addressed to the children about the glorification of death for the homeland. The chapter argues that the AKP has radically revolutionized the education system and introduced pro-martyrdom texts as part of an indoctrination campaign aimed at creating a new generation of lifelong AKP supporters, who are willing to die to 'defend' the regime, Turkey, Muslim World, Islam, and their leader Erdoğan.

The seventh chapter examines the use of martyrdom narratives in the AKP's management of blame avoidance. Blame avoidance is important to almost all regimes. However, the AKP—which has experienced a number of economic, political, and military disasters since coming to power—relies heavily on a number of blame avoidance strategies to avoid accountability and loss of popular support, thus, to maintain the stability of its authoritarian regime. An increasingly important aspect of the party's blame avoidance strategy, this chapter demonstrates, is its skilled use of martyrdom narratives. In fact, at the beginning, the AKP was accusing the bureaucratic establishment of using the martyrs as blame avoidance tools. This was the logic behind the whole 'solution process' regarding the Kurdish issue in the country as the AKP argued that the mothers should not cry (because their sons are martyred) so the Kurdish issue must be resolved. But eventually the AKP began to do the same thing it accused the Kemalist establishment of doing and mastered it. The chapter shows that the AKP regime uses two blame avoidance strategies, *presentational strategies* and *bargaining* via *rewards*, in managing blame avoidance and coping with crises that resulted in the deaths of soldiers and civilians. The party, the chapter contends, often attempts to turn blame into credit by framing the deaths of soldiers and civilians—which have occurred due to government failure—as martyrdom events in which ordinary people martyred themselves to protect the regime, the Turkish people, and Islam. Equally, the chapter contends that in *bargaining via rewards*, the second strategy, the AKP officeholders have widely used carrot and stick tactics to convince the families of its martyrs to support the regime's narratives. For example, the regime offers 'carrots' such as promises of financial aids including the extension and regulation of (civil) martyrdom, buying a house for the victim families, and allocating social privileges to families that support the martyrdom narrative, but finds ways to socially and economically punish families who attempt to hold the government to account for the death of their loved ones.

The eighth chapter argues that authoritarian governments, including the AKP in Turkey, use necropolitics and martyrdom narratives to create stability and perpetuate their rule. Like the Kemalists, the Erdoğanist AKP regime have been utilizing necropolitical martyrdom narratives for legitimation, repression, and mobilization as well as co-opting the far right opposition. The chapter shows how the AKP and Erdoğan construct their necropolitical narratives, which claim that the nation is facing existential threats that can only be tackled by sacrificing lives. To create stability and longevity, authoritarian regimes, such as the AKP, must repress their enemies (opposition, dissidents, human rights advocates, journalists and undesired minorities). To successfully repress their enemies, this chapter contends, the party weaponizes—among other things—a civilizational populist necropolitical martyrdom narrative, through which it securitizes and ultimately criminalizes its political opponents. The AKP frames its political enemies as an existential threat to Turkey, Islam, Ummah and Allah, and therefore showers with praise the martyrs who have died fighting the nation's, religion's and Allah's enemies. The chapter also shows how the AKP uses necropolitical martyrdom narratives to not only repress political opposition, but to legitimize its rule and actions, and at times co-opt other political parties and organizations, thereby extending its power over other political parties and ultimately Turkish society. The tacit ranking in martyrdom is also revealing its necropolitical use. The chapter is significant in that it also shows that in the Turkish context a martyr is worthy of remembering and being praised depending only on his/her usefulness in the AKP's discourse: for instance, there is a big difference between a 15 July martyr, or a soldier martyred by a Russian bombing in Syria.

The ninth chapter examines the reception the AKP's civilizational populist necropolitical narrative has received within Turkish society, and especially among its grassroots supporters and the families of the people it deems martyrs. The chapter begins with a discussion of authoritarian personality cults in Muslim majority regions, and the manner in which they have incorporated Islamic notions to encourage citizens to become willing to die for the leader. Following this, the chapter discusses how Islam is instrumentalized to advance a cult of personality around Erdoğan, and to encourage Turkish people to die for Erdoğan and his AKP regime, highlighting how the pro-AKP crowds at the AKP meetings chant and ask Erdoğan, 'Tell us kill, we will kill; tell us to die, we will die.' The chapter shows also how families of AKP-designated martyrs have repeated the party's martyrdom narrative and praised their martyred family member for giving their life to defend Turkey and Erdoğan. The chapter furthermore contends that the power of the AKP's civilizational populist narrative lies in its ability to help the party create an atmosphere in which dying for the regime—often under the guise of protecting Islam or the homeland—is perceived to be a high honour to be rewarded in the afterlife.

The final chapter draws together our arguments and research and describes how the AKP's assertion of power over Turkish television, schools, and Islam through its ally Diyanet has allowed it to propagate a partially new necropolitics in Turkey, which merges Islamism and Turkish nationalism and encourages citizens to die in the service of the AKP regime. The chapter describes how the party fused elements of Kemalist necropolitics with Islamism, civilizational populism and a personality cult around Erdoğan to create a new martyrdom narrative in which the deaths of Turkish civilian citizens and soldiers are framed as praiseworthy religious events that please Allah. Martyrdom in Turkey under the AKP rule, the chapter contends, is framed as an event ordained by God, rather than as a tragic accident and the result of government mistakes. Equally, chapter argues that the AKP has created an atmosphere of paranoia of existential fear in Turkey and encouraged citizens to believe that their country and religion are threatened by 'dark forces' (especially the West) outside their country and traitorous internal enemies, (i.e. the dissident, opposition and undesired minorities). In response, the AKP claims that to end this crisis and defeat Turkey's, Islam's and Ummah's enemies the Turkish people must rise to fight and, if need be, willingly martyr themselves in battle against their nation's, the Muslim World's and religion's external but especially internal enemies. Finally, the chapter underlines how the AKP uses its control over television, Diyanet, and the education system to create a generation of seemingly pious Muslims who will not question AKP rule, who view President Erdoğan as a national saviour, and who are willing to become martyrs for their nation, religion, and ultimately to perpetuate the rule of Erdoğan and the AKP.

REFERENCES

Açıksöz, Salih Can. 2012. 'Sacrificial Limbs of Sovereignty: Disabled Veterans, Masculinity, and Nationalist Politics in Turkey: Disabled Veterans, Masculinity, and Nationalist Politics in Turkey.' *Medical Anthropology Quarterly* 26 (1): 4–25. https://doi.org/10.1111/j.1548-1387.2011.01194.x.

Ahmetbeyzade, Cihan. 2008. 'Gendering Necropolitics: The Juridical-Political Sociality of Honor Killings in Turkey.' *Journal of Human Rights* 7 (3): 187–206. https://doi.org/10.1080/14754830802286095.

Akıncı, Eylül Fidan. 2018. 'Sacred Children, Accursed Mothers: Performativities of Necropolitics and Mourning in Neoliberal Turkey'. In *Performance in a Militarized Culture*, edited by Sara Brady and Lindsey Mantoan, 47–65. London; New York, NY: Routledge, an imprint of the Taylor & Francis Group.

Albertazzi, Daniele, and Duncan McDonnell. 2007. (eds.) *Twenty-First Century Populism: The Spectre of Western European Democracy*. New York: Springer.

Altinay, Ayşe Gül. 2006. *The Myth of the Military-Nation: Militerism, Gender, and Education in Turkey*. New York: Palgrave Macmillan.

Anderson, Benedict. 1983. *Imagined Communities*. London: Verso.

Azak, Umut. 2007. 'A Reaction to Authoritarian Modernization in Turkey: The Menemen Incident and the Creation and Contestation of a Myth, 1930—31'. In *The State and the Subaltern: Modernization, Society and the State in Turkey and Iran*, edited by Touraj Atabaki, 143–158. London and New York: I.B. Tauris.

Bakıner, Onur. 2019. '"These Are Ordinary Things": Regulation of Death under the AKP Regime'. In *Turkey's Necropolitical Laboratory*, edited by Banu

Bargu, 25–45. Edinburgh University Press. http://www.jstor.org/stable/10.3366/j.ctvs32r1g.6.

Bargu, Banu. 2016. 'Another Necropolitics'. *Theory & Event* 19 (1). muse.jhu.edu/article/610222.

Bargu, Banu, ed. 2019. *Turkey's Necropolitical Laboratory: Democracy, Violence and Resistance.* Edinburgh: Edinburgh University Press.

Barton, Greg, Ihsan Yilmaz, and Nicholas Morieson. 2021. 'Religious and Pro-Violence Populism in Indonesia: The Rise and Fall of a Far-Right Islamist Civilisationist Movement.' *Religions* 12 (6): 397. https://doi.org/10.3390/rel12060397.

Baykan, Toygar Sinan, Yaprak Gürsoy, and Pierre Ostiguy. 2021. 'Anti-Populist Coups d'état in the Twenty-First Century: Reasons, Dynamics and Consequences'. *Third World Quarterly* 42 (4): 793–811. https://doi.org/10.1080/01436597.2020.1871329.

Bayulgen, Oksan, Ekim Arbatli, and Sercan Canbolat. 2018. 'Elite Survival Strategies and Authoritarian Reversal in Turkey.' *Polity* 50 (3): 333–365. https://doi.org/10.1086/698203.

Bircan, D. 2014. 'Çanakkale İçinde Kurdular Beni: Şehitlik İmgesi Üzerinden Toplumsal Bedenin İnşası.' In *'Öl Dediler Öldüm' Türkiye'de Şehitlik Mitleri*, edited by S. De¯girmencio¯glu. Istanbul: İletişim Yayınları.

Bişkin, H. 2017, July 15. '15 Temmuz sonrası nerelerin adı değişti?' https://www.gazeteduvar.com.tr/gundem/2017/07/15/15-temmuz-sonrasi-nerelerin-adi-degisti. Gazete Duvar. https://www.gazeteduvar.com.tr/gundem/2017/07/15/15-temmuz-sonrasi-nerelerin-adi-degisti. Accessed 25 August 2021.

Bosworth, A.B. 2000. 'The Historical Context of Thucydides' Funeral Oration'. *The Journal of Hellenic Studies* 120 (November): 1–16. https://doi.org/10.2307/632478.

Bowersock, G.W. 1995. *Martyrdom and Rome*, 1st ed. Cambridge University Press. https://doi.org/10.1017/CBO9780511518546.

Brubaker, R. 2017. 'Between Nationalism and Civilizationism: The European Populist Moment in Comparative Perspective'. *Ethnic and Racial Studies* 40 (8): 1191–1226. https://doi.org/10.1080/01419870.2017.1294700.

Carney, Josh. 2018. 'Resur(e)Recting a Spectacular Hero: Diriliş Ertuğrul, Necropolitics, and Popular Culture in Turkey.' *Review of Middle East Studies* 52 (1): 93–114. https://doi.org/10.1017/rms.2018.6.

Castelli, Elizabeth A. 2004. *Martyrdom and Memory: Early Christian Culture Making*. Gender, Theory, and Religion. New York: Columbia University Press.

Davenport, Christian. 2007. *State Repression and the Domestic Democratic Peace*. New York: Cambridge University Press.

1 THE AKP'S CIVILIZATIONAL POPULIST... 25

Değirmencioğlu, Serdar. 2014. 'Kurgunun Deşifresi: Şehitlik Söylemini Anlamak.' In *Öl Dediler Öldüm: Türkiye'de Şehitlik Mitleri*, 177–202. Istanbul: İletişim.

Dorraj, Manochehr. 1997. 'Symbolic and Utilitarian Political Value of a Tradition: Martyrdom in the Iranian Political Culture.' *The Review of Politics* 59 (03): 489–521. https://doi.org/10.1017/S0034670500027698.

Erdoğan, R. Tayyip. 2017, July 12. 'July 15 Has Become One of the Symbols of Our National History.' *Presidency of the Turkish Republic*. https://www.tccb.gov.tr/en/news/542/78898/sokakta-aranan-adaletin-adi-intikamdir-sonu-da-vandalliktir. Accessed 8 April 2019.

Erkara, Busra. 2017, March 10. 'Propaganda in Istanbul.' *The New York Times*. https://www.nytimes.com/2017/03/10/opinion/sunday/propaganda-in-istanbul.html. Accessed 8 April 2019.

Erturk, Omer F. 2022. 'Anatomy of Political Islam in Republican Turkey: The Milli Görüş Movement as a Legacy of Naqshbandism.' *Contemporary Islam* 16 (2–3): 295–320. https://doi.org/10.1007/s11562-022-00500-x.

Escribà-Folch, Abel. 2013. 'Repression, Political Threats, and Survival Under Autocracy'. *International Political Science Review* 34 (5): 543–560. https://doi.org/10.1177/0192512113488259.

Gerschewski, Johannes. 2013. 'The Three Pillars of Stability: Legitimation, Repression, and Co-Optation in Autocratic Regimes.' *Democratization* 20 (1): 13–38. https://doi.org/10.1080/13510347.2013.738860.

Gidron, Noam, and Bart Bonikowski. 2013. 'Varieties of Populism: Literature Review and Research Agenda.' In Weatherhead Working Paper Series, Weatherhead Center for International Affairs, Harvard University, No. 13–0004. https://papers.ssrn.com/sol3/papers.cfm?abstract_id=2459387.

Gruber, C. 2013. 'The Martyrs' Museum in Tehran: Visualizing Memory in Post-Revolutionary Iran.' In *Unburied Memories: The Politics of Bodies of Sacred Defense Martyrs in Iran*, 68–97. London and New York: Routledge.

Grzymala-Busse, Anna, Kuo, Didi, Fukuyama, Francis, and McFaul, Michael. 2020. *Global Populisms and Their Challenges*. Freeman Spogli Institute for International Studies.

Hammond, Timur. 2020. 'Making Memorial Publics: Media, Monuments, and the Politics of Commemoration Following Turkey's July 2016 Coup Attempt.' *Geographical Review* 110 (4): 536–555. https://doi.org/10.1080/00167428.2019.1702429.

Hatina, Meir. 2014. *Martyrdom in Modern Islam: Piety, Power, and Politics*. New York: Cambridge University Press.

Hobsbawm, Eric. 2012. Introduction: Inventing Traditions. In *The Invention of Tradition*, edited by E. Hobsbawm and T. Ranger. Cambridge: Cambridge University Press.

Holdo, Markus. 2019. 'Cooptation and Non-Cooptation: Elite Strategies in Response to Social Protest.' *Social Movement Studies* 18 (4): 444–462. https://doi.org/10.1080/14742837.2019.1577133.

Islekel, Ege Selin. 2017. 'Absent Death: Necropolitics and Technologies of Mourning.' *Philosophia* 7 (2): 337–355. https://doi.org/10.1353/phi.2017.0027.

Jung, Dietrich, 2003. 'The Sèvres Syndrome.' *American Diplomacy*, August 2003, https://americandiplomacy.web.unc.edu/2003/08/the-sevres-syndrome/.

Klausner, Samuel Z. 1987. 'Martyrdom'. In *Encyclopaedia of Religion*, vol. 9, edited by Mircea Eliade, 230–237. New York: Macmillan.

Kriesi, Hanspeter, and Takis S. Pappas. (eds.). 2015. *European Populism in the Shadow of the Great Recession*. Colchester: ECPR Press.

Küçük, Bülent, and Buket Türkmen. 2020. 'Remaking the Public Through the Square: Invention of the New National Cosmology in Turkey.' *British Journal of Middle Eastern Studies*, 47 (2): 247–263. https://doi.org/10.1080/135 30194.2018.1491295.

Kyle, Jordan, and Gultchin, Limor. 2018, 13 November. Populism in Power Around the World. Available at SSRN: https://ssrn.com/abstract=3283962 or https://doi.org/10.2139/ssrn.3283962.

la Torre, Carlos de. 2019. 'Is Left Populism the Radical Democratic Answer?' *Irish Journal of Sociology* 27 (1): 64–71. https://doi.org/10.1177/079160 3519827225.

Maerz, Seraphine F. 2020. 'The Many Faces of Authoritarian Persistence: A Set-Theory Perspective on the Survival Strategies of Authoritarian Regimes.' *Government and Opposition* 55 (1): 64–87. https://doi.org/10.1017/gov. 2018.17.

Mbembe. 2019. *Necropolitics*. Translated by Steve Corcoran. Durham: Duke University Press.

Mbembe, Achille. 2003. 'Necropolitics'. Translated by Libby Meintjes. *Public Culture* 15 (1): 11–40.

Mosse, George L. 1990. *Fallen Soldiers: Reshaping the Memory of the World Wars*. Oxford and New York: Oxford University Press.

Mudde, Cas. 2004. 'The Populist Zeitgeist.' *Government and Opposition* 39 (4): 541–563.

Muno, Wolfgang and Christian Pfeiffer. 2022. 'Populism in Power—A Comparative Analysis of Populist Governance.' *International Area Studies Review*, 25 (4): 261–279. https://doi.org/10.1177/22338659221120067.

Özkan, Behzat. 2012. *From the Abode of Islam to the Turkish Vatan: The Making of a National Homeland in Turkey*. New Haven, London: Yale University Press.

Özyürek, Esra. 2016, August 18. 'Commemorating the Failed Coup in Turkey.' *Jadaliyya* - جدلية. http://www.jadaliyya.com/Details/33489. Accessed 19 April 2019.

Pappas, Takis S. 2014. 'Populist democracies: Post-authoritarian Greece and post-communist Hungary.' *Government and Opposition* 49 (1): 1–23.

Rolston, Bill. 2020. 'When everywhere is Karbala: Murals, martyrdom and propaganda in Iran.' *Memory Studies*, Feb 1, vol. 13 (1): 21.

Saleem, Raja M. Ali. 2021. 'Hinduism, Hindutva and Hindu Populism in India: An Analysis of Party Manifestos of Indian Rightwing Parties.' *Religions* 12 (10): 803. https://doi.org/10.3390/rel12100803.

Schneider, Carsten Q., and Seraphine F. Maerz. 2017. 'Legitimation, Cooptation, and Repression and The Survival of Electoral Autocracies.' *Zeitschrift für Vergleichende Politikwissenschaft* 11 (2): 213–235. https://doi.org/10.1007/s12286-017-0332-2.

Sluka, Jeffrey A. 1997. 'From Graves to Nations: Political Martyrdom and Irish Nationalism'. In *Martyrdom and Political Resistance Movements: Essays on Asia and Europe*, edited by Joyce J.M. Pettigrew. Amsterdam: VU University Press.

Soboul, Albert. 1989. *Understanding the French Revolution*. The Merlin Press.

Soileau, Mark. 2017. 'Hızır Pasha Hanged Us: Commemorating Martyrdom in Alevi Tradition.' *The Muslim World* 107 (3): 549–571.

Solomonovich, N. 2021. "Democracy and National Unity Day" in Turkey: The Invention of a New National Holiday. *New Perspectives on Turkey*, 1–26. https://doi.org/10.1017/npt.2020.33.

Swenson, Jill Diane. 1985. 'Martyrdom: Mytho-Cathexis and the Mobilization of the Masses in the Iranian Revolution.' *Ethos* 13 (2): 121–149.

Szyska, Christia. 2004. 'Martyrdom: A Drama of Foundation and Tradition'. In *Martyrdom in Literature: Visions of Death and Meaningful Suffering in Europe and the Middle East from Antiquity to Modernity*, edited by Friederike Pannewick, 29–46. Wiesdanden: Reichert.

The New York Times. 2018, February 26. Erdogan Tells a Weeping Girl, 6, She'd Receive Honors if Martyred. https://www.nytimes.com/2018/02/26/world/europe/turkey-erdogan-girl-martyr.html. Accessed 25 August 2021.

Verdery, Katherine. 2000. *The Political Lives of Dead Bodies: Reburial and Postsocialist Change*. New York: Columbia University Press.

von Soest, Christian, and Julia Grauvogel. 2017. 'Identity, Procedures and Performance: How Authoritarian Regimes Legitimize Their Rule.' *Contemporary Politics* 23 (3): 287–305.

Walzer, Michael. 2004. *Arguing About War*. New Haven and London: Yale University Press.

Yanık, Lerna K., and Fulya Hisarlıoğlu. 2019. 'They Wrote History with Their Bodies': Necrogeopolitics, Necropolitical Spaces and the Everyday Spatial

Politics of Death in Turkey.' In *Turkey's Necropolitical Laboratory: Democracy, Violence and Resistance*, edited by Banu Bargu, 46–70. Edinburgh University Press.

Yilmaz, Ihsan. 2005. 'State, Law, Civil Society and Islam in Contemporary Turkey.' *Muslim World* 95 (3) (July): 385–411.

Yilmaz, Ihsan. 2009. 'Muslim Democrats in Turkey and Egypt: Participatory Politics as a Catalyst.' *Insight Turkey* 11 (2) (April): 93–112.

Yilmaz, Ihsan. 2018. 'Islamic Populism and Creating Desirable Citizens in Erdogan's New Turkey.' *Mediterranean Quarterly* 29 (4): 52–76. https://doi.org/10.1215/10474552-7345451.

Yilmaz, Ihsan. 2021. *Creating the Desired Citizens: State, Islam and Ideology in Turkey*. Cambridge and New York: Cambridge University Press.

Yilmaz, Ihsan and Nicholas Morieson. 2021. 'A Systematic Literature Review of Populism Religion and Emotions.' *Religions* 12 (4): 272. https://doi.org/10.3390/rel12040272.

Yilmaz, Ihsan and Nicholas Morieson. 2022. 'Civilizational Populism: Definition Literature Theory and Practice.' *Religions* 13 (11): 1026. https://doi.org/10.3390/rel13111026.

Yilmaz, Ihsan and Omer Erturk. 2022. 'Authoritarianism and Necropolitical Creation of Martyr Icons by Kemalists and Erdoganists in Turkey.' *Turkish Studies* 23 (2): 243–260 4. https://doi.org/10.1080/14683849.2021.1943662.

Yilmaz, Ihsan, Caman, Mehmet Efe and Galib Bashirov. 2020. 'How an Islamist Party Managed to Legitimate Its Authoritarianization in the Eyes of the Secularist Opposition: The Case of Turkey.' *Democratization* 27 (2): 265–282 6 https://doi.org/10.1080/13510347.2019.1679772.

Yilmaz, Ihsan, Ahmed, Zahid, Bashirov, Galib, Morieson, Nicholas and Kainat Shakil. 2022. "Islamist Populists in Power: Promises, Compromises and Attacks on Democratic Institutions." *Populism & Politics*. European Center for Populism Studies (ECPS). August 7. https://doi.org/10.55271/pp0013.

Yilmaz, Ihsan, and Omer F. Erturk. 2021. 'Populism, Violence, and Authoritarian Stability: Necropolitics in Turkey.' *Third World Quarterly* 42 (7): 1524 1543. https://doi.org/10.1080/01436597.2021.1896965.

York, Tripp. 2007. *The Purple Crown: The Politics of Martyrdom*. Scottdale, Pa: Herald Press.

Zengin, Asli. 2016. 'Violent Intimacies. Tactile State Power, Sex/Gender Transgression, and the Politics of Touch in Contemporary Turkey.' *Journal of Middle East Women's Studies* 12 (2): 225–245.

PART I

Civilizational Populist Necropolitical Propaganda

CHAPTER 2

Martyrdom and Martyr-Icons in Turkish Politics

INTRODUCTION

The literature on martyrdom has shown that martyrdom transforms itself flexibly to any condition by adopting either secular or religious references (Sluka 1997, 49). This was the case in Turkey under secularist and nationalist governments. To a great extent, Erdoğan and his AKP have been using the religio-nationalist martyrdom understanding and concept inherited from the secularist Kemalists. Thus, it is important to discuss this background before moving on the analyse the Erdoğanist period.

In the following sections, we first look at the fears and traumas of the Kemalists, their response to these, establishment of the Turkish Republic, the militarist political culture, and use of education and religion to propagate the Kemalist militarism and necropolitics with a focus on martyrdom. Then, we will analyse the process of the Kemalist martyr-icon construction in the republican period until the AKP, and its necropolitical use: Kubilay, the military officer beheaded by a fanatical pro-Caliphate crowd protesting the secularist reforms in the town of Menemen, İzmir in 1930. To understand the use of necropolitical culture in the Turkish politics is vital to analyze the martyrdom politics of the AKP today, which is the main focus of this book.

© The Author(s), under exclusive license to Springer Nature Singapore Pte Ltd. 2023
I. Yilmaz and O. Erturk, *Populism, Authoritarianism and Necropolitics*, https://doi.org/10.1007/978-981-19-8292-7_2

31

Kemalism and Martyrs

To a great extent, the Turkish national psyche is under the influence of trauma of the gradual loss of a glorious empire and its eventual humiliating collapse. For the first time in its history the Ottomans lost territory with the Treaty of Karlowitz in 1699 and their self-confidence was shaken. Starting with the Treaty of Kuchuk-Kainarji in 1774, the Empire's capital would consistently receive one piece of devastating news after another. In the lands of the Empire there are now 26 countries in Europe and the Caucasus, 14 countries in the Middle East, and 22 countries in Africa. The gradual collapse took 220 years and left its traumatic mark on the national memory. In the nineteenth century, millions of Muslims escaped from ethnic cleansing in the lost territories in Crimea, the Balkans, and the Caucasus and poured into the shrinking Ottoman heartlands, creating additional trauma for the forced migrants as well as the receiving communities (Yilmaz 2021). All these traumas, anxieties, and fears have been perpetuated in education (especially history), media, popular culture, and official religious narrative propagated by its directorate of religious affairs (Diyanet) to create desired citizens (Yilmaz 2021), warn them against external and internal existential threats, mobilize them for the state's protection and get them sacrifice their lives for the country's and state's defence.

A 'chosen trauma' is the selective recollection of a calamity experienced by the predecessors of a national or ethnic group. Chosen traumas co-exist in the psyche of the groups with their diametrically opposite counterparts: 'chosen glories' that are used to bolster a group's self-esteem and to provide comforting narratives in times of intense ontological insecurity and existential anxiety (Volkan 1997, 81). Employing chosen traumas in new situations brings with it powerful emotions of loss, humiliation, vengeance, and hatred that in turn trigger unconscious defence mechanisms that attempt to reverse these emotions (Volkan 1997, 82). Chosen traumas and chosen glories are deeply connected to the narratives of the nation and religion (Kinnvall 2004, 756). The Kemalists used the chosen trauma of the collapse of the Ottoman Empire and invasion of Turkey by the Allies as well as the Greece to make sense of the defeats and challenges they faced. They sought refuge in a narrative about the existence of external forces, internal citizen enemies, and constant anti-Turkish conspiracies, traps, plot, and games.

Turkish Republic's establishment in 1923 was on the remnant of the Ottoman Empire that faced a humiliated defeat during the First World War and the real possibility of almost total dismemberment. The secret Sykes–Picot–Sazanov agreement of 1916 proposed the dismemberment of the Ottoman Empire into several pieces and the United States President, Woodrow Wilson, called for the Ottoman Empire's dismemberment. The Armistice of Mundros in 1918 pushed the Ottomans to give up the Arab provinces. Meanwhile, Armenia sought to annex parts of Eastern Anatolia and the Kurds asked for independence. The Ottoman Empire state lost its independence and the Great Powers occupied the Turkish heartlands in Anatolia in 1919. The Empire's capital Istanbul was occupied by the British.

Turkish resistance under the leadership of Young Turks and Mustafa Kemal started the Turkish War of Independence (1919–1922) and established a government in Ankara, disobeying the Sultan in Istanbul. After 3 years, the Ankara government won the War of Independence and signed the Treaty of Lausanne on 24 July 1923 that defined Turkey's borders, except for Antioch (now Hatay province) that joined Turkey in 1939.

All these anxieties, insecurities, and victimhood (Yilmaz 2017) worsened by siege mentality have become part of the Turkish national psyche, maintained, augmented, and emotionally reproduced in everyday life (Scheff 1994) through discourses in the public sphere, pop culture, textbooks, and other politico-cultural apparatuses such as newspapers, movies, TV series, and narratives of the elites (Yilmaz 2021). The state continually stoked citizens' fear of the outside enemy, a fear directed towards Western countries that allegedly sought to undermine Turkish unity and destroy the nation, just as they had dismembered the Ottoman Empire and divided the spoils during World War I (White 2017, 28). As a popular Turkish saying goes, 'Turks have no other friends but Turks' (White 2017, 28).

Mustafa Kemal declared establishment of the Turkish Republic on 29 October 1923 and was elected as the head of the state. He abolished the Caliphate in 1924. His ideology was inherited from the previously ruling Young Turks to a great extent. This evolved as Kemalism which has never been a well-defined ideology but was the constitutionally official ideology. Being a flexible concept, it has changed over time and vacillated between contradictions.

Secularism was among the defining characteristics of the Kemalists who believed, management and control of Islam was imperative for progress vis-à-vis the Islamists, who wanted restoration of the caliphate and sultanate. So, they tried to create a Kemalism-friendly version of nationalist Turkish Islam by using the state's Directorate of Religious Affairs (Diyanet) (Yilmaz 2005, 2013, 2016). In parallel with the rise of Stalinist threat, Kemalists became more hospitable to Islam during the cold war era against the communist ideology. Especially after the 1980 coup, Kemalism became even more religious. Thus, Sunni Islam increasingly became integrated into the state nationalist ideology (Yilmaz 2005).

Mustafa Kemal's choice of 'Atatürk' (Father of Turks) was the culmination of a personality cult that had been taking shape from the late 1920s. In 1921 the title Gazi, which was an Ottoman title for military officers of high rank—as well as a fighter for the Islamic faith—was conferred upon Mustafa Kemal. On the one hand, Atatürk is the Gazi, the prototypical religious fighter for the rights of (Turkish) Muslims. But on the other hand, he is also the incarnation of what the Turks are to become: a part of European modernity (Berger 2020, 122).

Public education was used not only to foster the personality cult of Atatürk by the Kemalists but also to engender a change of identity (Zorlu-Durukan 2006). They 'approached education as a vehicle for enforcing social discipline, inculcating morality…uniformity, order, and obedience' (Fortna 2010, 23–24). This 'also meant that the Islamic and imperial referents were replaced with the cult of the Turkish nation and, gradually, that of Mustafa Kemal, whose sayings and image were with time inserted into the set texts and the iconography of schooling' (Fortna 2010, 21).

Altınay notes (2004, 23) that three main issues stand out in these textbooks and population policies of the Turkish Republic from the 1930s onward: (1) the development of an ethnic/racial understanding of culture; (2) the glorification of the Turkish race as the basis of civilization and high culture in world history; and (3) the formation of a dual geographic framework whereby Central Asia is the main homeland, while Anatolia is claimed to have Turkish origins reaching back long before the Ottoman Empire arrived (Altınay 2004, 23, see also Copeaux 1998, 2002).

Sunnism was particularly emphasized in religion textbooks. Within this context, 'we' was constructed as the 'Sunni Muslim Turk' (Babahan 2014, 286). As Üstel (2011) has shown, the Kemalists' insecurities, anxieties, siege mentality, and narrative of Turkey's internal and external enemies have been a consistent feature of the textbooks even after the 1980s (see in detail Üstel 2011, 212–214, 297–299, 328; see also Gürpınar 2013).

Based on a content analysis of 77 of the published 110 textbooks used in primary, secondary (middle), and high schools' disciplines such as history, sociology, civics, and religion between 1924 and 1950, Babahan (2014, 284) shows that the dominant discourse, in the first sub-period (1924–1931), is based on the idea that Islam and Turkishness are two complementary components that form the basis of national identity and nationalism. In the second sub-period, between 1931 and 1939, a strict secular nationalism is seen in the textbooks, but during the third and last sub-period, covering the years between 1939 and 1950, reference to religion in textbooks once again became more prominent, the strict secularism of the second sub-period being replaced with a Turkish identity strongly associated with Islam (Babahan 2014, 284).

More recent analyses of textbooks through the lens of militarism show also 'the creation and continuous reinforcement of the intricate link between the nation and the military in the Turkish nationalist project' (Kancı and Altınay 2007, 7). In addition to the myth of the military nation, glorification of martyrdom has been significant of the state ideology in Turkey. Sacrificing lives to protect the homeland, the nation, and its symbols is 'not only a duty, but in fact a defining feature of being a Turk' (Keyman and Kancı 2011, 327). The education system emphasizes that attachment to the nation is what makes an individual's life meaningful and complete (Bayar 2014, 82).

Themes of suffering and self-sacrifice have struck powerful chords with generations of children who at the start of each school day chanted that they loved their country more than themselves: 'I offer my existence to the existence of the Turkish nation as a gift' (White 2015). This is called *Andımız* (Our Pledge). In the elementary school assemblies before the class, it was auditioned by a boy or a girl and repeated by all other students. So, it is not surprising that the most frequently used words in high school texts about Turkish literature and language were self-sacrifice, death, war, and hero.

As historian Eric-Jan Zürcher (2010, 66) eloquently puts it, Abdulhamid II's regime in the late nineteenth century, the Young Turks in the beginning of the twentieth century, the earlier Kemalists and their 1980s version of the military regime of General Kenan Evren all argued for a case of 'true Islam: loyal to the Caliph in Abdulhamid's case, open to science in that of the Young Turks, private and non-political in that of the Kemalists and nationalist with Chief of the General Staff General Kenan Evren' the head of the 1980 military coup.

The Kemalists tried to create a reformed official version of Turkish Islam, 'Diyanet Islam' (Yilmaz 2021), a Turkish nationalist Islam separated from the faith's transnational connections, revered the nation-state, and closed to dialogue with other religions and religious communities (Yilmaz 2005, 404–405). The Diyanet aimed at providing a basis for a civic morality reinforcing the holistic spirit of Turkish nationalism, which subordinated the individual to society (Türkmen 2009, 382).

Until the consolidation of the AKP's power in 2010, the Kemalist version of Diyanet Islam, i.e., Diyanet Islam 1.0 (Yilmaz 2021), was in full action and its main tenets in relation to high politics issues such as national unity, solidarity, love of the homeland, Turkish nationalism, existential threats to the nation, militarism, reverence of the state and Mustafa Kemal Atatürk, and deep respect for the martyr had not changed.

Books and sermons produced by the Diyanet officials aimed to create good citizens with civic responsibility towards the state: to promote respect for law and order, hard work for the development of Turkey, love of homeland, and the sacredness of the military service and martyrdom (Gözaydın 2008, 223). These texts create a link between religiosity and obedience to the state (Gürpınar and Kenar 2016, 74) and manipulate Islam to argue that 'the defence of the country is a religious duty, since an attack on the homeland and the nation is considered an attack on Islam (which implies an attack on God and the Prophet as well) and thus on the dignity of the Muslims' (Flöhr 2020, 57).

Friday sermons written at the Diyanet headquarters and delivered verbatim in every mosque in Turkey every Friday constantly warned the congregation against the enemies of the nation and tried to inculcate militarist values in them (Gürpınar and Kenar 2016, 66–67). A study on the sermons delivered in years 2003, 2004, and 2005 shows the word 'war' was presented in a positive context 135 times as in, 'A person must sacrifice their own life, for their honour, values, and national dignity', while it was presented in a negative context only nine times (Akyeşilmen 2011, 20). The Diyanet's audience was constantly told that 'military service is a form of worship, and martyrdom is the highest status which secures entrance to heaven' (Gürpınar and Kenar 2016, 67; see also Ongur 2020, 444). Militarist triumphs of the nation were persistently commemorated in the Diyanet sermons. Especially four of them were never skipped: 'the conquest of Istanbul by Mehmed II in 1453, the Battle of Gallipoli in 1915, the Battle of Dumlupınar in the Turkish War of Independence in 1922 and the Battle of Manzikert in 1071' (Gürpınar and Kenar 2016, 69).

Diyanet Islam of the Kemalist state, in its most ideal form, envisioned a religious Sunni Muslim type (Homo Diyanetus 1.0) (Yilmaz 2021) who revered the state and Atatürk, who loved the homeland, who was a Turkish nationalist and militarist, and who was aware of the existential threats posed to the nation, homeland, and the state. Homo Diyanetus believed that being a nationalist Turk was a requirement of faith, and being a Muslim was a requirement of Turkishness. Homo Diyanetus knew that defending the state and the nation was a religious duty; that many Turks in the past sacrificed their lives defending the nation, homelands, and the state and became martyrs (Yilmaz 2021).

Kemalists' Martyr Hero Icon Kubilay

The manner in which martyrdom was used by Kemalist elites in Turkey to produce ideological 'myths' and 'icons' for the new secular regime has already been studied. Bureaucratizing and ritualizing martyrdom as an official memory and through the exemplary model of Kubilay was a defining feature of the Kemalist regime. Even recently, the icon of martyr 'Kubilay has been revived by Kemalist associations, the army, and the mainstream media as a way to express and restore citizens' dedication to the secularist regime' (Azak 2008, 38–39; 2007, 143–158; Yilmaz and Erturk 2022). Who was Kubilay and what happened to him?

On 23 December 1930, a group gathered under the leadership of Derviş Mehmet, who was allegedly affiliated with the Naqshbandi Sufi order (see Erturk 2022a, b), and protested the Kemalist regime and its secularist reforms in the town of Menemen, İzmir, demanding the restoration of Shari'a and Caliphate. A squad of soldiers under the command of Lieutenant Mustafa Fehmi Kubilay attempted to intervene and quell the protesters. During the fight, Kubilay and two guards were killed, along with many of the protesters. The incident was shockingly violent: Kubilay was beheaded, and the protesters reportedly placed his head on a pole as a symbol of victory, parading it around the town.

In reaction to the incident, the Kemalist regime initiated a series of repressive steps. This violent incident gave legitimacy to the state's enacting of emergency measures and extrajudicial acts around the country.

38   I. YILMAZ AND O. ERTURK

The US ambassador's report to Washington at the time depicts the event as a 'golden opportunity for the regime', showing it was well understood how this incident could be turned into repression of the opposition (Azak 2007, 145). In this oppositional camp, there were three main groups: Naqshbandis, supporters of the Free Republican Party (*Serbest Cumhuriyet Fırkası*, [FRP], which included some of Mustafa Kemal's old fellows-in-arms), and leftists, including Zekeriya Sertel and Nazım Hikmet, and their media outlets (Goloğlu 2011, 334; Sertel 2001).

When addressing the army, President Mustafa Kemal said in 1930 that 'Kubilay's pure blood will refresh and strengthen the vitality of the Republic' (Azak 2010, 38; 2007, 155). In a speech during his visit to the Menemen cemetery on 28 December 1930, Şükrü Kaya, the Minister of Interior, described the incident as '[a] crime, committed against the martyrs, the Revolution and the fatherland' (Azak 2010, 32). The regime itself aimed to institutionalize legitimacy through the martyr discourse and wanted to prolong it over time. Thus, the incident and Kubilay as a revolutionary martyr were enshrined in textbooks, official commemorations, statues, and murals. On 23 October 1933, the tenth anniversary of the Republic, a monument of revolutionary martyrdom was erected in Menemen, with the words 'they believed, fought, and died; we are the guardians of the trust they left behind' engraved on the pedestal (Azak 2010, 41).

Along with political, judicial, and military measures, the media mouthpieces of the regime, such as *Cumhuriyet* (Republic) or *Hakimiyet-i Milliye* (Sovereignty of Nation) (Weiker 1973, 31), established by Atatürk himself, immediately began to propagandize and glorify Kubilay's martyrdom. Regime propagandists such as Necip Fazıl Bey (Kısakürek) frequently emphasized that 'Kubilay was the exemplar of martyrdom who bestowed his life for us, thousands, millions of Turkish citizens' (Kısakürek 1931b). Kısakürek urged people, especially the youth, to pour out into the streets and spread fear of the religious reactionaries and massacre them; otherwise, if not, they would meet a similar end to Kubilay:

> If you do not protect and save the reforms, if you do not represent the heart, concerns, and nerves of the reforms, you will be watching one day what predestined to Kublay's head, cut with the back of the knife within twenty minutes. You shall dry up the green blood of *softa* (pious)

2 MARTYRDOM AND MARTYR-ICONS IN TURKISH POLITICS 39

and *mürteci* (religious reactionary) population on the logs in Turkey. (Kısakürek 1931b)

Along with martyrdom (şehadet), Kısakürek also represented Kemalist reaction to Menemen incident as the 'jihad of civilization' (*uygarlık cihadı*). In an article titled '*Kublay'ın Başı*' (the Head of Kublay), Kısakürek was encouraging the regime to spill the *şeriatçı* blood freely in return for Kublay's head, while legitimating state violence: 'We are cleaning up our country from the *irtica* circles who have a tarred soul written on [Qur'anic verse] *innafetahnaleke* [lit. we opened to you]' (Kısakürek 1931a). Kısakürek resembles the *irticacıs* and others to a black snake and writes that this snake should be exterminated forcefully by the regime, claiming imprisoning them is not sufficient: 'the black snake hisses: you showed me a hole lest I die in it. [...] Unless you crush my head with a stone, unless you burn me with oil, unless you hurl my ashes to the wind, I shall not leave you alone' (Kısakürek 1931a). In another piece, published on 5 January 1931, Kısakürek frames Kubilay's martyrdom in an authoritarian manner: 'If Kublay was not beheaded, we would not be able to take action [...] Therefore, who is responsible here? It is not Derviş Mehmet and his friends' (Kısakürek 1931b). The journal states that this incident is just the tip of the iceberg and there are people behind this incident who opposed the reforms like that and other reforms of Atatürk (Kısakürek 1931b). According to the journal, it is possible to recognize the instigators and real criminals simply by analysing their 'way of walk', 'way of sights' though they self-deny that they have nothing to do with the crime and even if they did not support it indeed, since they were wearing formerly head turban (*sarık*). For the journal, Kublay is the exemplar of martyrdom who bestowed his life for 'us' instead of thousands, millions (Kısakürek 1931b).

The use of the martyr Kubilay and the incident of his death continued during the post-single-party era as a repressive tool. For example, the 1952 Islamist assassination attempt on a secularist Kemalist journalist, known as the Malatya Incident, was directly equated with Kubilay by the Kemalists. The gunman was a close friend of Kısakürek and a member of Islamist Greater East Movement (*Büyük Doğu Hareketi*), which was allegedly led and masterminded by Necip Fazıl Kısakürek, who became now a fervent Islamist leader against the Kemalists in the 1950s. Following the incident, depictions and photos of Kubilay immediately appeared in Kemalist journals (Azak 2008, 39) and the link was

40   I. YILMAZ AND O. ERTURK

echoed in secularist circles. Soon, under the pretext of state security, the incident led to mass incarceration and operations launched in various cities, mostly targeting the *Nurcus*, followers of the Islamic scholar Said Nursi (Salihoğlu 2013). 'Kubilay was remembered as a martyr, especially during social and ideological tensions which resulted in violent social clashes, such as those in 1969 and 1978' (Azak 2008, 39). We can add 1960 military coup, 1997 post-modern coup, and 2007 internet memo to these events. Thus, we see that the use of martyrdom of Kubilay by the Kemalist hegemony reached paramount before the military coups or military memos staged by the Kemalist elites. Many incidents and many political murders between 1950 and 2006 were likened to Menemen incident and Kubilay the exemplary martyr. Kubilay, martyr of the revolution, became a memory, a blue print or a pattern, and a signal of threat. The list of martyrs of the Kemalist revolution after Kubilay who died struggling with the *gericis* (religious reactionaries) is quite long; Uğur Mumcu in 1993, Muammer Aksoy in 1990, Bahriye Uçok in 1990, Çetin Emeç in 1990, Ahmet Taner Kışlalı 1999, Necip Hablemitoğlu in 2002, Mustafa Yücel Özbilgin in 2006 were declared as 'martyrs of secularism' referring to Kubilay (Azak 2008, 39). The dichotomy between Kubilay and Derviş Mehmet was maintained vividly. For example, after the assault of the Council of State (Danıştay), Mustafa Yücel Özbilgin (Bacik and Salur 2007) the incident was announced as an incident of Kubilay by pro Kemalist judiciary, military and CHP (Hurriyet Daily 2006a, b; Arıkan 2006). In the commemoration of Danıştay assault, held in 2010, 7th Chamber president of Danıştay Turgut Candan stated:

> You are Kubilay O Mustafa! The Kubilay of the judiciary...Kubilays who were lit in order to expel the darkness are never forgotten. Neither will we forget you, nor will we forget Derviş Mehmets who slaughtered Kubilays. (Radikal 2006)

CONCLUSION

In this chapter we have shown how necropolitics has played an important role in legitimizing authoritarian rule in Turkey throughout the history of the Republic. The glorification of martyrdom in the service of the state, and death and blood narratives, are mostly used in non-democratic regimes as a tool for building collective memory, rituals, symbols, myth-making, and mass mobilization. This has taken place in Turkey since the foundation of the Republic, in which martyrdom narratives have been used as a powerful official tool to produce desired political action and encourage nationalist struggles against elements of the previous regime. The power of martyrdom narratives stems from its flexibility; while we might conceive of martyrdom as a 'religious' concept, both secularist regime of the Kemalists and the AKP employed religious and nationalist martyrdom narratives to produce regime legitimacy, new national myths and identities, and to mobilize supporters. The Menemen incident turned out to be a great opportunity to strengthen the Kemalists' authoritarian rule through the necropolitical use of martyrdom as in the form of the exemplary Kemalist martyr-icon of Kubilay. In the following chapter, we discuss how the AKP has built on this necropolitical culture, how it followed very similar tactics to create its own necropolitical martyr role models and icons to legitimize and strengthen its authoritarianism.

REFERENCES

AA. 2018. 'Asım Safitürk: Şehidimizin Kanı Kimsenin Yanında Kalmamıştır.' February 4. https://www.aa.com.tr/tr/turkiye/asim-safiturk-sehidimizin-kani-kimsenin-yaninda-kalmamistir/1053811.

Ahmetbeyzade, C[idot]han. 2008. 'Gendering Necropolitics: The Juridical-Political Sociality of Honor Killings in Turkey.' *Journal of Human Rights* 7 (3): 187–206.

Akıncı, EylülFidan. 2018. 'Sacred Children, Accursed Mothers: Performativities of Necropolitics and Mourning in Neoliberal Turkey.' In *Performance in a Militarized Culture*, edited by Sara Brady and Lindsey Mantoan, 47–65. London and New York, NY: Routledge, an imprint of the Taylor & Francis Group.

Altınay, Ayşe Gül. 2004. *The Myth of the Military-nation: Militarism, Gender, and Education in Turkey*. New York: Palgrave Macmillan.

Akyeşilmen, Nezir. 2011. 'Diyanet Hutbelerinde İnsan Hakları.' *Hülasa* 1 (1): 19–21.

Arıkan, Fahir. 2006. 'İkinci Kubilay olayı.' *Hürriyet*, May 18. http://www.hurriyet.com.tr/gundem/ikinci-kubilay-olayi-4432623.

Azak, Umut. 2007. 'A Reaction to Authoritarian Modernization in Turkey: The Menemen Incident and the Creation and Contestation of a Myth, 1930–31.' In *The State and the Subaltern: Modernization, Society and the State in Turkey and Iran*, edited by Touraj Atabaki, 143–158. London; New York: I.B. Tauris.

———. 2008. 'Kubilay: Icon of Secularism.' *ISIM Review* 21 (1): 38–39.

42   I. YILMAZ AND O. ERTURK

———. 2010. *Islam and Secularism in Turkey: Kemalism, Religion and the Nation State*. International Library of Twentieth Century History. London; New York: I.B. Tauris.

Babahan, Ali. 2014. *Nationalism and Religion in the Textbooks of the Early Republican Period in Turkey*. Unpublished PhD thesis. Ankara: METU.

Bacik, Gokhan, and Sammas Salur. 2007. 'Deconstructing the Multiple Readings of a Terrorist Event in Turkey: The Case of the Council of State (Danıştay) Assault of 2006.' *Terrorism and Political Violence* 19 (4): 529–544. https://doi.org/10.1080/09546550701606556.

Bakıner, Onur. 2019. '"These Are Ordinary Things": Regulation of Death under the AKP Regime.' In *Turkey's Necropolitical Laboratory*, edited by Banu Bargu, 25–45. Edinburgh University Press. http://www.jstor.org/stable/10.3366/j.ctvs32r1g.6.

Bargu, Banu, ed. 2019. *Turkey's Necropolitical Laboratory: Democracy, Violence and Resistance*. Edinburgh: Edinburgh University Press.

Bayar, Yeşim. 2014. *Formation of the Turkish Nation-State, 1920–1938*. New York: Palgrave Macmillan.

Bayulgen, Oksan, Ekim Arbatli, and Sercan Canbolat. 2018. 'Elite Survival Strategies and Authoritarian Reversal in Turkey.' *Polity* 50 (3): 333–365. https://doi.org/10.1086/698203.

BBC. 2016. 'Turkey Shuts More than 130 Media Outlets,' July 28, sec. Europe. https://www.bbc.com/news/world-europe-36910556.

Berger, Lutz. 2020. 'The Leader as Father. Personality Cultsin Modern Turkey.' In *Kemalism as a Fixed Variable in the Republic of Turkey*, edited by Lutz Berger and Tamer Düzyol, 119–18. Baden-Baden: Ergon.

Bircan, Düzcan. 2014. 'Çanakkale İçinde Kurdular Beni: Şehitlik İmgesi Üzerinden Toplumsal Bedenin İnşası.' In *'Öl Dediler Öldüm' Türkiye'de Şehitlik Mitleri*, edited by Serdar Değirmencioğlu. Istanbul: İletişim Yayınları.

Bosworth, A. B. 2000. 'The Historical Context of Thucydides' Funeral Oration.' *The Journal of Hellenic Studies* 120 (November): 1–16. https://doi.org/10.2307/632478.

Bowersock, G. W. 1995. *Martyrdom and Rome*. 1st ed. Cambridge University Press. https://doi.org/10.1017/CBO9780511518546.

Boynukalın, Abdurrahim. 2016a. 'O kadar mutmain ki. "Ne kadar ferasetli adam" demek bile garip geliyor insana. Biz kimiz ki kanaat bildiriyoruz böyle bir baba hakkında.' Twitter, November 11. https://twitter.com/A_Boynukalin/status/797001817695588352.

Boynukalın, Abdurrahim. 2016b. 'Rabbim bize de nasipetsin. Şehitolalım, göçe-limbudiyarlardan. Dünyayaşanılacakyerdeğil.' Twitter, November 11. https://twitter.com/A_Boynukalin/status/797001989959913472.

2 MARTYRDOM AND MARTYR-ICONS IN TURKISH POLITICS 43

Caman, Mehmet Efe. 2020. 'Authoritarianization and Human Rights in Turkey: How the AKP Legitimizes Human Rights Violations.' https://doi.org/10.13140/RG.2.2.20616.57603.

Carney, Josh. 2018. 'Resur(e)Recting a Spectacular Hero: Diriliş Ertuğrul, Necropolitics, and Popular Culture in Turkey.' *Review of Middle East Studies* 52 (1): 93–114. https://doi.org/10.1017/rms.2018.6.

Castelli, Elizabeth A. 2004. *Martyrdom and Memory: Early Christian Culture Making. Gender, Theory, and Religion.* New York: Columbia University Press.

Champion, Mark. 2016. 'Coup Was "Gift From God" for Erdoğan Planning a New Turkey.' *Bloomberg*, July 18. https://www.bloomberg.com/news/articles/2016-07-17/coup-was-a-gift-from-god-says-Erdoğan-who-plans-a-new-turkey.

Copeaux, Etienne. 1998. *Tarih Ders Kitaplarında (1931–1993): Türk Tarih Tezinden Türk-İslam Sentezine.* Istanbul: Tarih Vakfı Yurt Yayınları.

Copeaux, Etienne. 2002. 'Religious Identities in Turkish Textbooks.' In *Clio in the Balkans: The Politics of History Education*, edited by C. Kolouri, 300–312. Thessaloniki: Center for Democracy and Reconcialiation in Southeatern Europe.

Dorraj, Manochehr. 1997. 'Symbolic and Utilitarian Political Value of a Tradition: Martyrdom in the Iranian Political Culture.' *The Review of Politics* 59 (3): 489–521. https://doi.org/10.1017/S0034670500027698.

Duvar, Gazete. 2017. '"Halisdemir Bylokçu" iddiası mahkemeyi karıştırdı.' Text, May 6. https://www.gazeteduvar.com.tr/gundem/2017/06/05/halisdemir-bylokcu-iddiasi-mahkemeyi-karistirdi.

Erdoğan, R. Tayyip. 2017. 'July 15 Has Become One of the Symbols of Our National History.' *Presidency of the Turkish Republic.* https://www.tccb.gov.tr/en/news/542/78898/sokakta-aranan-adaletin-adi-intikamdir-sonu-da-yan dalliktir.

Erkara, Busra. 2017. 'Propaganda in Istanbul.' *The New York Times*, March 10, sec. Opinion. https://www.nytimes.com/2017/03/10/opinion/sunday/propaganda-in-istanbul.html.

Erturk, Omer. 2022a. 'The Myth of Turkish Islam: The Influence of Naqshbandi-Gümüşhanevi Thought in Turkish Islamic Orthodoxy.' *British Journal of Middle Eastern Studies* 49 (2): 223–247. https://doi.org/10.1080/13530194.2020.1782727.

Erturk, Omer. 2022b. 'Anatomy of Political Islam in Republican Turkey: The Milli Görüş Movement as a Legacy of Naqshbandism.' *Contemporary Islam* 16: 295–320. https://doi.org/10.1007/s11562-022-00500-x.

Fortna, Benjamin C. 2010. 'The Ottoman Educational Legacy.' In *Turkey's Engagement with Modernity: Conflict and Change in the Twentieth Century*, edited by Celia Kerslake, Kerem Öktem and Philip Robins, 15–26. London and New York: Palgrave.

44   I. YILMAZ AND O. ERTURK

Flöhr, Benjamin. 2020. '"Love of one's homeland is part of faith"—Islam and Nationalism in Ahmet Hamdi Akseki's 'catechism' for the Military.' In *Kemalism as a Fixed Variable in the Republic of Turkey*, edited by Lutz Berger and Tamer Düzyol, 45–73. Baden-Baden: Ergon.

GazeteKarınca. 2018. 'Safitürk davasını haberleştiren gazeteci Nalin Öztekin tehdit edildi.' *GazeteKarınca (blog)*, October 23. https://gazetekarinca.com/2018/10/safiturk-davasini-haberlestiren-gazeteci-nalin-oztekin-tehdit-edildi/.

Gazetesi, Evrensel. 2020. 'Kaymakam Fatih Safitürk'ün ağabeyi tehdit edildiğini açıkladı.' Evrensel.net, October 6. https://www.evrensel.net/haber/417322/kaymakam-fatih-safiturkun-agabeyi-tehdit-edildigini-acikladi.

Gürpınar, Doğan. 2013. *Ottoman/Turkish Visions of the Nation, 1860–1950*. London: Palgrave Macmillan.

Gürpınar, Doğan and Ceren Kenar. 2016. 'The Nation and its Sermons: Islam, Kemalism and the Presidency of Religious Affairs in Turkey.' *Middle Eastern Studies* 52 (1): 60–78.

Goloğlu, Mahmut. 2011. *TürkiyeCumhuriyetiTarihi - I 1924–1930: DevrimlerveTepkileri*. 3rd ed. İstanbul: Türkiye İş Bankası Kültür Yayınları.

Gözaydın, İştar B. 2008. 'Diyanet and Politics.' *The Muslim World* 98 (2–3): 216–227.

Gruber, Christiane. 2013. 'The Martyrs' Museum in Tehran: Visualizing Memory in Post-Revolutionary Iran.' In *Unburied Memories: The Politics of Bodies of Sacred Defense Martyrs in Iran*, edited by Peddram Khosronejad, 68–97. London New York: Routledge.

Gurcan, Metin. 2016. 'Turning a True Turkish Hero into a Commodity.' *Al-Monitor*, November 10. https://www.al-monitor.com/pulse/originals/2016/11/turkey-coup-attempt-turning-hero-commercial-commodity.html.

Hammond, Timur. 2020. 'Making Memorial Publics: Media, Monuments, and the Politics of Commemoration Following Turkey's July 2016 Coup Attempt.' *Geographical Review* 110 (4): 536–555. https://doi.org/10.1080/00167428.2019.1702429.

Hatina, Meir. 2014. *Martyrdom in Modern Islam: Piety, Power, and Politics*. New York: Cambridge University Press.

Hurriyet Daily. 2006a. 'Kenan Evren: Danıştay'a saldırı Menemen olayının bir eşi.' *Hürriyet*, May 19. http://www.hurriyet.com.tr/gundem/kenan-evren-danistaya-saldiri-menemen-olayinin-bir-esi-4443170.

———. 2006b. 'Hakime kurşun Kubilay olayıdır.' July 8. http://www.hurriyet.com.tr/gundem/h-kime-kursun-kubilay-olayidir-4717728.

Islekel, Ege Selin. 2017. 'Absent Death: Necropolitics and Technologies of Mourning.' *PhiloSOPHIA* 7 (2): 337–355. https://doi.org/10.1353/phi.2017.0027.

2 MARTYRDOM AND MARTYR-ICONS IN TURKISH POLITICS   45

Kancı, Tuba, and Ayşe Gül Altınay. 2007. 'Educating Little Soldiers and Little Ayşes: Militarised and Gendered Citizenship in Turkish Textbooks.' In *Education in 'Multicultural' Societies. Turkish and Swedish Perspectives*, edited by Marie Carlson, Annika Rabo and Fatma Gök, 51–70. Stockholm: Swedish Research Institute in Istanbul.

Keyman, E. Fuat, and Tuba Kancı. 2011. 'A Tale of Ambiguity: Citizenship, Nnationalism and Democracy in Turkey.' *Nations and Nationalism* 17 (2): 318–336.

Kısakürek, Necip Fazıl. 1931a. 'Kublay'ın Başı.' *HakimiyetiMilliye*, January 1.

———. 1931b. 'Necip Fazıl Beyin Nutku.' *HakimiyetiMilliye*, January 5.

Kinnvall, Catarina. 2004. 'Globalization And Religious Nationalism: Self, Identity, and the Search for Ontological Security.' *Political Psychology* 25 (5): 741–767.

Klausner, Samuel Z. 1987. 'Martyrdom.' In *Encyclopedia of Religion*, edited by Mircea Eliade, 9: 230–237. New York: Macmillan.

Küçük, Bülent, and Buket Türkmen. 2020. 'Remaking the Public through the Square: Invention of the New National Cosmology in Turkey.' *British Journal of Middle Eastern Studies* 47 (2): 247–263. https://doi.org/10.1080/135 30194.2018.1491295.

Milli Gazete. 2020. 'Şehit Kaymakamın ağabeyinden flaş iddialar: İyileşecekti, vali...' *Milli Gazete*, October 6. https://www.milligazete.com.tr/haber/557 5603/sehit-kaymakamin-agabeyinden-flas-iddialar-iyilesecekti-vali.

Milliyet. 2016. 'Şehit kaymakam Muhammed Fatih Safitürk son yolculuğuna uğurlandı.' *Milliyet*, November 2016. https://www.milliyet.com.tr/gun dem/sehit-kaymakam-muhammed-fatih-safiturk-son-yolculuguna-ugurlandi-2343866.

———. 2017. 'Şehit Kaymakam Safitürk'ün Adı 30 İlde Yaşatılıyor.' November 10. https://www.milliyet.com.tr/yerel-haberler/sakarya/sehit-kaymakam-saf iturkun-adi-30-ilde-yasatiliyor-12393721.

Muižnieks, Nils. 2016. 'Memorandum on the Human Rights Implications of the Measures Taken Under the State of Emergency in Turkey.' Visit Memorandum CommDH(2016)35. Strasbourg: Commissioner for Human Rights. https://www.coe.int/en/web/commissioner/view/-/asset_publis her/ugj3i6qSEkhZ/content/the-commissioner-publishes-a-memorandum-on-the-human-rights-implications-of-the-emergency-measures-in-turkey.

Ongur, Hakan Övünç. 2020. 'Performing through Friday khutbas: Reinstrumentalization of Religion in the New Turkey.' *Third World Quarterly* 41 (3): 434–452.

Öztekin, Nalin. 2018. 'Kaymakam Safitürk suikastinde önemli iddialar.' *Arti Gerçek*, 15 October. https://artigercek.com/haberler/kaymakam-safiturk-sui kastinde-onemli-iddialar.

46   I. YILMAZ AND O. ERTURK

Öztürk, Saygı. 2016. 'Ailesi de kahraman.' *Sözcü*, August 28. https://www.sozcu.com.tr/2016/gundem/ailesi-de-kahraman-1368049/.

Özyürek, Esra. 2016. 'Commemorating the Failed Coup in Turkey.' Jadaliyya - 18 جدلية. August 2016. http://www.jadaliyya.com/Details/33489.

Radikal. 2006. 'Özbilgin son Kubilay'dır.' *Radikal*, May 18. http://www.radikal.com.tr/turkiye/ozbilgin_son_kubilaydir-997407/.

Rice, Cecil A., and Jarlath F. Benson. 2005. 'Hungering for Revenge: The Irish Famine, the Troubles and Shame-Rage Cycles, and Their Role in Group Therapy in Northern Ireland.' *Group Analysis* 38 (2): 219–235. https://doi.org/10.1177/0533316405052380.

Roberts, Jennifer Talbot. 2012. 'Mourning and Democracy.' In *Thucydides and the Modern World: Reception, Reinterpretation and Influence from the Renaissance to the Present*, edited by Katherine Harloe and Neville Morley. Cambridge: Cambridge University Press.

Rosoux, Valérie. 2004. 'The Politics of Martyrdom.' In *Martyrdom: The Psychology, Theology and Politics of Self-Sacrifice*, edited by Rona M. Fields, 83–116. Westport: Praeger Publishers.

Sabah Daily. 2017. '250 şehidimiz bizim güneşlerimiz.' *Sabah*, July 16. https://www.sabah.com.tr/gundem/2017/07/16/sehidimiz-bizim-guneslerimiz .

Salihoğlu, M. Latif. 2013. 'Malatya HadisesiveNur(Cu)Lar.' *Yeni Asya*. 11 April 2013. http://www.yeniasya.com.tr/m-latif-salihoglu/malatya-hadisesi-ve-nur-cu-lar_210637.

Sanalbasın. 2017. 'Bekçi mülakatında 15 Temmuz sorusuna "Kaymakam tepkisine" Valilik el koydu.' *Bekçi mülakatında 15 Temmuz sorusuna 'Kaymakam tepkisine' Valilik el koydu*, December 30. http://www.sanalbasin.com/bekci-mulakatinda-15-temmuz-sorusuna-kaymakam-tepkisine-valilik-el-koydu-22907086.

Scheff, Thomas. 1994. *Bloody Revenge: Emotions, Nationalism, War*. Boulder, CO: Westview.

Sertel, Zekeriya. 2001. *Hatırladıklarım*. İstanbul: Remzi Kitabevi.

Sluka, Jeffrey A. 1997. 'From Graves to Nations: Political Martyrdom and Irish Nationalism.' In *Martyrdom and Political Resistance Movements: Essays on Asia and Europe*, edited by Joyce J. M Pettigrew. Amsterdam: VU University Press.

Solomonovich, Nadav. 2021. '"Democracy and National Unity Day" in Turkey: The Invention of a New National Holiday.' *New Perspectives on Turkey*, January, 1–26. https://doi.org/10.1017/npt.2020.33.

Swenson, Jill Diane. 1985. 'Martyrdom: Mytho-Cathexis and the Mobilization of the Masses in the Iranian Revolution.' *Ethos* 13 (2): 121–149.

Szyska, Christia. 2004. 'Martyrdom: A Drama of Foundation and Tradition.' In *Martyrdom in Literature: Visions of Death and Meaningful Suffering in Europe and the Middle East from Antiquity to Modernity*, edited by Friederike Pannewick, 29–46. Wiesdanden: Reichert.

2 MARTYRDOM AND MARTYR-ICONS IN TURKISH POLITICS 47

T24. 2016. 'Sözleşmeli öğretmen alımı mülakatlarından: Reis denilince aklına kim geliyor; Ömer Halisdemir kimdir?' *T24*, 1 October 2016. https://t24. com.tr/haber/sozlesmeli-ogretmen-alimi-mulakatlarindan-reis-denilince-akl ina-kim-geliyor-omer-halisdemir-kimdir,362640.

T.C. Geyve Kaymakamlığı. 2017. 'GEDEP Projesi Kapsamında Asım Safitürk Hocamız Konferans Verdi.' 20 December 2017. http://geyve.gov.tr/gedep-projesi-kapsaminda-asim-safiturk-hocamiz-konferans-verdi.

T.C. Hizan Kaymakamlığı. n.d. 'Asım Safitürk İlçemizde Konferans Verdi.' Accessed 6 November 2020. http://www.hizan.gov.tr/asim-safiturk-ilcemi zde-konferans-verdi.

Türkmen, Buket. 2009. 'A Transformed Kemalist Islam or a New Islamic Civic Morality? A Study of "Religious Culture and Morality" Textbooks in the Turkish High School Curricula.' *Comparative Studies of South Asia, Africa and the Middle East* 29 (3): 381–397. Duke University Press.

Üstel, F. (2011). *"Makbul Vatandaş" ın Peşinde: II. Meşrutiyet'ten Bugüne Türkiye'de Vatandaş Eğitimi* (5. baskı.). İstanbul: İletişim.

Volkan, Vamık. 1997. *Bloodlines: From Ethnic Pride to Ethnic Terrorism*. Boulder, CO: Westview.

Weiker, Walter F. 1973. *Political Tutelage and Democracy in Turkey: The Free Party and Its Aftermath*. Leiden: Brill.

White, Jenny B. 2015. 'The Turkish Complex.' *American Interest* 10 (4). https://www.the-american-interest.com/2015/02/02/the-turkish-com plex/.

White, Jenny B. 2017. 'Spindle Autocracy in the New Turkey.' *Brown Journal of World Affairs* 24 (1): 23–37.

Worley, Will, and Samuel Osborne. 2016. 'Erdoğan Government Reasserts Itself as 2,700 Judges Purged—As It Happened.' *The Independent*, July 16. http://www.independent.co.uk/news/world/europe/turkey-coup-live-Erdoğan-dead-killed-istanbul-ankara-military-take-over-martial-law-latest-upd ates-a7140371.html.

Yanık, Lerna K., and Fulya Hisarlıoğlu. 2019. '"They Wrote History with Their Bodies": Necrogeopolitics, Necropolitical Spaces and the Everyday Spatial Politics of Death in Turkey.' In *Turkey's Necropolitical Laboratory: Democracy, Violence and Resistance*, edited by Banu Bargu, 46–70. Edinburgh University Press.

Yilmaz, Ihsan. 2005. 'State, Law, Civil Society and Islam in Contemporary Turkey.' *Muslim World* 95 (3, July): 385–411.

Yilmaz, Ihsan. 2013. 'Homo LASTus and Lausannian Muslim: Two Paradoxical Social-Engineering Projects to Construct the Best and the Good Citizens in the Kemalist Panopticon.' *Turkish Journal of Politics* 4 (2, December): 107–126.

Yilmaz, Ihsan. 2016. *Muslim Laws, Politics and Society in Modern Nation States: Dynamic Legal Pluralisms in England, Turkey and Pakistan.* Reprint. London and New York: Routledge.

Yilmaz, Ihsan. 2021. *Creating the Desired Citizens: State, Islam and Ideology in Turkey.* Cambridge and New York: Cambridge University Press.

Yilmaz, Ihsan and Omer Erturk. 2022. 'Authoritarianism and Necropolitical Creation of Martyr Icons by Kemalists and Erdoganists in Turkey.' *Turkish Studies* 23 (2): 243–260. https://doi.org/10.1080/14683849.2021.1943662.

Yilmaz, Ihsan and Galib Bashirov. 2018. 'The AKP after 15 Years: Emergence of Erdoğanism in Turkey.' *Third World Quarterly* 39 (9): 1812–1830. https://doi.org/10.1080/01436597.2018.1447371.

Yilmaz, Ihsan, Mehmet Efe Caman, and Galib Bashirov. 2020. 'How an Islamist Party Managed to Legitimate Its Authoritarianization in the Eyes of the Secularist Opposition: The Case of Turkey.' *Democratization* 27 (2): 265–282. https://doi.org/10.1080/13510347.2019.1679772.

Yilmaz, Zafer. 2017. "The AKP and the Spirit of the 'new' Turkey: Imagined Victim Reactionary Mood and Resentful Sovereign." *Turkish Studies* 18 (3): 482–513. https://doi.org/10.1080/14683849.2017.1314763.

York, Tripp. 2007. *The Purple Crown: The Politics of Martyrdom.* Scottdale, Pa: Herald Press.

Zengin, Aslı. 2016. 'Violent Intimacies: Tactile State Power, Sex/Gender Transgression, and the Politics of Touch in Contemporary Turkey.' *Journal of Middle East Women's Studies* 12 (2): 225–245.

Zorlu-Durukan, Şefika Akile. 2006. *The Ideological Pillars of Turkish Education: Emergent Kemalism ve the Zenith of Single-Party Rule.* PhD thesis, University of Wisconsin-Madison.

Zürcher, Eric-Jan. 2010. *Young Turk Legacy and Nation Building: From the Ottoman Empire to Atatürk's Turkey.* London: I. B. Tauris.

CHAPTER 3

Martyrdom in the Erdoğanist AKP's Politics

INTRODUCTION

Similar to the Kemalists, the AKP has also been trying to create its alternative versions of martyr-icons, who provide an Islamist alternative to the secularist martyr-icons created by the secular Kemalist regime (Yilmaz and Erturk 2022). Following the 15 July attempted mysterious coup, the AKP regime produced its own counter martyr-icons out of the deaths of especially Ömer Halisdemir and later Muhammed Fatih Safitürk, two men who the regime claimed had died protecting the government, people of Turkey, Islam and Allah, and were therefore worthy of admiration and imitation. In creating these martyr-icons, the AKP leaders were themselves imitating their secular predecessors, who had used the Menemen incident to create a martyr-icon in the form of Kubilay, who was held up as a paragon of virtue and a person worthy of imitation insofar as he was willing to die for the Kemalist regime. And just as Kubilay was to feature in educational texts produced by the Kemalists over many decades, and moreover used to create national myths and collective memories that serve to legitimize the regime and advance its agendas, so too have Halisdemir and Safitürk—among many others—been instrumentalized by the AKP to legitimize its authoritarian rule and advance its Islamist agenda. The lives of Halisdemir and Safitürk, alongside other stories of martyrs, have prominent places in the textbooks of the current era, in which they are framed as defenders of Islam, democracy and the fatherland who did not

© The Author(s), under exclusive license to Springer Nature
Singapore Pte Ltd. 2023
I. Yilmaz and O. Erturk, *Populism, Authoritarianism and Necropolitics*,
https://doi.org/10.1007/978-981-19-8292-7_3

hesitate to sacrifice their lives for the survival of their nation, and who fought against various internal enemies and their external supporters. It thus appears that the AKP is trying to consolidate, via necropolitical use of martyrdom, a new foundational myth and collective memory based on the events of 15 July 2016 and its aftermath, to legitimize the Erdoğanist regime and justify its growing authoritarianism.

Erdoğanism and Martyrs

The Kemalists consciously prioritized Diyanet Islam (Yilmaz 2005, 2021) and demonized the Turkish-Islamist thought, which is largely confined with tariqa formations, by creating alternative narratives and institutions, such as creating a distinction between regressive and progressive Islam (Cizre 2008, 27). The state tried to leave no official room for private and civil interpretations of Islam believing that they were the representatives of the anicent regime, the Ottoman Sultanate and Caliphate, which was defined as backwardness. Thus, Islamists had to keep a very low profile. With the start of the multiparty era in 1946, Turkish Islamists came back from the shadows.

Under the leadership of some of the Naqshbandi shaykhs and Necmettin Erbakan, Turkish Islamists started to establish political parties around a movement named Milli Görüş Hareketi (National Outlook Movement, NOM) that would become coalition partners in 1970s: (1) National Order Party (*Milli Nizam Partisi*—MNP, 1970–1971); (2) National Salvation Party (*Milli Selamet Partisi*—MSP, 1972–1980); (3) Welfare Party (*Refah Partisi*—RP, 1983–1998); (4) Virtue Party (*Fazilet Partisi*—FP, 1997–2001); (5) Felicity Party (*Saadet Partisi*—SP, 2001–present); and (6) Justice and Development Party (*Adalet ve Kalkınma Partisi*—AKP, 2001–present) (Erturk 2022a, b; Yilmaz 2021).

In the narrative of the Turkish Islamists, the West regarded Islam as an obstacle to its exploitation of the Muslim world and thus was working in tandem with Zionism to inject the idea of imitating the West into the minds of the Turkish people (Erturk 2022a). As a result, two main ideological camps were seen to exist in Turkey: The NOM that represented the pure, Muslim, and innocent people against the infidel and evil elite, who were the blind imitators of the West and were represented by all the other political parties (Erturk 2022a, b; Eligür 2010, 145). Erbakan did not see those who did not vote for him as Muslims, because he believed himself to be the sole leader who represented Islam in a fierce battle of 'truth against error' (Çınar 2006, 477; Erturk 2022b; Yıldız 2003, 193). Erbakan and his followers accused their opponents as either mouthpieces of the USA or CIA agents as they believed that their political party meant religion and accordingly those Muslims who did not lend support to the party were sinners. Erbakan was celebrated with chants of *mujahid* (the one who is engaged with holy struggle, *jihad*) in party demonstrations that were perceived as a holy struggle by the participants (Tuğal 2009, 46). A recent ground-breaking research on the books of Erbakan's *Naqshbandi* sheikh Zahid Kotku and Kotku's master Gümüşhanevi shows decisively that Erbakan's (and also Erdoğan's) spiritual's masters had radical Salafist and jihadist views in relation the doctrine of loyalty and disavowal (*al-wala' wal-bara'*), apostasy (*takfir*) (apostasy), *jihad*, Islamic state and source of sovereignty (*hakimiyya*), women, and art and philosophy (see in detail Erturk 2022a). Erturk shows that this ideological and radical Islamist views were transferred into the politics through Necmettin Erbakan and then his loyal disciple Tayyip Erdoğan, who grew within the Naqshbandi milieus of İsmailağa, Erenköy and İskenderpaşa brotherhoods (Erturk 2022b).

In 1996, as the major partner in a coalition government with the secular, right of centre True Path Party (*Doğru Yol Partisi*, DYP), Erbakan became Turkey's first Islamist prime minister. However, the Kemalists led by the military forced Erbakan to resign on 18 June 1997.

As a Naqshabndi disciple and a student of Erbakan, Erdoğan was the mayor of Istanbul at that time, but he was also punished after reading an emotional, religious and militarist poem. The poem reads as:

The mosques are our barracks,
The minarets are our bayonets.
The faithful are our soldiers,
God is great. God is great.

The Islamist political void created after the banning of RP was later filled by the Virtue Party (*Fazilet Partisi*, FP). The reformist younger generation of the party led by Erdoğan argued that Erbakan's Islamism 'reached an impasse because it let religious issues dominate its political agenda, it underplayed the importance of consensus-seeking and dialogue-building with the other sectors of the society, and it did not address itself to a broader public' (Cizre and Çınar 2003, 326). The Constitutional Court closed the FP on 22 June 2001 on the grounds it was an extension of the Islamist RP. Following this, the reformist wing within the FP publicly declared that they would not join the new Islamist party of Erbakan, the Felicity Party (*Saadet Partisi*, SP). Members of the breakaway group declared that they 'took off their Islamist National Outlook shirt' and merged with other politicians from the centre-right to establish the Justice and Development Party (*Adalet ve Kalkınma Partisi*, AKP) on 14 August 2001, declaring the party's ideology to be conservative democratic (Yilmaz 2009). In the November 2002 election, the AKP formed a single-party government by winning 34.43 per cent of the votes and 365 parliamentary seats, while the traditionalist Islamist SP gained only 2.49 per cent of the votes and no seats.

After forming the government, the AKP vowed to pursue the necessary steps for Turkey to qualify for EU accession negotiations. The prospect of EU membership provided a vision, which the majority of Turkish society shared, and the AKP leadership realized that the EU could be of critical assistance in its effort to gain political legitimacy.

The AKP and its supporters were heterogeneous. It had created a broad coalition of resentful liberals, democrats, Muslim and non-Muslim groups, ethnic minorities, and civil society organizations that were victimized by the Kemalists for decades. The Kemalist/militarist mindset was so scary to the undesired citizens of the country that until the Gezi Protests, Erdoğan's authoritarian tendencies had been apologetically swallowed as the lesser of two evils (Özpek and Yaşar 2018, 206–207). That is why not only Gülenists but also liberals, democrats, Kurds, and leftists, in the hope of curbing the Kemalist hegemony over bureaucracy and of democratizing the bureaucratic oligarchy, wholeheartedly endorsed the constitutional referendum in 2010 that was only objected by the Kemalists. The referendum in fact terminated the Kemalist hegemony within the judiciary and limited the military's influence on politics, but at the same time weakened checks on Erdoğan's power.

After winning 50 per cent of the vote in the 2011 election, the AKP's reformist and democratizing agenda increasingly weakened. Erdoğan was re-elected as prime minister, but thereafter he began to react to political challenges in a growingly demagogic, populist, and autocratic manner (Yilmaz 2018). After a series of shocks, the AKP had faced, beginning with the Gezi Protests in mid-2013 and 17–25 December police probes in 2013 accelerated the degradation in democratic norms. After the Gezi, 'his discourse has become more nationalist and statist in tone, as well as more divisive and hostile, targeting anyone opposing his rule and alienating many former supporters' (Sawae 2020, 259).

In order to convince their supporters and conceal the scandals, Erdoğanists spread disinformation and fake stories (Özen 2020, 12) mainly based on the civilizational populist conspiracy theory that the country's nationalist and Islamic values and beliefs were under attack. Erdoğan and his media claimed that a coup was staged by the Gülenist police and bureaucracy. During the Gezi protests, which began after the probe scandals, this time they 'repeatedly accused the protesters of consuming alcohol inside a mosque near Gezi, entering it wearing shoes, and repeatedly claimed that a head-covered woman with a baby was attacked and assaulted by a group of "drunken" Gezi protesters. This conspiratorial rhetoric appealed to the popular base of the AKP' (Özen 2020, 12). As a result, Erdoğan convinced his voters that 'the protests were posing a direct and substantial threat to conservative/religious way of life' (Özen 2020, 12).

The 15 July 2016 mysterious coup attempt was a turning point in Turkey's history. This event has affected Turkey enormously by cementing Erdoğan's power to socially engineer the masses. SADAT, Erdoğan's alleged paramilitary army led by the Naqshbandi retired general Adnan Tanrıverdi, and various Islamist and Naqshbandi communities had a vital role in the clashes and so-called suppression of the coup attempt. It is no surprise that Erdoğan has called it 'a gift from God'. On 24 June 2018, Erdoğan was re-selected as president with 52.39 per cent of the votes. This referendum in 2017 and the presidential election in 2018 allowed for the parliamentary system to fall within the presidential one, making Erdoğan not only the de facto but also the *de jure* hegemon.

Since the coup attempt, a new civilizational populist narrative about the victory of national will, resembling the victory of the War of Independence, has been created and propagated by the AKP. According to that narrative, Atatürk was the founding father after the first War of Independence, but Erdoğan is the new father of Turkey and leader of the Muslim World, as he challenged the 2016 abortive coup attempt. In this narrative, he is constructed as the leader and hope of the Muslim communities in the world, ummah. His supporters in the media, social media, TV dramas, and movies compare him to the pan-Islamist Sultan of the Ottoman Empire, the Abdulhamid II. In an obvious attempt to replace Atatürk's personality cult with Erdoğan's, the state under the

54   I. YILMAZ AND O. ERTURK

rule of Erdoğanists has been working hard to consolidate this civilizational populist narrative. As the leader of the 'New Turkey' and the Muslim World, Erdoğan has been transformed into a cult personality and has been presented by the AKP as 'a man of the people', 'lover of God', 'leader of the Ummah', and 'light of hope for the millions'. Since Erdoğan embodies the nation, any accusation against him is an assault on the nation (Taş 2015, 785). In this narrative, the fate of the country depends on Erdoğan's political success and 'if Erdoğan falls, Turkey will fall' (Taş 2015, 785). He has been constantly 'divinised by partisan voters and elites, and as such a personality cult around him has been entrenched' (Lancaster 2014, 1680–84). This personality cult of Erdoğan has reached such levels that many AKP officials utters statements such as 'I swear by God that Erdoğan has been Turkey's president eternally since the past (*ezeli*, i.e. one of God's attributes) and will stay as president forever (*ebedi*, i.e. another attribute of God)'; 'To belong to AKP means to be officially wedded to Erdoğan'; 'I recognize Erdoğan as the caliph and submit my recognition'; 'We will obey him to death'; 'Erdoğan is my forefather'; 'Prayer of thanks must be said for Erdoğan every day'; '"To do what Erdoğan does is *sunnah* (body of Islamic custom and practice based on Prophet Muhammad's words and deeds)'; 'Spring has come. Both nature and history are rising to greet our prime minister'; 'Even touching Erdoğan is an act of worship'; 'Erdoğan is the glad tidings our Creator sent to humanity'; 'Erdoğan is the shadow of God on this earth'; and 'Erdoğan is a leader who combines all attributes of God' (Taş 2014, Gürsel 2014). In 2016, the former AKP spokesperson and lawmaker, sociology professor Yasin Aktay told that whenever they mention Erdoğan's name, they say '*salli ala Muhammad*' (O Allah, raise the rank of the Prophet Muhammad). Generally, in the Sunni Islamic culture, this prayer is recited whenever the Prophet Muhammad's name is mentioned not anyone else's. Even Erdoğan himself mimicked God and said 'our (read as my) mercy has transcended our wrath' (Taş 2014). Originally, in the Islamic tradition, it is believed that this is a statement made by Allah as reported by the Prophet Muhammad. His fans have 'welcomed him wearing white shrouds, symbolizing that they are ready to die for him and go to the grave' (Akyol 2014).

Continuing what he learned from his master, Erbakan, and Naqshbandi shaykhs, in the Erdoğanist narrative opponents are conspiring enemies made up of everyone from Zionists, international bankers, interest lobby, Islamophobes, the CIA, the American ambassador, CNN, Twitter, and the Gülen Movement (GM) (Cook 2017, 118–119; Erturk 2022a, b). These labels have been used interchangeably but the government has also accused the GM of working with the CIA, Mossad, MI6, PKK, and other organizations to destroy Turkey from within and without (Yilmaz and Shipoli 2022).

The insecurities, anxieties, and fears of the AKP are not much different from the Kemalist ones. Like their Kemalist counterparts, Turkey's Islamists harbour their own insecurities, victimhood, fears, and siege mentality vis-à-vis the West whom they blame for the downfall of the two institutions they venerate and glorify: The Ottoman Empire and the Caliphate (Akkoyunlu and Öktem 2016, 510). Nevertheless, in the Islamist, and hence Erdoğanist psyche and narrative, Kemalists are seen as products of Western cultural imperialism and the self-colonizing pawns of the 'godless' West that are fixated on destroying Turkey's Islamic identity and Turkey's Muslims (Akkoyunlu and Öktem 2016, 510).

Erdoğan has skilfully turned the coup attempt into an extraordinary popular support with a rally around the flag effect. Maybe more importantly, he has solidified the staunch support of the conservative religious and conservative nationalist segments with the articulation of a civilizational populist discourse that has ignited fear and anxiety among these masses by portraying all opposition and criticism of as detrimental to their interests, lifestyles, and even existence (Özen 2020, 1–3). He has consistently strongly argued that:

> There are all kinds of *traps*, all kinds of *attacks*, all kinds of *conspiracies*, all kinds of *betrayal*, all kinds of pain and all kinds of trouble. The Turkish Nation, with its citizens and security forces, is carrying out its struggle for its independence and future, step by step to victory. We are determined to continue this struggle forever for the *future of all our friends and brothers* (the Muslim World) ... Yes, we, as a nation that *shed our sweat and blood*, when necessary, believe that we will be gifted with God's good tidings... We are well aware that the attacks that we have been experiencing for the last 7 years have aimed at *our belief*, history, culture, unity, togetherness, *adhan*, flag, and all our sacred values... It is our duty to pay our debt against this sacrifice of our nation by working with sacrifice, diligence and perseverance that will spoil all the *conspiracies*. (Erdoğan 2020)

As discussed above, to some extent conspiratorial anxieties and resentments of the pro-Erdoğanists 'related with the authoritarian secularism of Kemalism were not totally unfounded, given the social exclusions and different sorts of discriminations that they had been subjected before the rule of the AKP' (Özen 2020, 11). But Erdoğan has successfully manipulated these anxieties, fears, and resentments and used them for his own authoritarian civilizational populist purposes.

As nationalism and religion are intimately linked to chosen traumas and chosen glories, they are powerful identity signifiers in times of uncertainty by supplying a consistent structure and simple but comprehensive answers to complex questions (Kinnvall 2004, 757). In this process of resentment, hate becomes the link among the present, the future, and a re-written past and 'serves as a social chain for successive generations as a particular event or trauma becomes mythologized and intertwined with a group's sense of self' (Kinnvall 2004, 755). However, this resentful construction of self is almost always a way to frame superior and inferior beings. Superiors are those on the inside (of the religion or nation), while those on the outside are affected by pollution, falsity, ugliness, bad, and wrong (chaos) (Kinnvall 2004, 763).

Erdoğan's election speeches since the Gezi are full of the markers of populism: binary framework in which 'us', the 'native and authentic' members of the nation vis-a-vis minorities and the Kemalist establishment of the White Turks that has usurped political power to serve its own; his equation of himself and his party with the 'native and national (*yerli ve milli*) people'; and his constant on the threat of foreign and domestic enemies and their conspiracies (Sawae 2020, 260). As found in the political psychology study of Bar-Tal and Antebi (1992), Erdoğanist collective victimhood is accompanied by a 'siege mentality', the belief that the in-group is encircled by enemies and in existential need of self-defence (Bar-Tal and Antebi 1992; see now in detail Yilmaz 2021).

Thus, Erdoğan has been encouraging people to sacrifice their lives to protect the nation, Ummah and Islam against the conspiracies of these imagined existential enemies. For example, in August 2017, when addressing the crowds, he said that:

> With the inspiration we receive from our ancestors, we say with the highest tone that our voice can afford, coming from our hearts, you will not succeed. You will not be able to *divide our nation, lower our flag, silence our adhans, dismember our homeland, destroy our state*, strangle the voice of the righteousness and truth, or break the *last hope of the ummah*. As a nation that has *sacrificed so much blood for the sake of freedom and sacrificed many lives*, it is not appropriate to leave the square to these looters and

escape, is it? If necessary, are we ready for new Gallipolis, new 15 Julys on this path? Are we ready to defeat those who think they made us powerless and squeezed us into a corner? (BirGün 2017)

Like the Kemalists, Erdoğanists want to create their own myths, to re-write their own historical events and create their own symbols (Lüküslü 2016, 645). One of the important historical events used for restoratively nostalgic myth-creation is the annual celebration of the Battle of Manzikert in 1071 under the Seljuk Empire. On 26 August 2017, Erdoğan visited Manzikert (now Malazgirt), where he directed a celebration that had a nomadic aesthetic and official staff dressed in medieval style. Erdoğan tries to mark the importance of Muslim Turks' historical past and promotes himself as the successor to this history. In his speech during the Manzikert celebration on 26 August 2018, Erdoğan said 'the Battle of Manzikert foreshadowed the succeeding conquests of Bursa, Edirne, and Istanbul. He said the battle was the moment Turks emerged as a power in history and if Turkey forgets the spirit of Manzikert, it will lose its history and future' (Sabah 2018). According to Erdoğan, Turkey does not "have the luxury to display a moment of weakness... Vultures are always circling" (Sabah 2018). He also added that:

If Anatolia falls, Africa falls. The Caucasus falls. The Middle East falls. Central Asia falls... That's why we need to be strong in economy, diplomacy, military, industry and all relevant agencies and institutions. (Sabah 2018)

Using the glorification of the past, rewriting history and reconstruction of memory through commemorations have been widely used for nation-building (Gillis 1994; Nora and Kritzman 1997). Erdoğanists have been increasingly using this instrument since at least 2010 (Uzer 2018). Moreover, the previous narrative about Atatürk has been reconstructed from an Islamist perspective in which anti-Westernism is promoted in contrast to Kemalism's Westernism, and revolutionary reforms and Westernism is totally ignored. The new narrative focuses on Atatürk's Islamic characteristics, such as being a 'ghazi, an Islamic war hero'. This re-narration of Atatürk is pursued to accumulate greater powers into Erdoğan's hands (Alaranta 2016). He almost builds up his predecessor in his image, giving more weight to himself.

A new celebration that serves the Erdoğanist Turkish myth creation is the commemoration of 15 July as Democracy and National Unity Day. Erdoğan has tried to establish the 'July 15 Saga', as the myth that creates him as the new founding father of Turkey and the Turkish people above the military. As noted by Hoffman et al. (2018, 20), 15 July is the closest thing to a military victory Erdoğan has and this martial component is important, given many nationalist Turks' self-perception of Turkey as a military nation and the militaristic nature of Turkish history as taught in school curricula and presented in popular culture. Thus, through creating a myth around 15 July, Erdoğan is trying to bolster his 'legitimacy as the natural heir to Turkey's martial history, while elevating the people above the military, and secure hegemony over the country's dominant nationalist constituency' (Hoffman et al. 2018, 20).

Moreover, with this new myth, he is also trying to establish himself as the leader of the Muslim world, portraying himself as a Muslim warrior who fights with internal and external enemies of Islam and who protects Muslim minorities all over the world. On the fourth anniversary of the coup attempt on 15 July 2020, Erdoğan emphasized very strongly that:

> Whatever happened in Manzikert (1071) was on 15 July (2016). What happened in the Battle of Kosovo (1389), in the Battle of Nicopolis (1396) was on 15 July. What happened in the conquest of Istanbul (1453) was on 15 July. What happened in Gallipoli (1915), in the War of Independence (1919-1922) was on 15 July. In short, 15 July is the latest ring in the existential chain of struggles that we have been having in these lands. (Hurriyet 2020; Euronews 2020)

By referring to all these historical events, he is not only attempting to make sure that he is a hero like the leaders of these important wars, by selectively mentioning the Seljuk, Ottoman, and Turkish victories against the Christian states but omitting the victories against the Muslim Safavids or Mamluks, in a pure civilizational populist fashion, he is also implying that 15 July is about Muslims being attacked by the Crusader Christians.

Erdoğanists' Martyr-Icons

Like the use of the Menemen incident and the martyrdom of Kubilay, the failed coup of July 2016 and the martyrs of that night have been used by the Erdoğanists for myth building, legitimation, and justification for repression. Reminiscent of the Menemen incident for the Kemalist regime, in a live TV appearance, Erdoğan declared that the coup attempt was a 'gift from God [or God's grace]' that would help them to cleanse Turkey of enemies and terrorists from inside the state (Champion 2016). He also 'used many religious motifs, mentioning that those who participated in the coup were infidels (*kafir*), and that those who died trying to prevent it were martyrs' (Solomonovich 2021, 7).

Six days after the coup attempt, the AKP government declared a three-month state of emergency (SoE). This was more than the SoE prescribed in the Turkish constitution, in that it seriously violated even the most essential human rights and rule of law, such as *habeas corpus* and right to a fair trial including domestic remedies. During the SoE, with the resolution of the Council of Ministers headed by Erdoğan, a series of decrees were issued with the force of law. More than 160,000 government workers from the armed forces, the police, the judiciary, education, and media were purged while others were arrested or taken immediately into custody (Worley and Osborne 2016). The government added the designation 'purged' to the social security records of those that had been dismissed, making it impossible for them to find another job even in the private sector, essentially leading to lifelong deprivation or a civil death. More than 1,000 nongovernment organizations and 130 media outlets, including TV stations, newspapers, news agencies, radio stations, and publishers were disbanded or liquidated without any judicial proceedings (BBC 2016; See also the ninth paragraph of the memorandum published by Muižnieks 2016). The government also appointed trustees for municipalities in predominantly Kurdish-populated areas, replacing the democratically elected mayors that were members of the pro-Kurdish People's Democracy Party (*Halkların Demokartik Partisi*, HDP). Some of the deputies from the opposition CHP and the HDP were also taken into custody or arrested.

During the mysterious coup attempt, Erdoğan immediately called civilians to occupy city squares and airports to protest against the plotters. Soon, in response to Erdoğan's invitation, some members of the public tried to capture the Bosporus Bridge back from the soldiers, while others tried to occupy military bases in various cities. During these clashes, 251 civilians died and about 30 soldiers were either lynched to death or shot by unknown civilians. According to Erdoğan, the 251 martyrs of the coup attempt were Turkey's 'sun' because, 'in return for them', Erdoğan said 'we saved our future' (Sabah Daily 2017).

Among those martyrs, a sergeant, Ömer Halisdemir, became the initial paragon martyr of the AKP regime in its creating myth, in part due to his manner of death which has been personally praised by the highest echelons of the AKP and Erdoğan himself. For months, Halisdemir was vociferously propagated by the AKP media and government as the man 'who stopped the coup and saved the country' since he sacrificed himself, knowing he was going to be killed after he shot dead the 'coup plotter' Brig. Gen. Semih Terzi. It is claimed by the pro-AKP media and high-placed AKP members that if General Terzi had been able to take control of the Special Forces headquarters in Ankara the coup would have been successful.

Roughly 30 primary schools, high schools, and university campuses, and hundreds of streets, libraries, sport facilities, and city parks have since been renamed after Ömer Halisdemir (Gurcan 2016). In the four months after his death, a thousand new-born babies were named after him, and his grave became a pilgrimage site, which more than 300,000 people have visited (Gurcan 2016). It is recorded that in the second half of 2016, according to travel companies, Halisdemir's grave was among the most in-demand destinations in Turkey (Gurcan 2016). His name, his significance during the coup attempt, and the place where he was buried have been repetitively asked questions during the interviews in governor employments by the commission (T24 2017). Film producers from AKP circles documented Halisdemir's life in tragic and dramatic ways, such as in the pro-AKP filmmaker Mesut Genç's 'I, Omer', or pro-AKP and member of Menzil Naqshbandi religious community, Dursun Ali Erzincanlı's 'First Bullet, First Martyr: 30 Birds' (Gurcan 2016). Halisdemir's figure in depicting resistance is significant because it also has the additional role of legitimizing and drawing focus from radical jihadi groups organized by the AKP government, which also appeared on the night of the coup in Ankara and Istanbul.

However, the myth-making of July 15 around the exemplar of Halisdemir was not as clear-cut and complete as Kubilay. First, it has been revealed from the statements of soldiers and Terzi's wife that General Terzi did not die when Halisdemir shot him. Instead, as argued by Mrs. Terzi, who is a doctor that visited General Terzi that night at the hospital, he was mysteriously killed later at the hospital where he was taken. Later, it was argued that Halisdemir was on purge lists, since he had links with Gülenists, he was a Bylock user, a mobile application that was deemed as the strongest 'legal' evidence of having Gülenist ties, his children were going to Gülen-linked schools and he would have been declared a terrorist if he had survived (Duvar 2017). Also his family profile did not match with the profile of the AKP supporters, since it has been asserted that his family supports the CHP, and thus they did not accept any aid from the AKP after Halisdemir's death (Öztürk 2016).

Perhaps considering these shortcomings, the AKP attempted to bolster the martyr-icon narrative by creating additional martyr-icons. Several figures in addition to Halisdemir, such as Erol Olçok, and his son Abdullah Tayyip Olçok, have also been 'central to the narrative surrounding the coup attempt' (Hammond 2020). While not used as extensively as Halisdemir, they have also been constructed as martyr-icons by the AKP. What is more, in a surprisingly different political context, the AKP continued constructing martyr-icons. The case of Muhammed Fatih Safitürk is remarkable in this regard. Safitürk was newly appointed as a trustee governor for an HDP municipality in Derik, Mardin province, and he reportedly died during a PKK (Kurdistan Workers' Party) bombing in November 2016. His profile suggested he supported the AKP at this time. Moreover, he was killed during the intense clashes taking place because of the Kurdish struggle against the AKP over their incitement of nationalism-cum-Islamism, against the 'disbelieving' Kurdish PKK fighters, another important enemy for the AKP. At Safitürk's funeral ceremony, Erdoğan himself reminded attendees of the importance of martyrdom in Islam, reciting Qur'anic verses. Erdoğan said:

> Oh, my brothers! ... As recited in the Qur'anic verses, in the name of Allah, *kullu nafsin dhaiqat ul mawt thumma ilayna turjaoon* [Q 29:57], meaning we will return to God Himself. You know, martyrdom is the greatest of the ranks after the Prophethood. And we believe that our brother Muhammet Fatih is one of those who reached to that rank ... My dear brothers, I would like to clearly state that these soils are not ordinary soils. Martyrs have always gushed out from these soils ... This nation has given many martyrs for his land. (Milliyet 2016)

As in the case of Halisdemir, the AKP attempted to create a myth and collective memory by renaming schools and streets and increasing the visibility of the name Safitürk in the public sphere. Immediately following his death, for instance, about 30 schools, bus stops, social facilities, Qur'anic schools, libraries, and student dormitories were renamed as 'martyr governor Muhammet Fatih Safitürk' (Milliyet 2017).

Safitürk's other significance for the AKP was that his father, wearing gown and turban, was one of the vicegerents of the radical Islamist İsmailağa Naqshbandi community. Similar to other Naqshbandi communities, the community is known for its ultimate support for the AKP, and its close links with President Erdoğan (Erturk 2022a, b). Taking advantage of these facts, the AKP turned the 'martyrdom' into a political propaganda; Safitürk's father was invited to many AKP events following his son's death and shown as an exemplary martyr father. Quoting Erdoğan's favourite quatrain on the blood and flag, as reiterated by the father Safitürk at the funeral, AKP's deputy Minister Abdurrahim Boynukalın posted a tweet that eulogizes the father's way of embracing his son's martyrdom. Boynukalın defines the elder Safitürk as an ideal father who is 'wise and mature' enough in the face of embracing his son's death (Boynukalın 2016a). In another supportive Twitter post, Boynukalın eulogizes self-sacrifice and death by saying: 'May God predestine [martyrdom] for us as well. Let us be martyred, let us move from this earth. The world is not such a place to live for' (Boynukalın 2016b). The senior Safitürk has also been invited to many educational conferences and events organized by the National Ministry in various cities around Turkey to address youth and teachers on the importance of martyrdom and the homeland, during the government's military operations against the Kurdish people both in Turkish eastern cities and Northern Syria (T.C. Hizan Kaymakamlığı, n.d.; T.C. Geyve Kaymakamlığı 2017). To underscore the importance of Turkey's Olive Branch military operation in the Northern Syrian Kurdish provinces, for example, Safitürk, as an exemplar martyr father, resonated with the pro-AKP media, saying:

> We are sacrificing our children for the homeland. Not only our children, but also, we are ready to die, we are continuously ready to join to the front line. Owing to the fact that we sacrifice martyrs, we can easily perform our prayers [at mosques], we sleep at home, and walk in the downtown and the in the market. (AA 2017)

As in the case of Halisdemir, schools, streets, and official buildings were named after martyr Muhammet Fatih Safitürk. However, within two years, as trials of the coup suspects proceeded, some controversial news began to appear. For example, Safitürk's brother Ali Haydar Safitürk has said that he has deep suspicions that the police tampered with forensic evidence, casting doubt on the official narrative (Öztekin 2018). He also explained that his brother was knowingly and forcefully transferred to the wrong hospital department and then to a hospital in Gaziantep from Mardin under the command of the provincial governor after he was initially transferred to a hospital in Mardin, though the doctors did not want Safitürk to be transferred to another city (Milli Gazete 2020). Safitürk's brother lodged a complaint against the chief of police and the city governor. Brother Ali Haydar Safitürk later explained that he was 'threatened' with the removal of his brother Muhammet Fatih's official status of martyrdom unless he dropped his complaint about the chief of police (Evrensel 2020). Later it was also revealed that a journalist following the case was threatened and told to stop reporting on the trial (GazeteKarınca 2018).

CONCLUSION

The AKP uses the civilizational populist necropolitical martyrdom narrative to legitimize its rule and in particular its use of violence against 'enemies'. By turning the failed coup and the deaths of Halisdemir, and Safitürk, into a new national myth, Erdoğan and AKP were able to give new legitimacy to their authoritarian regime by framing their rule as the choice of the people and blessed by God and portraying the coupists as murderous criminals hated by God. By portraying all political opposition as accessories to the failed coup attempt Erdoğan is able to frame himself as the saviour and protector of the Turkish people and Muslim Ummah, further legitimizing his position as the leader of Turkey and the Muslim World. At the same time, the necropolitical martyrdom narrative allows the AKP to frame all its actions—including mass arrests and the intimidation of political opposition—as necessary to protect the causes that the martyrs' died protecting.

The lives and deaths of Halisdemir and Safitürk, alongside other stories of AKP approved martyrs, now appear in the Turkish school textbooks, in which the men are framed as admirable martyrs and defenders of Allah, Islam, democracy and the fatherland. By elevating these particular deaths to martyrdom events, the AKP is trying to consolidate, via a necropolitical use of martyrdom, a new foundational myth for the Turkish Republic and a powerful civilizational populist collective memory based on the events of 15 July 2016 to legitimize the Erdoğanist regime and justify its authoritarian Islamist rule. Ironically, despite their diametrically opposed imaginings of the Turkish state, both the Kemalists and

Erdoğanists have embraced necropolitics and martyrdom narratives to achieve political and discursive hegemony in Turkey.

REFERENCES

AA. 2017. 'Cumhurbaşkanı Erdoğan: Bizim Aradığımız Adalet, 250 Şehidimizin Kanıdır'. 20 June 2017. https://www.aa.com.tr/tr/gunun-basliklari/cumhur baskani-Erdoğan-bizim-aradigimiz-adalet-250-sehidimizin-kanidir/845777.

Akkoyunlu, Karabekir and Kerem Öktem. 2016. 'Existential Insecurity and the Making of a Weak Authoritarian Regime in Turkey.' *Southeast European and Black Sea Studies* 16 (4): 505–527.

Akyol, Mustafa. 2014. 'Turkey's Warring Personality Cults'. *Al Monitor*. 28 February 2014. https://www.al-monitor.com/pulse/originals/2014/02/tur key-personality-cult-war-erdogan-gulen.

Alaranta, Toni. 2016. 'Turkish Islamism and Nationalism Before and After the Failed Coup Attempt'. *Turkey Analyst*, 1 December. https://www.turkeyana lyst.org/publications/turkey-analyst-articles/item/569-turkish-islamism-and-nationalism-before-and-after-the-failed-coup-attempt.

Bar-Tal, Daniel and Dikla Antebi. 1992. 'Beliefs about Negative Intentions of the World: A Study of the Israeli Siege Mentality'. *Political Psychology* 13 (4): 633–645.

BBC. 2016a. 'Turkey Coup Attempt: Erdoğan Signals Death Penalty Return'. *BBC News*, 19 July 2016, sec. Europe. https://www.bbc.com/news/world-europe-36832071.

———. 2016b. 'Turkey Shuts More than 130 Media Outlets', 28 July 2016, sec. Europe. https://www.bbc.com/news/world-europe-36910556.

BirGün. 2017. https://www.birgun.net/haber/erdogan-yeni-15-temmuz-lara-var-miyiz-174499.

Boynukalın, Abdurrahim. 2016a. "O kadar mutmain ki.. 'Ne kadar ferasetli adam' demek bile garip geliyor insana. Biz kimiz ki kanaat bildiriyoruz böyle bir baba hakkında.." *Twitter*, November 11, 2016. https://www.turkeyana lyst.org/publications/turkey-analyst-articles/item/569-turkish-islamism-and-nationalism-before-and-after-the-failed-coup-attempt.

Boynukalın, Abdurrahim. 2016b. 'Rabbim bize de nasip etsin. Şehit olalım, göçelim bu dıyarlardan. Dunya yaşanılacak yer değil'. *Twitter*, November 11, 2016. https://twitter.com/A_Boynukalin/status/797001989959913472.

Champion, Mark. 2016. 'Coup Was "Gift From God" for Erdogan Planning a New Turkey'. *Bloomberg*, July 18, 2016. https://www.bloomberg.com/ news/articles/2016-07-17/coup-was-a-gift-from-god-says-erdogan-who-plans-a-new-turkey.

Çınar, Menderes. 2006. 'Turkey's Transformation Under AKP Rule'. *The Muslim World* 96 (2–3): 469–486.

3 MARTYRDOM IN THE ERDOĞANIST AKP'S POLITICS 65

Cizre, Ümit. 2008. 'Ideology, context and interest: The Turkish military'. In *The Cambridge History of Turkey*, ed. R. Kasaba, 301–332. Cambridge: Cambridge University Press.

Cizre, Ümit and Menderes Çınar. 2003. 'Turkey 2002: Kemalism, Islamism and Politics in the light of February 28 Process'. *The South Atlantic Quarterly* 102 (2–3): 309–332.

Cook, Steven A. 2017. *False Dawn: Protest, Democracy, and Violence in the New Middle East*. New York: Oxford University Press.

Duvar. 2017. '"Halisdemir Bylokçu" iddiası mahkemeyi karıştırdı'. Text. *Duvar*, May 6, 2017. https://www.gazeteduvar.com.tr/gundem/2017/06/05/hal isdemir-bylokcu-iddiasi-mahkemeyi-karistirdi.

Eligür, Banu. 2010. *The Mobilization of Political Islam in Turkey*. New York: Cambridge University Press.

Erdoğan, Recep Tayyip. 2020. *Türkiye Cumhuriyeti Cumhurbaşkanı Recep Tayyip Erdoğan Cumhurbaşkanlığı Kabinesi 2. Yıl Değerlendirme Toplantısı*. Ankara: TCBB. https://www.tccb.gov.tr/assets/dosya/kabine/kabine.pdf.

Erturk, Omer. 2022a. 'The Myth of Turkish Islam: The influence of Naqshbandi-Gümüşhanevi thought in Turkish Islamic orthodoxy'. *British Journal of Middle Eastern Studies*. https://doi.org/10.1080/13530194.2020.1782727.

Erturk, Omer. 2022b. 'Anatomy of political Islam in Republican Turkey: the Milli Görüş Movement as a legacy of Naqshbandism'. *Contemporary Islam* 16 (2–3): 295–320. https://doi.org/10.1007/s11562-022-00500-x.

Euronews. 2020. https://tr.euronews.com/2020/07/15/Erdogan-istanbul-un-fethinde-ne-olmussa-15-temmuz-da-o-oldu.

Evrensel. 2020. 'Kaymakam Fatih Safitürk'ün ağabeyi tehdit edildiğini açıkladı'. *Evrensel*, October 6, 2020. https://www.evrensel.net/haber/417322/kay makam-fatih-safiturkun-agabeyi-tehdit-edildigini-acikladi.

Gazete Karınca. 2018. 'Safitürk davasını haberleştiren gazeteci Nalin Öztekin tehdit edildi'. *Gazete Karınca* (blog), October 23, 2018. https://gazetekar inca.com/2018/10/safiturk-davasini-haberlestiren-gazeteci-nalin-oztekin-teh dit-edildi/.

Gillis, J. R. (ed.) 1994. *Commemorations: The Politics of National Identity*. Princeton, NJ: Princeton University Press.

Gurcan, Metin. 2016. 'Turning a True Turkish Hero into a Commodity'. *Al-Monitor*. November 10, 2016. https://www.al-monitor.com/pulse/origin als/2016/11/turkey-coup-attempt-turning-hero-commercial-commodity.

Gürsel, Kadri. 2014. 'The Cult of Erdoğan'. *Al Monitor*, 6 August 2014. https://www.al-monitor.com/pulse/fr/originals/2014/08/gursel-tur key-social-peace-erdogan-cult-polarization-akp.

Hammond, Timur. 2020. 'Making Memorial Publics: Media, Monuments, and the Politics of Commemoration Following Turkey's July 2016 Coup

66 I. YILMAZ AND O. ERTURK

Attempt'. *Geographical Review* 110 (4): 536–555. https://doi.org/10.1080/00167428.2019.1702429.

Hoffman, Max, Michael Werz, and John Halpin. 2018. *Turkey's 'New Nationalism' Amid Shifting Politics Further Analysis of Polling Results*. Washington, DC: Center for American Progress.

Hurriyet. 2020. https://www.hurriyetdailynews.com/Erdogan-urges-unity-for-strong-turkey-156586.

Kinnvall, Catarina. 2004. 'Globalization and Religious Nationalism: Self, Identity, and the Search for Ontological Security'. *Political Psychology* 25 (5): 741–767.

Lancaster, Caroline. 2014. 'The Iron Law of Erdoğan: The Decay from Intra-Party Democracy to Personalisti Rule'. *Third World Quarterly* 35 (9): 1672–1690.

Lüküslü, Demet. 2016. 'Creating a Pious Generation: Youth and Education Policies of AKP in Turkey'. *Southeast European and Black Sea Studies* 16 (4): 637–649.

Milli Gazete. 2020. 'Şehit Kaymakamın ağabeyinden flaş iddialar: İyileşecekti, vali...' *Milli Gazete*, October 6, 2020. https://www.milligazete.com.tr/haber/5575603/sehit-kaymakamin-agabeyinden-flas-iddialar-iyilesecekti-vali.

Milliyet. 2016. 'Şehit kaymakam Muhammed Fatih Safitürk son yolculuğuna uğurlandı'. *Milliyet*, November 2016. https://www.milliyet.com.tr/gundem/sehit-kaymakam-muhammed-fatih-safiturk-son-yolculuguna-ugurlandi-2343866.

Milliyet. 2017. 'Şehit Kaymakam Safitürk'ün Adı 30 İlde Yaşatılıyor'. *Milliyet*, 10 November 10 2017. https://www.milliyet.com.tr/yerel-haberler/sakarya/sehit-kaymakam-safiturkun-adi-30-ilde-yasatiliyor-12393721.

Muižnieks, Nils. 2016. 'Memorandum on the Human Rights Implications of the Measures Taken Under the State of Emergency in Turkey'. *Visit Memorandum. Strasbourg: Commissioner for Human Rights*, October 7, 2016. https://www.coe.int/en/web/commissioner/view/-/asset_publisher/ugj3i6qSEkhZ/content/the-commissioner-publishes-a-memorandum-on-the-human-rights-implications-of-the-emergency-measures-in-turkey.

Nora, P., and L. D. Kritzman. 1997. *Realms of Memory: The Construction of the French Past*. New York: Columbia University Press.

Özen, Hayriye. 2020. 'Reproducing "hegemony" Thereafter? The Long-term Political Effects of the Gezi Protests in Turkey'. *Southeast European and Black Sea Studies*. https://doi.org/10.1080/14683857.2020.1745417.

Özpek, Burak B., and Nebahat Tanriverdi Yaşar. 2018. 'Populism and Foreign Policy in Turkey Under AKP Rule'. *Turkish Studies* 19 (2): 198–216.

Öztekin, Nalin. 2018. 'Kaymakam Safitürk suikastinde önemli iddialar'. *Arti Gerçek*, October 15, 2018. https://artigercek.com/haberler/kaymakam-safiturk-suikastinde-onemli-iddialar.

Öztürk, Saygı. 2016. 'Ailesi de kahraman'. *Sözcü*, August 28, 2016. https://www.sozcu.com.tr/2016/gundem/ailesi-de-kahraman-1368049/.

Sabah. 2017. '250 şehidimiz bizim güneşlerimiz'. *Sabah*, 16 July 2017. https://www.sabah.com.tr/gundem/2017/07/16/sehidimiz-bizim-guneslerimiz.

Sabah. 2018. https://www.dailysabah.com/turkey/2018/08/26/Erdogan-top-officials-mark-947th-anniversary-of-battle-of-manzikert.

Sawae, Fumiko. 2020. 'Populism and the Politics of Belonging in Erdoğan's Turkey'. *Middle East Critique* 29 (3): 259–273.

Solomonovich, Nadav. 2021. '"Democracy and National Unity Day" in Turkey: The Invention of a New National Holiday'. *New Perspectives on Turkey*. January 15, 2021, 1–26.

T24. 2017. 'Erdoğan: Vatan için, istikbal için akıtılacak çok kanımız var; 16 Nisan bunun için çok önemli'. T24. 23 March 2017. https://t24.com.tr/haber/Erdoğan-vatan-icin-istikbal-icin-akitilacak-cok-kanimiz-var-16-nisan-bunun-icin-cok-onemli,395248.

Taş, Hakkı. 2014. 'Yeni Türkiye'nin yeni kültü'. *Radikal*, 27 April 2014. https://www.radikal.com.tr/radikal2/yeni-turkiyenin-yeni-kultu-1188716/.

Taş, Hakkı. 2015. 'Turkey—from Tutelary to Delegative Democracy'. *Third World Quarterly* 36 (4): 776–791.

T.C. Geyve Kaymakamlığı. 2017. 'GEDEP Projesi Kapsamında Asım Safitürk Hocamız Konferans Verdi'. *T.C. Geyve Kaymakamlığı*, 20 December 2017. https://geyve.gov.tr/gedep-projesi-kapsaminda-asim-safiturk-hocamiz-konferans-verdi.

T.C. Hizan Kaymakamlığı. n.d. 'Asım Safitürk İlçemizde Konferans Verdi'. *T.C. Hizan Kaymakamlığı*. n.d. Accessed 6 November 2020. https://www.hizan.gov.tr/asim-safiturk-ilcemizde-konferans-verdi.

Tuğal, Cihan. 2009. *Passive Revolution: Absorbing the Islamic Challenge to Capitalism*. Stanford: Stanford University Press.

Uzer, Umut. 2018. 'Glorification of the Past as a Political Tool: Ottoman History in Contemporary Turkish Politics'. *The Journal of the Middle East and Africa* 9 (4): 339–357.

Worley, Will, and Samuel Osborne. 'Erdogan Government Reasserts Itself as 2,700 Judges Purged—as It Happened'. *The Independent*. July 16, 2016. https://www.independent.co.uk/news/world/europe/turkey-coup-live-erdogan-dead-killed-istanbul-ankara-military-take-over-martial-law-latest-updates-a7140371.

Yıldız, Ahmet. 2003. 'Politico-Religious Discourse of Political Islam in Turkey: The Parties of National Outlook'. *Muslim World* 93 (3): 187–210.

Yilmaz, Ihsan. 2005. 'State, Law, Civil Society and Islam in Contemporary Turkey'. *Muslim World* 95 (3): 385–411.

Yılmaz, Ihsan. 2009. 'The Role of Liberalized Autocracy and Democratic Learning in Islamists' Transformation to Muslim Democrats in Turkey and Egypt'. *Insight Turkey* 11 (2): 93–112.

Yılmaz, Ihsan. 2018. 'Populism, Erdoğanism and Social Engineering Through Education in Turkey'. *Mediterranean Quarterly* 29 (4): 52–76.

Yılmaz, Ihsan. 2021. *Creating the Desired Citizen: Ideology, State and Islam in Turkey*. 1st ed. Cambridge University Press. https://doi.org/10.1017/978 1108961295.

Yilmaz, Ihsan and Erdoan Shipoli. 2022. 'Use of Past Collective Traumas, Fear and Conspiracy Theories for Securitization of the Opposition and Authoritarianisation: The Turkish case'. *Democratization* 29 (2): 320–336. https://doi.org/10.1080/13510347.2021.1953992.

Yilmaz, Ihsan and Omer Erturk. 2022. 'Authoritarianism and Necropolitical Creation of Martyr Icons by Kemalists and Erdoganists in Turkey'. *Turkish Studies* 23 (2): 243–260. https://doi.org/10.1080/14683849.2021. 1943662.

CHAPTER 4

Necropolitical Sermons

Introduction

Similar to the Kemalists, the AKP has given great importance to the Diyanet in its policies (Yilmaz 2021). The Diyanet's importance to the AKP is demonstrated in the scale of its funding and support by the AKP government. In 2020, according to a five-year plan, 2 billion USD were released to the Diyanet, and this sum will gradually increase to 2.6 billion USD by 2023 (Ahval 2019; Duran and Bellut 2019). This huge budget allowed the Diyanet to establish radio and television channels and thus expanded its sphere of influence. Furthermore, this new budget has provided for the Diyanet to deliver religious services outside mosques, for example, in state institutions such as hospitals, schools, prisons, retirement homes, and women's shelter (Duran and Bellut 2019). To support its activities, some 107,000 employees are on the payroll, across 36 countries and publications in 28 languages (Duran and Bellut 2019).

This mutual and symbiotic relationship between mosque and state reached new heights under the current radical Islamist Diyanet President Ali Erbaş and his predecessor Mehmet Görmez, who were appointed by President Erdoğan in 2017 and 2011, respectively. The Diyanet, because of the efforts of its recent Islamist presidents, is now deliberately and systematically at the AKP's service. In the hands of Görmez and Erbaş, this institute, in tune with AKP's civilizational populist and authoritarian policies, has been radicalized, becoming exclusivist and divisive

© The Author(s), under exclusive license to Springer Nature Singapore Pte Ltd. 2023
I. Yilmaz and O. Erturk, *Populism, Authoritarianism and Necropolitics*,
https://doi.org/10.1007/978-981-19-8292-7_4

69

(see for instance, Öztürk 2016; Yilmaz and Barry 2020; Ongur 2020; Yilmaz and Albayrak 2022). In line with its increasing autocratization, the AKP has resorted to civilizational populist necropolitical use of death and martyrdom in the political and Islamist context in order to suppress, intimidate, and ward off its opponents (Yilmaz and Erturk 2021a, b; Yilmaz and Erturk 2022).

In this chapter, we subject Diyanet sermons to qualitative content and discourse analysis. Though Friday sermons are delivered orally (read verbatim from the centrally written text) in mosques in Turkish, they are also posted on the Diyanet's official website. Thus, the research in the present chapter is based on textual sources of Diyanet sermons gathered from its official website. We conducted content analysis for sermons, focusing on the use of militarism, jihad, and martyrdom (sacrificing one's life for 'religious' values such as religion, Allah, ummah, and the homeland).

The chapter proceeds as follows. First, before moving on to the analysis of necropolitics in the Friday sermons, we will briefly discuss the importance of the Diyanet for the Turkish state and explain the Friday sermons. This will be followed by our analysis of primary data: the weekly Friday sermon texts since the early 2010s when AKP's autocratization started and its Islamism became obvious, focusing especially the post-2016 coup attempt period. The empirical analysis section has three interrelated sections: militarism, jihadism, and Islamist glorification of martyrdom in the Friday sermons.

Militarism in the Friday Sermons from Kemalist to Erdoğanist Times

Despite the secularist claims of the state, the Turkish state and national identity have always been fused with Islamic identity. In fact, Islam was institutionalized in a government agency at the birth of the republic and integrated into the government structure with the Directorate of Religious Affairs (the Diyanet) (Yilmaz 2005, Muslim World journal). This continued an Ottoman state strategy, in which the sultan's authority subordinated to the clergy's authority (Toprak 1981; Berkes 1998; Bein 2011). The Diyanet has a prominent place in the constitutions of 1924, 1961, and 1982. The current constitution, from 1982, mentions the Diyanet in Article 136, stating that it functions in accordance with the principle of secularism, stays out of all political discussions, and works towards fostering national solidarity and unity. The main task of the Diyanet was 'to control and to shape Islam in accordance with the needs of the secular nation-state to the effect of creating a secular, modern, national, and official Islam' (Yilmaz 2005, 389).

Friday sermons play a significant role in the Diyanet's dissemination of the pro-state religio-political message. In Islam, Friday prayer, unlike other prayers, is a congregational prayer, obligatory for every adult male and can be only performed at the mosques and together with the congregation. The Friday sermon (*khutbah*) lasts about 15 minutes and is a crucial part of the Friday prayer. According to a catechism published by the Diyanet, speaking to each other, looking around, or not listening to the sermon is *makruh* (reprehensible) (Karagöz and Altuntaş 2011). Besides the sermons' contribution to people's religious and moral life, many political leaders have a fundamental understanding of the socio-political dimension of the sermons. This aspect of sermons has encouraged many leaders to unite the people around their policies with the help of powerful sermons, in the form of 'speech acts'. For this reason, it has been common for caliphs throughout history to ask religious officials to read sermons on their behalf and pray for their health, leadership, and power at the end of each sermon in Muslim majority regions (Baktır 1998, 426). About 60 per cent of Turkish adult males attend Friday prayers (AA 2014). The Diyanet centrally prepares 54 sermon texts every year, for the 52 weeks plus two religious festival sermons. These are delivered in Diyanet-controlled mosques, which now number around 90,000 in Turkey plus the many thousands abroad in Turkish diaspora communities, especially Western democracies (Yilmaz and Albayrak 2021; Yilmaz and Albayrak 2022; Yilmaz et al. 2022).

Historically the Diyanet has been no stranger to the army. The institution was formed by the Kemalists, who were the military guarantors of secularism in Turkey. Previously, the military was referred to using the word 'Mehmetçik', which is attributed a religious meaning (i.e. the little Muhammad), rather than with the word 'army', in both sermons and general discourse. However, this has changed as the army has come under the control and guardianship of the AKP in recent years.

Having entered the orbit of the AKP government after 2010, the Diyanet has gradually become politicized and has not been shy of embracing the militarization efforts of its patron political party. The earliest examples of the Diyanet embracing the AKP's militaristic narrative can be seen when it transformed from an institution that played an active role in the solution of the Kurdish problem and rejected securitized approaches to the issue, to an institution that glorified war and martyrdom (Yilmaz and Erturk 2021b). In line with growing authoritarianism that gained momentum after the Syrian civil war erupted in 2011, the AKP's corruption and bribery scandal in 2013, the suspension of the Kurdish peace process in 2015, and the failed coup attempt in July 2016, the Diyanet was converted into a machine that would justify any wrongdoing and backsliding of the government.

Before 2015, sermons read on occasions such as Victory Day (August 30) and Martyrs' Day (March 18), examined notions of nationalist and militarist rhetoric in a positive manner, with little to do with conspiracy theories. In these sermons, heroism and Turkish nationalism prevailed, with 'saint ancestors' mentioned and a focus on 'obstacles will be overcome' as long as 'the spirit of Çanakkale' is kept alive by 'taking lessons from the past' (14 March 2014; 13 March 2013).[1] The importance of understanding 'the role of belief and spirit behind the victories' and having 'faith and submission' was also a focus of the sermons (14 March 2014).

In parallel with the increasing autocratic policies, bellicose and combative political discourse of the AKP, the Diyanet has increasingly adopted militaristic and aggressive Islamist terminologies in its sermons. The sermons seek sacrifice from the nation and prepare the audience for duty. Particularly the post-2015 sermons are directed towards AKP's perceived antagonists. But this was already evident before 2015, a sermon close to Victory Day in 2014 emphasized that it is the duty of current generations to 'protect the homeland they have entrusted by previous generations to hand them over to the next generations' by 'shedding their blood' (29 August 2014).

Significantly after 2016, the Diyanet sermons create a sense of fear and urgency among the congregation when they talk about 'a new war of independence' being a 'matter of survival' against 'the enemy'. This enemy—which includes pro-Kurdish politicians, Gülenists, and the opposing political parties, mainly the Republican People's Party (CHP)— is designated by the AKP and is otherized and demonized by the government. These notions have been conveyed in many Friday sermons.

---

[1] In our research, we will be giving only dates of the related sermons in parentheses. Diyanet's sermon archive can be found at the link below: https://dinhizmetleri.diyanet. gov.tr/kategoriler/yayinlarimiz/hutbeler/hutbe-ar%C5%9Fivi.

We see that some military concepts that had been used within the Kemalist context changed into Islamic as well. As of 2014, the term '*Mehmetçik*', which had been traditionally used to define Turkish soldiers, gained an Islamist character as it was being linked to the ummah at the macro level. For example, the sermon delivered on 14 March 2014, defines *Mehmetçik* as the 'common name' of the Islamic army, irrespective of their race, place, or colour. In line with this shift in the Diyanet, Erdoğan also defined the Turkish Army as the 'Muhamedan army' in his October 2019 Twitter, which he posted in the Arabic language. Since 2019, it has been declared that Turkish soldiers have the duty to emancipate all the oppressed nations from suppressors, appointing a sort of private international mission to the Turkish Army. For example, in the sermon delivered on 25 October 2019, following the Peace Spring military campaign, *Mehmetçik* were spoken as:

> On the front for the good to prevail in the world and for the sake of humanity. [...] they are rushing and struggling, [...] for the oppressed and the victimized who are deprived of their rights and freedoms.

In the same vein, the sermon delivered on 11 October 2019 states that

> [we] will fight for diminishing the evil and for establishing the good on earth [and] our nation will continue to be the remedy for the remediless people, be there for those people who has nobody by their side and be the hope and safe haven for the victimized and the refugees.

Similarly, another sermon, delivered on 28 February 2020, entitled 'Our Fight, and Spirit of Unity and Solidarity in the Cause of Allah', says:

> Our soldiers have been and will always be standing by the oppressed against the oppressors. They are at the battlefronts for the good of the world and shield their chests for humanity. They are mobilized to rush to help of those whose rights are infringed and removed from them.

Sermons have not only increased the frequency of mentioning the army but have begun to glorify its sacrifices. In one sermon, as an example of the merits of Mehmetçik it was proclaimed:

> While running from front to the front, he sometimes leaves a leg, sometimes an arm, sometimes an eye behind; but always keeps the love of the homeland in the front. 'Long live homeland!' he would say, 'As long as

74   I. YILMAZ AND O. ERTURK

the homeland is secure [I am ready to lay down my life for]'! (25 October 2019)

Surrounded and engulfed in 'the ring of fire' is the army, according to the Diyanet, that defends the people and their faith. The growing AKP-led military presence is thus rationalized as a necessary step for Turkey to ensure its safety, while it masks Ankara's growing expansionist and irredentist ambitions.

Overall, the Diyanet's sermons have increasingly employed a heavy militaristic language, as the Turkish Army has become subordinate to the AKP and been a part of its Islamist policies after the 15 July 2016 coup attempt. In the next part, we will scrutinize how jihadism has been used in sermons since the AKP regime's militaristic shift.

JIHADISM IN FRIDAY SERMONS

Perhaps one of the most important indicators of the change and transformation that the Diyanet has experienced in recent years has been the use of the controversial concept of *jihad*, which is open to different interpretations. In the past, under the surveillance of the Kemalist army, the guarantor of secularism, it was ensured that jihad was not widely espoused by congregations. The concept of jihad was not commonly invoked and when it was used, it meant the Sufistic inner spiritual struggle and self-discipline. Only in the Diyanet's recent repositioning in compliance with Turkey's authoritarian government has it adopted a bellicose concept of *jihad* and included it in the official discourse.

This controversial Islamic term, jihad, epistemologically and literally means 'struggle', or more broadly, to achieve something on the path of God (Özel 1993, 527). However, the term has also been interpreted as a fight or battle, traditionally and historically, by the Islamic jurisprudence. Over the course of time, the term has been split into two, *jihad al-akbar* (greater fight), meaning inner struggle against the self, and *jihad al-asghar* (lesser fight), meaning to fight against disbelievers. It is still a debated question whether jihad, in an armed sense, is defensive or offensive (Bukay 2008, 77–99; Sabbaghchi 2014). Outside of these debates, in the context of Sufi Islam, which has been considered the backbone of Turkish Islamic understanding since the eleventh century, it is asserted that the term jihad is mostly taken as a peaceful, spiritual, and moral ethos, of Islam: to fight with the self (Erturk 2022). According to Sufi ethos, inner struggle is the 'greater jihad', and a true Muslim should discipline and criticize himself (*ana, nafs*) first, rather than impose jihad or judgement on others (Sonbol 2009, 297).

Following the 2010 constitutional referendum, in which Erdoğan freed himself from the Kemalist 'threat', the Diyanet began to use the term jihad in the offensive and emancipatory context, rather than spiritual or defensive, as discussed above. For instance, the sermon delivered on 18 March 2016 says:

> Our hero ancestors sacrificed their blood and their lives for God and Islam. They defended the oneness of God, the honour of Islam and the dignity of Muslims.

Previously, rather than God, Islam, and ummah, only the nation and homeland would have been emphasized in sermons about sacrificing lives. Unlike under the Kemalists, the Diyanet sermons delivered during the post-coup Erdoğanist era contain civilizational populist, revisionist and irredentist character, together with a transnational use of jihad. This is much clearer in the examples of the Friday and Eid sermons delivered amid the increased Islamist rhetoric of Erdoğan and the AKP, during military operations such as in Syria and Azerbaijan, or freeing Quds, which is accompanied by anti-Semitic discourse.

In these sermons, Turkish Muslims are addressed as the 'the hope of the oppressed', and Turkey is defined as 'the home (refuge/ safe haven) of the miserable' (14 May 2021). Additionally, the sermon underlines the significance of Quds (Jerusalem) and Masjid al-Aqsa, wanting all Muslims around the world to strive to protect such places under occupation. This transnational use of jihad using the example of Quds was also seen in the Eid al-Fitr sermon in 2021, delivered by the head of Diyanet, Ali Erbaş, holding a sword in his hand in the pulpit as a sign of jihad and conquest during the sermon. Erbaş said:

> The issue of al-Quds is a shared issue that concerns not only Palestinians, but also all Muslims [...] For the sake of this Eid morning, may Allah the Almighty (swt) grant salvation to all oppressed people, and all victimized people forced out of their homes and lands. May He (swt) enable us to strengthen our spirit of being ummah and of brotherhood in faith. May He (swt) enable us to see true days of Eid when al-Quds, the Masjid al-Aqsa, and all Islamic lands and places under occupation can freely celebrate. (13 May 2021)

In the same manner, the term jihad has been defined and propagated as an armed conflict by the Diyanet as of 2016. A sermon entitled 'Jihad: The Struggle in Allah's Cause with One's Life and Wealth' on 16 February 2018, was issued following the Afrin Military Operation in Syria. In these sermons, we see that the peaceful and violent use of jihad was combined as one jihad. For instance, though the sermon begins with the peaceful explanation of jihad, that is striving 'against his own soul', it finishes with the explanation of the external, armed jihad, which is underscored as the 'true meaning of jihad'. The sermon declared that 'the highest level of the jihad is the armed struggle'. The sermon sees the Turkish Army's Afrin Military Operation as a matter of life and death for Turkish Muslims and subliminally defines Muslim majority Kurdish people living in Afrin as 'enemies of Islam':

> If a believer succeeds in the jihad with one's own should, then s/he will succeed in the jihad against the enemies of Islam as well. [...] Today, we are striving with our lives and our wealth for existence as a nation. [...] We all have our responsibilities in this struggle for survival [...] O Allah! Grant victory to our heroic army who has been fighting for our independence and our future, for our unity and solidarity. (16 February 2018)

In the same fashion, the sermon entitled 'For Our Soldiers (Mehmetçik) are All Our Prayers' delivered on 25 October 2019, is a good example of an irredentist and transnational use of jihad. The sermon was addressing the Turkish Army's 'Peace Spring' military campaign, defining it as a jihad that would emancipate the oppressed Muslims from the disbelievers. The sermon starts with a *hadith* (sayings of the Prophet), underlining the need to carry jihad on the path and the cause of Allah, in an armed manner, then continues:

> Mehmetçik has hit the road once again [...]. To bring peace to those victimized by terrorism, to bring tranquillity to those at unease, to lighten those whose hearts are in flames [...]Mehmetçik rewrites the history with his sweat and blood. Along the borders he protects, not only is our homeland safe, but also the fate of humanity is saved from chaos. (25 October 2019)

The head of the Diyanet, Ali Erbaş, preached this same sermon while on a trip to the southern Hatay province where he met with military officials coordinating the assault on the US-backed Kurdish People's Protection

Units (YPG) in Afrin, who also fought against the ISIS in the region (Diken 2018). Also, during an opening ceremony of a Qur'anic School, Ali Erbaş reportedly said,

> I beg God's mercy and grace for our martyrs, and I beg God that our veterans heal very soon. We are opening Qur'anic Schools. They continue *jihad* over there and we do here, too. (Diken 2018)

A month later, on 16 March 2018, there was another Diyanet sermon on *jihad* and fighting, at the commemoration of the War of Gallipoli. The title of the sermon distributed nationwide was 'Our Nation's Struggle for Existence: The Victory of Çanakkale'. Amid the Afrin operation debates and the excessive politicization of martyrdom, the sermon opens with a Qur'anic verse and a hadith that underscores the importance of *jihad*,

> Our Almighty Lord enjoins: Those who [...] were harmed in my cause or fought or were killed – I will surely remove from them their misdeeds, and I will surely admit them to gardens beneath which rivers flow as reward from Allah.

The Hadith transmitted in the same sermon reads:

> Allah guarantees to the person who carries out *Jihad* for His Cause and to confirm the *Kalimah al-Tawhid* that He will either admit him into Paradise or return him with his reward or the booty he was earned to his residence from where he went out. (16 March 2018)

The actions of the Turkish Army, including its various operations in Syria, sanctioned by the AKP, are increasingly being presented in sermons as holy war waged by Turkey. To introduce this concept of *jihad*, which is highly controversial and open to different interpretation, the Diyanet had to step in. The concept of jihad has found an increasingly secure place both in supportive statements of Ali Erbaş, the current President of the Diyanet, in regard to operations in Syria, and in relevant Diyanet sermons. The mosque's presence in this political arena clearly shows that Turkey, facing the repercussions of the Syrian crisis and being driven into the vortex of this crisis, activated this concept of *jihad* as a political move. The AKP government has been criticized for its strategy since the beginning of the Syrian crisis. In recent years, Turkey's presence, and the rationality of Turkey's operations in Syria has been questioned by the public. In the face of these questions, the regime has been in search of ways to legitimize its policies and tried to convince the Turkish people of the rationality of its policies. In this context, the narrative of *jihad* has played an important role in conveying the message, both domestically and abroad, that the Turkish Army is in *jihad* against 'those who pursue mischief and corruption' and 'tyranny'. Showing the operations of the Turkish Army as equivalent to *jihad*, one of the sermon reads as follows:

> Today, as a nation, we are fighting for survival with our lives and property. Our *Mehmetçik* shows once again to the whole world that we can sacrifice our existence for the sake of our faith, our flag, and our homeland. (16 February 2018)

The deaths of 33 members of the Turkish Army from an attack by the Syrian Arab Army during Operation Peace Spring and Idlib operation in 2020, which were launched by the Turkish Army to create a safe zone in northern Syria, were explained to the public using the concept of *jihad*. During this period, in relation to the operations in Syria, the message given to the public from the pulpits was that the Turkish Army launched these operations not only to protect the people of Turkey from attacks and threats, but also, to deliver peace to the regions that are overwhelmed by terrorism, to be the hope of those innocents whose hope are consumed, and to deliver peace to those aggrieved ones whose peace has been abducted. (28 February 2020).

In addition, with the start of Operation Peace Spring, the *surah* Al Fath from the Qur'an (meaning 'Victory', chapter 48 of the Qur'an, with 29 verses) was read after the morning prayer in all mosques, and prayers were said for the Turkish Army. Erbaş, as head of the Diyanet, performed the morning prayer in Ankara, defending the operation with the words:

> Against the plans of the cruel and tyrannical forces that attempted to occupy every corner of the Islamic world, the peace of the nation and the region, the establishment of peace and security, the honour of the ummah.

After the Idlib attack in Syria, again, the concept of *jihad* was used in the sermon in response to indignant questioning by the public. The following Friday, Erbaş led prayer and delivered the sermon in Hatay, the border city of Turkey with Syria. In the sermon, Erbaş again described the cross-border operations of the Turkish Army using the concept of *jihad*:

Our Mehmetçik, by following the call of our Prophet, who says 'do Jihad with your hands, your tongues and your possessions,' says 'stop' to the shameless raid of the enemy...Mehmetçik, who set out on an expedition to deliver peace to the geographies tired of terrorism, hope to the innocents whose hope was consumed, and peace to the aggrieved ones whose peace was lost. (28 February 2020)

To summarize, the Diyanet's emphasis on jihad, in line with the AKP's civilizational populism and aggressive policies abroad, has shifted from national to a transnational and global level, as seen in the sermons. The Turkish Army's military operations have been defined as jihad for the first time in Diyanet's history. Additionally, the sermons' use of jihad—which means struggle—has been taken more radically, as an armed fight, and defined as one of the essential tenets of the Turkish Army in its current role.

MARTYRDOM IN FRIDAY SERMONS

In line with the autocratization of the AKP as of 2015, when it lost its majority in the general elections, we see that the use of necropolitics to consolidate support and deflect attention from public issues has also evolved and matured. In the hey-day of the Kurdish 'peace process', both the AKP government and the Diyanet arguably strived to ensure that concepts such as martyrdom were not glorified, with the then-famous slogan of the AKP at the time, 'Don't let mothers cry anymore!' This slogan clearly referred to the mothers of martyrs (Turkish soldiers killed by the PKK) and killed members of the outlawed PKK. So, while trying not to intimidate its conservative and mildly nationalist base, the AKP propagated themes of unity, togetherness, tolerance, and cohabitation as it maintained dialogue with Kurdish parties including the HDP and PKK. Erdoğan, during this phase, stressed the importance of 'the peace process' by referring to the mistakes of former governments, hailing the prospect of fully resolving the Kurdish issue by the end of the process, while pursuing the Muslim Democratic model. In this regard, arguably the most notable statement of Erdoğan was about martyrdom. In 2012, Erdoğan tweeted: 'A logic of accepting and swallowing a certain number of martyrdoms every year is neither humanistic nor conscientious', amid mounting criticism by extreme nationalists of 'the peace process' (Bir

Gun 2020). This statement is in deep contrast to more recent necropolitical attitudes of the party's leadership regarding the sacrificial endurance of the nation.

During the AKP's peace process period, martyrdom was not a popular subject in Friday sermons. Between 2010 and 2015, very few sermons referred to martyrdom, including those preached on 18 March, Martyrs' Day, and August 30, Victory Day. However, martyrdom has become one of the most striking and recurring themes of the Diyanet sermons since 2015. While martyrdom had been used in many sermons in the context of wishing God's mercy for all ancestors and martyrs, as a show of gratitude from current generations, the intensity of references to martyrdom in sermons over recent years points to a shift in the sermon's discourse.

As will be seen in the following examples taken from sermons over the past decade, the use of the martyrdom narrative has been transformed, from a phenomenon that should be avoided, to a precious and glorified status that every honourable and patriotic citizen should seek and desire. The AKP has promoted necropolitics through this marriage between martyrdom and its glorification (Yilmaz and Erturk 2021a, b; Yilmaz and Erturk 2022). The use of martyrdom in sermons and politics has two aims: it not only glorifies self-sacrifice, but also addresses opposition inside and outside the country as traitors and disbelievers that must be fought. Thus, in essence, the AKP and Diyanet coalition has been determining 'who may live and who must die', the necropolitics's core definition (Mbembe 2003, 11; 2019, 66), while at the same time using the narrative 'for the production of collective memory' (Bargu 2019, 17).

As the political environment in Turkey has become harsher and security issues once again came to occupy centre stage of the political agenda after the collapse of 'the peace process' in the aftermath of the June 2015 elections, the Diyanet repositioned itself vis-à-vis the new reality and, since then, coverage of martyrdom has also proliferated. Not only has the Diyanet's embraced this theme as the new normal in Turkey, but it also shifted rhetoric in sermons towards more a nationalist, civilizational populist and conservative discourse, mirroring the AKP's transformation in this period. The Diyanet joined AKP in promoting martyrdom as not only an inevitable cost that the nation must bear to protect is independence and sovereignty in the face of mounting civilizational attacks from 'the external forces' that 'employ various plans and traps against the nation's survival, independence, and future', but also a phenomenon that must be embraced and appreciated for the sake of security and well-being of the homeland (*vatan*), Ummah and religion.

The sermons usually praise the uniqueness of Turkey and Turks, who not only 'sacrificed their lives and irrigated this territory with their blood' to render it homeland, without blinking, and but also constituted 'the last hope' of the Muslim world. The sermons then exalt the sacrifices of 'the noble nation (*Necip millet*)' today:

> As a nation, we passed through great troubles and heavy tests. Just yesterday in Çanakkale, Sakarya, and Dumlupınar, the remorseless powers that lost their mercy and humanity came to us to wipe us from the stage of history. We were subjected to one of the biggest betrayals of our history on July 15th. We had tremendous strength that made us victorious in these difficult days. This power was our unwavering faith in God. It was our love for homeland, adhan, flag and independence. It was our love for Martyrdom and veteran. (26 January 2018)

Citing the civilizational 'challenges and threats' this 'noble nation' has been facing recently, this sermon continued:

> We live without food and water, when necessary, but we never compromise our freedom and independence, and dignity. We cover our bodies for the sake of our sacredness, but we do not give up even an inch of our homeland. (26 January 2018)

However, according to the sermons, martyrdom is a religious obligation as much as a patriotic duty. Usually, sermons promoting martyrdom begin by referring to Qur'anic verses and *hadiths* and then stressing its religious imperative. A sermon preached on 18 March, Martyrs' Day, defined martyrdom as a divine status:

> Martyrdom is such an exalted place that it was praised by our Lord and desired by our Prophet. Martyrdom is to reveal its existence so that right, truth, and justice prevail on earth. It is to witness goodness and peace in the face of evil and cruelty. The reward of this martyrdom is honour in the life of this world and heaven in the hereafter. (16 March 2018)

Furthermore, the glorification of martyrdom is not confined to exalting the sacrifices, courage, or glories of former generations, or to highlighting what martyrdom corresponds to in Islam. The term 'martyr' has also been traditionally 'sweetened' to associate it with something that arouses a desirable taste in the subconsciousness of people (Yilmaz and Erturk 2021a). In many sermons, martyrdom is coupled with '*sherbet*', a sweet Turkish drink, in order not to let martyrdom evoke a negative meaning like loss of life. In one sermon, for example, this rhetoric was re-visited while explaining what homeland means:

> Homeland is a sacred trust left to us by those who sacrificed their lives, their loved ones and all their wealth and drink martyrdom [*sherbet*], and those who give up their existence and become veterans. (30 August 2019)

'Drinking sherbet of martyrdom' was mentioned in 10 sermons between 2014 and 2020. As of 2011, it is now seen as vital to learn and teach the significance of martyrdom in sermons. For instance, it was said that 'we must explain the heroism and sacrifices of our martyrs and veterans to our children and teach the value of our cherished homeland and our lofty values' (18 March 2011). In the same vein, another sermon says:

> It is a fact that those who cannot grasp the spirit of martyrdom and veteranship are doomed to remain in captivity of the enemies. Next generations must be introduced to this spirit and raised with this spirit. (16 March 2012)

In the same fashion, as mentioned above, the use of martyrdom in politics and sermons simultaneously plays another role in line with Mbembe's essential formulization of necropolitics: it spreads fear into opposition circles inside and outside the country, targeting those who must be fought and killed. For instance, Erdoğan, addressing the main opposition party CHP's Kemal Kılıçdaroğlu—in a manner reminiscent of Mustafa Kemal's order to his soldiers in the real battlefield 'I order you to die'—stated 'there will be no heads on their shoulders' following the Spring Shield military operation in Syria (Yeni Şafak 2020). Then, Erdoğan addressed the leader of the opposition with his first name and implied that he is not even a Muslim:

> O Mr. Kemal! We have given these martyrs in Uhud, Khandaq (the Prophet Muhammad's battles) [...] and will continue to give them from now on. But you don't know what martyrdom is and what it is to be a martyr. It is impossible for you to comprehend this!

The Diyanet sermons also often invoke praise for the courage and heroism of Husayin, the grandson of the Prophet, who is usually referred to as Master (*sayyid*) of the martyrs, and his companions who drank 'sherbet of martyrdom', and their martyrdom has also been interpreted as sacrifice for the sake of religion and sacred values (23 October 2015). Although martyrdom is mentioned in the national context in these sermons, it is implied that all martyrs sacrifice their lives for the same values and purposes, thereby making a connection between nationalist and *ummatic* discourse (6 September 2019).

The loss of civilian lives in the mysterious 2016 coup attempt in Turkey brought a new meaning to the notion of martyrdom in the Friday sermons. The 15 July coup attempt, and notions of martyrdom helped the AKP to renew the allegiance of its base and strengthen its grip on public institutions, including the Diyanet. This unwritten allegiance could constitute a new model of engagement in which the transformation of emotion is produced both in the individual and in societal consciousness. In this understanding, the martyrs of 15 July are alive. The resistance against this coup attempt is immortalized in religious, cultural, and social terms by the government and in Friday sermons, while the bond between the normal citizen and the AKP government has deepened (Taş 2018). The coup attempts and the notion of martyrdom, which is increasingly found in the memory of every demographic of Turkish society, has become the site of symbolic immortality in the collective consciousness. The glorious pages of Turkish history, like the Battle of Manzikert, battles of Sakarya and Dumlupınar, and Turkish War of Independence, even the battles of the Prophet Muhammad that have led the course of Islamic history (such as Badr and Uḥud) are increasingly being understood in relation to 15 July. The sermon preached on the first anniversary of the 15 July coup attempt, mentioned these 'historic turning points' as the occasions when it became apparent God was helping Turkey and then stated that the nation witnessed God's help on July 15 too (14 July 2017).

In another example, we see that martyrdom has become a motive and propagation in the sermon delivered on 28 February 2020, the anniversary of so-called Kemalist soft coup staged in 1997, 'It is the desire to fall martyr in the cause of Allah or live on as a veteran that we have deep in our hearts' (28 February 2020).

In line with Erdoğan's heavy martyrdom discourse as of 15 July 2016, and particularly since 2017 (Kurdish operations), and claims that there would be more martyrs and blood, we simultaneously see these sentiments reflected in the Diyanet sermons, with the use of martyrdom and self-sacrifice within Islamist civilizational populist discourse (T24 2018). For the first time since at least 2010, dying for the state and becoming a martyr has appeared in the March 2019 sermon quoted above. The March 2019 sermon has another novelty. Previously, martyrdom was mentioned in reference to the past. Younger generations were emphasized, but only in the context of teaching them the spirit of martyrdom. As of 2019, the sermons have started using martyrdom in the prospective context, rather than retrospective one. In 2019, for the first time, the sermon stated that, if need be, there will be many more martyrs:

> In case of a necessity, many souls shall pass away for such sake; however, no impure hand shall be able to touch upon what is sacred for us. Those who have designs against damaging the unity and solidarity of our nation, in servitude to Allah only, shall never be able to succeed. (15 March 2019)

This message was strengthened in the 11 October 2019 sermon:

> Those who set their eyes on our homeland, every inch of which is watered by the blood of our noble martyrs, and who aim to scatter our nation are doomed to lose today, too, just as in the past. (11 October 2019)

Similarly, we see that martyrdom and sacrificing oneself has become a daily motif, and a reality in the sermons, which has been mostly integrated with a siege mentality, that puts Turkey, Islamic civilization and the 'Islamic world' on the brick of existential attack by 'infidels'. For instance, the sermon delivered on 11 October 2019 notes that 'the world today was turned into a place full of dark and evil traps' and '[t]hose who plan to dig pits of fire in all around the Islamic world have used weapons of sedition, terrorism, and betrayal to cause brothers to hit one another'. And the one delivered on 28 February 2020 preaches:

> We as a nation are facing great challenges and going through heavy tests today [...] We will not let anybody pull our national flag down the post, silent our adhans, or tread on our homeland. [...] It is the desire to fall martyr in the cause of Allah or live on as a veteran that we have deep in our hearts. [...] Allah the Almighty gives the good news to those who, with this great love, have sacrificed their lives in this cause.

We see that martyrdom, together with a siege mentality, and paradoxically *i'la kalimatillah*, an Islamic goal or principle whose aim is to promote and disseminate the words of Allah, has begun to be used in the sermons. The sermon delivered on 15 March 2019 says that glorifying and disseminating Islamic belief and making it dominant in the world is significant, together with *shahadah*, 'which is the base of religion'. The sermon continues by stating that 'in case of a necessity, many souls shall pass away for such sake'.

Like the use of jihad, martyrdom has gained a transnational Islamist civilizational populist character, elevated from the micro to the macro level, in line with Erdoğan's caliphal dreams and the political-Islamist idealization of Erdoğan. For example, the sermon entitled 'The Turkish Victory of the Battle of Gallipoli and the Esprit de Corps', delivered on 15 March 2019 says:

> The martyrdom [...] is one of the most supreme positions since a martyr takes the risk of abandoning all such beloved ones as his mother, father, wife, and children for the sake of religion, homeland, nation, state, and freedom.

Overall, the empirical evidence shows that the radical use of martyrdom both inside and outside the country in both Islamist civilizational populist and nationalist senses has been employed by the Diyanet sermons, simultaneous with the AKP's and Erdoğan's increasing civilizational populism, authoritarianism and intensive rhetoric on martyrdom.

CONCLUSION

Diyanet, long a tool of the Turkish state, has devolved into a client of the AKP, which acts as its patron. The Directorate has been increasingly instrumentalized by AKP over the two decades of its rule, but especially after the party's authoritarian turn in the 2010s. The role of Diyanet in contemporary AKP ruled Turkey is to propagandize on behalf of the regime. Because the party uses Islamist civilizational populist martyrdom narratives, Diyanet has increasingly encouraged Turkish people to view martyrdom in a positive light and praised those who supposedly martyred themselves in the name of God, religion and the state. Through its religious authority, Diyanet sermons quote Islamic literature praising martyrdom, and use it to frame the deaths of Turkish soldiers in Syria as a somewhat positive event, insofar as the dead willingly sacrificed themselves for their nation and religion and should therefore be commemorated.

In this chapter we conducted content analysis on the Diyanet's Friday sermons to see how necropolitical use of militarism, jihadism, and martyrdom, which already existed during the secularist Kemalist Diyanet era, have been heavily used by the Islamist civilizational populist AKP government. The analysis shows that there has been a dramatic shift from micro national level to the macro transnational level with the use of Islamic values such as jihad and martyrdom, and even the military through the re-definition of the *Mehmetçik* as a transnational army of Islam.

The findings show that jihadism has become a commonplace notion in Diyanet sermons, where it is used to encourage the Turkish people to perceive the world around them through an Islamist civilizational populist lens in which the enemies of Islam are persistently attacking Muslims, whose duty is to defend their religion and homeland, as well as the other Muslim majority lands. This positive portrayal of violent jihad is part of the global ambitions of the AKP regime, which encourages Turkish people to feel pride in their history and in their ancestors, who fought for Islam, and sacrificed themselves for God and Islam. As part of this narrative, Turkish people who died performing armed Jihad are praised in Diyanet sermons, and Turkish people are encouraged to imitate the jihadis. At the same time, Diyanet sermons encourage congregants to perceive Turkey's military action in Syria as part of a jihad, and therefore as a praiseworthy and noble enterprise against the enemies of Turkey and Islam. This kind of jihad, previously considered the lesser form, is increasingly portrayed as the highest level of jihad in Diyanet sermons to normalize death in the service of the regime and portray it as an honour. Once death in the service of the regime is framed in this manner, it becomes possible to portray all deaths of soldiers during the AKP's military actions as righteous and holy deaths, rather than as evidence that the regime is pursuing a foolish and dangerous path in its military interventions.

Diyanet emphasizes the afterlife and its rewards as part of its encouragement of jihadism and martyrdom. Indeed, martyrdom is claimed to be something very sweet in sermons, in order to both portray death in the service of the nation and Islam (though in reality the AKP) as desirable, but also to persuade the broader public that they should not hold the Turkish government responsible when Turkish soldiers are killed in Syria or in other conflicts, but should rather praise and envy the soldiers for seeking and achieving martyrdom. This is part of the AKP regime's civilizational populist necropolitics, in which death is to be welcomed if it occurs as part of jihad, and thus in defence of Islam, the Muslim World, Allah and not just the homeland. Diyanet portrays death in this manner to protect its patron—the AKP—and advance its Islamist civilizational populist agenda. The directorate also attempts to normalize death to protect its patron from criticism over its failure to protect its own soldiers or civilians, and thus frames all deaths caused in part or whole by the AKP government as 'glorious' and the dead as 'martyrs'.

In a pure Islamist civilizational populist fashion, the Diyanet's martyrdom narratives posit that the world is divided into good Muslims and their enemies, who pose an existential threat and who therefore must be fought—even if it means the death of an individual. Therefore, glory is given to those who die for Turkey and God, and they will be rewarded in the next life. While most necropolitics is about giving death to enemies and preserving the lives of the 'good people', the AKP's necropolitics, insofar as it is promulgated in Diyanet sermons, is based around the notion that not merely do the enemies of God and Turkey deserve death, but to die in the name of Turkey and Islam is the highest honour, and that the dead will be rewarded in the next life and remembered by future generations on Earth.

The empirical evidence derived from the sermons shows that, under the rule of the AKP, the use of militaristic elements, jihad, and martyrdom have gained significant emancipatory, irredentist, revisionist, and Islamist civilizational populist meanings since 2015. The role and status of the Turkish Army has also been Islamized in Diyanet sermons and has become an important part of the AKP's jihad and necropolitical narratives.

REFERENCES

AA. 2014. *'Türkiye'de Dini Hayat Araştırması'*. 15 July 2014. https://www.aa. com.tr/tr/yasam/turkiyede-dini-hayat-arastirmasi/141424.

Ahval. 2019. "Turkey's top religious body to spend $11 billion by 2023." *Ahval.* December 29, 2019. https://ahvalnews.com/directorate-religious-affairs/tur keys-top-religious-body-spend-11-billion-2023.

Baktır, Mustafa. 1998. *Hutbe, Türkiye Diyanet Vakfı İslam Ansiklopedisi*, Volume XVIII. İstanbul: Diyanet Vakfı.

Bargu, Banu. ed. 2019. *Turkey's Necropolitical Laboratory: Democracy, Violence and Resistance*. Edinburgh: Edinburgh University Press.

88   I. YILMAZ AND O. ERTURK

Bein, Amit. 2011. *Ottoman Ulema, Turkish Republic: Agents of Change and Guardians of Tradition*. First edition. Stanford, California: Stanford University Press.

Berkes, Niyazi. 1998. *The Development of Secularism in Turkey*. London: Hurst.

Bir Gun. 2020. 'Erdoğan contradicted his words 7 years ago.' *Bin Gun*. Mar. 4, 2020. https://www.birgun.net/haber/Erdoğan-7-yil-onceki-sozleriyle-cel isti-290451?__cf_chl_captcha_tk.

Bukay, David. 2008. *From Muhammad to Bin Laden: Religious and Ideological Sources of the Homicide Bombers Phenomenon*. New Brunswick, N.J: Transaction Publishers.

Diken. 2018. 'Diyanet'e göre Afrin harekatı 'cihat''. *Diken*. Jan. 29, 2018. http://www.diken.com.tr/diyanete-gore-afrin-harekati-cihat/.

Duran, E. Aram, and Bellut, Daniel. 2019. 'Diyanet: The Turkish religious authority that makes millions'. *DW*. September 20, 2019. https://www.dw.com/en/diyanet-the-turkish-religious-authority-that-makes-millions/a-505 17590.

Erturk, Omer. 2022. 'The Myth of Turkish Islam: the influence of Naqshbandi-Gümüşhanevi thought in Turkish Islamic orthodoxy'. *British Journal of Middle Eastern Studies* 49 (2): 223–247. https://doi.org/10.1080/135 30194.2020.1782727.

Karagöz, İsmail, and Halil Altuntaş. 2011. *Namaz İlmihali*. Fourth edition. Ankara: DİB Yayınları. https://diniyayinlar.diyanet.gov.tr/Docume nts/namaz-ilmihali.pdf.

Mbembe, Achille. 2003. 'Necropolitics'. Translated by Libby Meintjes. *Public Culture* 15 (1): 11–40.

———. 2019. *Necropolitics*. Translated by Steve Corcoran. Durham: Duke University Press.

Ongur, Ö. Hakan. 2020. 'Performing through Friday khutbas: Re-instrumentalization of Religion in the New Turkey.' *Third World Quarterly* 41 (3): 434–452.

Özel, Ahmet. 1993. 'Cihad'. In *TDV İslâmAnsiklopedisi*, 7: 527–31. Ankara: TDV İslâm Araştırmaları Merkezi.

Öztürk, Ahmet Erdi. 2016. 'Turkey's Diyanet under AKP Rule: From Protector to Imposer of State Ideology?' *Southeast European and Black Sea Studies* 16 (4): 619–635.

Sabbaghchi, Yahya. 2014. 'Starting a War: Advised or Forbidden? An Islamic Viewpoint'. In *The Changing Places and Faces of War*, edited by Sarah A. Wagner and Peter Mario Kreuter, 137–54. BRILL. https://doi.org/10. 1163/9781848882966_008.

Sonbol, Amira. 2009. 'Norms of War in Sunni Islam'. In *World Religions and Norms of War*, edited by VesselinPopovski, Gregory M. Reichberg, and Nicholas Turner, 282–302. Tokyo, Japan; New York: United Nations University Press.

Taş, Hakkı. 2018. 'The 15 July abortive coup and post-truth politics in Turkey.' *Southeast European and Black Sea Studies* 18 (1): 1–19. https://doi.org/10.1080/14683857.2018.1452374.

Toprak, Binnaz. 1981. *Islam and Political Development in Turkey.* Leiden: Brill.

T24. 2018. 'Erdoğan'dan "Kan dökülmesin" diyenlere tepki: Ne diyorsun sen ya, bu süreçte gazi de olur, kan da olur!'. *T24.* 21 January 2018. https://t24.com.tr/haber/Erdoğandan-kan-dokulmesin-diyenlere-tepki-ne-diyorsun-sen-ya-bu-surecte-gazi-de-olur-kan-da-olur,541028.

Yeni Şafak. 2020. 'Cumhurbaşkanı Erdoğan: Omuzların üzerinde baş kalmayacak'. Yeni Şafak. 2 March 2020. https://www.yenisafak.com/gundem/cumhurbaskani-Erdoğan-konusuyor-3527852.

Yilmaz, Ihsan. 2005. 'State, Law, Civil Society and Islam in Contemporary Turkey'. *Muslim World* 95 (3): 385–411.

Yilmaz, Ihsan. 2021. *Creating the Desired Citizen: Ideology, State and Islam in Turkey.* Cambridge and New York: Cambridge University Press.

Yilmaz, Ihsan, and James Barry. 2020. 'Instrumentalizing Islam in a "Secular" State: Turkey's Diyanet and Interfaith Dialogue'. *Journal of Balkan and Near Eastern Studies* 22 (1): 1–16. https://doi.org/10.1080/19448953.2018.1506301.

Yilmaz, Ihsan, and Ismail Albayrak. 2021. 'Religion as an Authoritarian Securitization and Violence Legitimation Tool: The Erdoğanist Diyanet's Framing of a Religious Movement as an Existential Threat'. *Religions* 12 (8): 574. https://doi.org/10.3390/rel12080574.

Yilmaz, Ihsan and Ismail Albayrak. 2022. *Populist and Pro-Violence State Religion: The Diyanet's Construction of Erdoğanist Islam in Turkey.* Singapore: Palgrave Macmillan.

Yilmaz, Ihsan, Ismail Albayrak, and Omer Erturk. 2022. 'Use of Religion in Blame Avoidance in a Competitive Authoritarian Regime: Turkish Directorate of Religious Affairs (Diyanet)'. *Religions* 13 (10): 876. https://doi.org/10.3390/rel13100876.

Yilmaz, Ihsan, and Omer Erturk. 2021a. 'Populism, Violence and Authoritarian Stability: Necropolitics in Turkey'. *Third World Quarterly* 42 (7): 1524–1543. https://doi.org/10.1080/01436597.2021.1896965.

Yilmaz, Ihsan, and Omer Erturk. 2021b. 'Pro-Violence Sermons of a Secular State: Turkey's Diyanet on Islamist Militarism, Jihadism and Glorification of Martyrdom'. *Religions.* https://doi.org/10.3390/rel12080659.

Yilmaz, Ihsan, and Omer Erturk. 2022. 'Authoritarianism and Necropolitical Creation of Martyr Icons by the Kemalists and Erdoganists in Turkey'. *Turkish Studies.* https://doi.org/10.1080/14683849.2021.1943662.

CHAPTER 5

The Use of TV Series for Civilizational Populist Necropolitical Propaganda

INTRODUCTION

As well-known, the mass media is a vital site of hegemonic struggle (Hall 1980; Herman and Chomsky 1988; Harvey 2005). There is a rich literature showing how television dramas have been exploited by nation-states in constructing their national identities (see for instance, Yoshimi 2003; Abu-Lughod 2005; and Porto 2011). Governments in Turkey too have tried to make use of media for their ideological programme and political agenda. However, none of them was as direct, bold, and interventionist as the AKP governments. Most people in Turkey watch and trust TVs and like the print press, and the AKP dominates the TVs.

According to a representative survey undertaken in April–May 2018 by the state's Radio and Television Supreme Council (Radyo ve Televizyon Üst Kurulu, RTÜK) on television watching trends, 69.2 per cent of the respondents trust television, 62.3 per cent of them the press, 62.2 per cent the radio, 59.1 per cent the internet news sites and 53.7 per cent trust social media as a news source (RTÜK 2018, 79). Average daily television viewing time is 3 hours 34 minutes (RTÜK 2018, 13). 86.7 per cent regularly watch television (RTÜK 2018, 93). The most watched programme type is 'the news' with average 24 days per month followed by 'native TV series' with an average of 15 days per month (RTÜK 2018, 53). 19.7 per cent state that their favourite TV channel is the pro-government ATV channel run by Erdoğan's son-in-law's brother. This is

© The Author(s), under exclusive license to Springer Nature
Singapore Pte Ltd. 2023
I. Yilmaz and O. Erturk, *Populism, Authoritarianism and Necropolitics*,
https://doi.org/10.1007/978-981-19-8292-7_5

91

followed by the fully partisan state TV, TRT with 17.5 per cent. Independent Fox TV is the favourite of only 14.3 of the respondents (RTÜK 2018, 52).

In this chapter, the TV series either produced by the AKP-controlled media or strongly supported by the AKP, Diriliş: Ertuğrul (Resurrection: Ertuğrul, 2014, TRT), Payitaht: Abdulhamid (TRT 2017), İsimsizler (The Nameless, 2017, Kanal D), Mehmetçik Kutül-Amare (TRT 2018) will be examined in terms of revealing how Islamist civilizational populist necropolitical propaganda has been implemented by the AKP regime. The time frame of this research is between 2011 and 2022.

The State's Use of TV Series from Kemalist to Erdoğanist Times

The AKP has increasingly used TV to propagate a populist, moralistic, and somewhat pastoral portrait of the socio-cultural imagery of Turkey's conservative hegemony (Emre-Çetin 2014, 2465; Coşar and Onbaşı 2016, 218). After the 2007 general elections, the AKP has started promoting a conservative religious, pro-AKP media bloc, and taming mainstream media outlets (Özçetin 2019a, 246; Özçetin 2019b; Yilmaz 2021).

The AKP realized that historical and/or political dramas produced by the Kemalists, leftists and secularists who have dominated the cultural sphere and filmmaking have been influencing people's interpretation of current socio-political events. The use of TV series as a political instrument began before the AKP came to power. The first one was a production named Deli Yürek (Crazy Heart) in 1998 (113 episodes). It was followed by Kurtlar Vadisi (Valley of the Wolves) (97 episodes) in 2003.

Having become quite popular among the society, thorough these fictive and quite conspiratorial content, people from all walks of life, even in the academic milieus, began speculatively believing that they began to learn actual political developments, carefully hidden by the corrupt elites, from these TV series.

The political and international events which the episodes handle were mostly interpreted by mainly the right-wing Kemalist nationalists from the point of national security and military. The essential theme in these series was that the truth was beyond what the news on the TV and the newspapers presenting to the Turkish community. These series were largely interpreting the politics and security over the conspiratorial and highly nationalistic views, frequently inspiring the audience that Turkey, as a most important country, had been prevented from being a wealthy and powerful state by some of the dark powers and their shadowy elements who infiltrated through the state apparatuses, mostly the security, intelligence, and business. The narrative went on to allege that these corrupt elites had been operating clandestinely on the account of their foreign, non-Turkish, and non-Muslim patrons. This theme, actually, has dominated the Turkish politics almost since the beginning of the Tanzimat, when the Ottoman state decided to adopt modernization in the 1800s.

In the second decade of its rule since 2011, the Justice and Development Party (Adalet ve Kalkınma Partisi, AKP) has decided to build on the Kemalist path by using the TV series for ideological and political propaganda by taking advantage of the media. This is quite the similar methodology and tactics adopted by the AKP in transformation of Diyanet that has helped the Islamist AKP's implementation of its political will, as clearly defined in the previous chapter.

These TV series mostly include necropolitical images such as martial, brutal, and bloody fighting or sacrificing scenes abundantly to increase their impact on the viewers, to stimulate their heroic, nationalists, and religious senses. Together with nationalist and militarist themes, which had been full of necropolitical images, and which had already become popular by the dramas such as *Deli Yürek* and *Kurtlar Vadisi*, the AKP reshaped this trend by inoculating Islamist, neo-Ottomanist and jihadi themes. In recent years, the AKP-controlled, state-owned television station, TRT, has produced TV series such as *Filinta*, *Diriliş Ertuğrul* (*Resurrection Ertuğrul*), *Bir Zamanlar Osmanlı* (*Once Upon a Time: The Ottoman Empire*), *Osmanlı Tokadı* (*The Ottoman Smack*), *Osmanlı'da Derin Devlet* (*Deep State in the Ottoman Empire*), *Kutül-Amare*, *Mehmetçik* and *Payitaht: Abdulhamid* (*The Last Emperor*). Other pro-AKP TV channels also have produced similar historical and political TV series such as *İsimsizler*, *Teşkilat*, *Alparslan: Buyuk Selcuklu*, *Seddulbahir 32 Saat*, *Uyanış Büyük Selcuklu*, *Yüz Yıllık Mühür: Genç Kahramanlar*, *Yüz Yıllık Mühür: Kadın Kahramanlar*, *Yüz Yıllık Mühür: Gayrı Müslim Kahramanlar*, *Kınalı Kuzular*, *Ya İstiklal Ya Ölüm*, and *Kızıl Elma*. All these also propagate the AKP's civilizational populist necropolitics of martyrdom, jihad, murder, and violence.

These TV shows have been directed to engage with Turkey's Ottoman roots, glorify the Ottoman emperors, and promote Ottoman cultural

94   I. YILMAZ AND O. ERTURK

heritage (Carney 2014, 2018, 2019). Through these series, the AKP reinforces the restorative nostalgia for the Ottoman Empire and the anti-Western political discourse. The main narrative of these historical drama series, 'the overarching theme of foreign plots, internal and external enemies of the Ottoman Empire, fits well with Turkey's contemporary political discourse that they too have enemies' (Çevik 2019, 237). Among them, *Diriliş Ertuğrul* (*Resurrection Ertuğrul*) seems to have been the most influential one and has been heavily promoted by the AKP, including its leader Erdoğan (Yilmaz 2021).

In his public speeches, Erdoğan has repeatedly underlined the importance of these TV series to teach the new generations the true history of the Turks and encourages the nation to watch them. When talking to an audience in which the Resurrection producers, director, and cast were present, Erdoğan referred to an incident at an award ceremony that when presenting the award to the Resurrection, a famous TV talk show programme presenter said that he had never watched the series and he will never watch:

> There is an African proverb that I love so much, 'Unless the lions write their own stories, we have to listen to the heroic stories of the hunters.' Therefore, lions will continue to write their own stories. Don't worry about them commenting like that, keep on going. *This nation* has embraced you. Does it matter if *they* (the White Turks, the corrupt elite) embrace you or not? (Sozcu 2016).

On another occasion he made clear his Islamist civilizational understanding of these TV series:

> To know history, you should watch the Abdulhamit the Last Emperor. The conspiracies against Sultan Abdulhamid exist in the present day. There is a Western plot against Turkey, and it is only the actors and the time that have changed… The Resurrection will, God willing, give the youth a new spirit. (Hurriyet 2017; Erdoğan 2017).

The TV Series as a Means of Necropolitical Re-Production

AKP-sponsored TV series are playing the most important role in the making of civilizational populist glorification of death and the mythicizing of martyrdom. Via TV series project, the politicized Islamist lexicons such as martyrdom, jihad, or tawhid (oneness), ornamented with nationalist and Ottomanist discourse, are being infiltrated directly into the houses, met families. Tawhid normally means having belief in the oneness of God. However, in Islamist terminology, it politically extended to the social level meaning that no place for diversity, pluralism, or opposition. These post-truth series in which the jihadi fighting and war scenes are abundant are used to make the Turkish society aware of ummah and nation (millet) consciousness, and martyrdom and jihad.

The media has been dominated 90 per cent by the AKP after 2016 by means of these series and the audience is being accessed in one way or another, exposed to heavy bombardment of necropolitical slogans, scenes, and engineering. AKP uses these series as a means of 'political technology', more than entertainment, or more than the series about the knowledge of the history. The AKP is trying to produce social support for its dominantly nationalist-conservative-authoritarian politics, through the newly fictitious interpretations of the past events (Sinanoğlu 2017). By the term 'siege mentality', AKP government is trying to instil that Turkish, Islamic community, is under attack by the enemies, who aim to divide and destroy the country by toppling Erdoğan as illustrated in the TV series (Sinanoğlu 2017). One of the main themes of the series' scenarios is that the 'infidels' are currently at work, trying to operate the same scenarios in Turkey, as occurred in history many times, trying to topple Erdoğan and conquest 'our' lands, just as what they had done to Ertuğrul Bey, the founder of the Ottoman Empire, or to Sultan Abdulhamid in the past or what their offspring have been doing over the last a few decades during the reign of the AKP government. These series are suggested by Erdoğan himself to Turkish society. Erdoğan frequently asks his audience if they watch and get informed from those series by stating that 'Turkey is fulfilling a sacred destiny under his presidency, returning to its historical role as a regional leader and global power' (Armstrong 2017). Erdoğan and high echelons of the AKP often reinterpret the political events by referring to those series, and thus build a bridge between fiction and non-fiction according to their own interests.

Blended with Islamism, the series 'express the idea that Turkey has a unique mission as the heir of a great empire' (Armstrong 2017), the sole and true heir of Caliphate in the Muslim world. During the party rallies, Erdoğan frequently slips into his favourite poems, which do not exceed two or three in total. He constantly reiterates some of the quotes from

96   I. YILMAZ AND O. ERTURK

those poems, and those lines also take place in the TV series. One of them is Yahya Kemal's civilizationalist poem 'August 26, 1922':

> The storm breaking out right now is the Turkish Army, oh God
> This is the army *dying* on the path of You, oh God .
> In order to raise your true name with the *adhan* [call to prayer]
> Make them victorious, for this is the last army of Islam.

Erdoğan's other favourite poem is 'Soldier's Pray'. Erdoğan was also jailed for four months in 1999 and banned from holding political office after reciting the following quartet of the poem (Matthews 2002). The part that Erdoğan recited, reads as follows: 'The minarets are our bayonets/The domes are our helmets/The mosques are our barracks/The believers are our soldiers, Allahu Aqbar.'

These TV series are also used to legitimate Turkey's expansionist military operations accross the border. For instance, a TV series Mehmetçik Kut'ül Amare began to broadcast on 18 January 2018, on state-run TRT-1 channel. Given the theme and the timing of the series, it is understood that it is aimed to provide legitimacy to Afrin Olive Branch military operation for the Turkish Army in Southern Syria against the Syrian Kurdish people, started two days after the series, on January 20. Before the broadcast, the trailer of the series had been shown nearly for two months repetitively in TRT channels. The Siege of Kut'ül Amare was between the Ottoman Empire and the British/Indian forces in Iraqi lands in 1916, which ended with the temporary victory of the Ottoman Empire. However, the siege in question was firstly politicized for civilizational populist necropolitical purposes by the AKP government in April 2016, and its 100th anniversary was officially celebrated. With the then-prime minister Ahmet Davutoğlu's statement, 'the Kut'ül Amare spirit' will not be forgotten once more until the doomsday, and 'we will act suitable with the memoirs of our martyrs and the honour of our homeland, which was remoulded with the blood' (Davutoğlu 2016). The series helps to consolidate the necropolitical frame built by the AKP. During the series, trailer, broadcast for two months, Erdoğan's famous poetic reference, that is 'minarets are bayonets' poem, which made him a downtrodden and a hero before his base, is vociferously recited by the Ottoman army in an inciting manner. The prominent quotes from the series showing the necropolitical references are as follows:

Ottoman commander: our mission is difficult. Our dreams are great. Either we win, or we die![1]
Ottoman Soldier: Your order sir!
(Back voice: The fate charges different missions to each generation. From now on, we should tightly prepare ourselves for the campaign)
Ottoman commander: if we are not betrayed from inside, we will be victorious of this battle.
Another Ottoman soldier: I am ready to give up my right of freedom for the future of the Islamic lands, Turan soils. I am among the ones who think that martyrdom is an honour on this path. While we are defeating their armies at the fronts, you shall wage fight within their cities as well. The only Islamic free country is the land of Ottoman Empire on this earth. If it falls, the world ends for the whole Muslims.

The trial ends with the voice of an Ottoman soldier, who make the battalion repeat after him the 'minarets are our bayonets' quartet, in which all the soldiers shout Allahu Aqbar, Allahu Aqbar at the end (TRT 2017).

As seen in the excerpt, the nationalistic images such as Turan (Turkish utopia to create a unified Turkic empire), and Islamic ones such as Islamic country, Islamic land, etc., synthesized as successfully done in the other series. However, in his speeches and rallies, Erdoğan only takes the issue to a fully Islamist civilizational populist and jihadi manner, rather than nationalist or Kemalist context. For instance, before the above-mentioned military operation, Erdoğan announces that by 'Olive' they mean the God's promise in the Qur'an 95:1–3 for the Muslims given the fact that the region they operated in Syria is full of olive trees. Erdoğan interprets the verse in question as a sign and legitimacy from God for his military campaign against Kurdish people of Afrin in Syria, who are Muslim majority. Citing the related verse 'I call to witness fig and the olive', Erdoğan says: 'I call to witness the olive that we will finish them off' (Erdoğan 2018). What is more, Diyanet has somehow religiously approved Erdoğan's statement stating that 'Erdoğan showed his determination by pointing Quranic verse of 95:1', through its TV channel named TRT Diyanet (TRT-DİYANET 2018).

---

[1] This is one of the mottos of Erdoğan he repetitively recites in his speeches. (@RT_Erdoğan July 13, 2017, 11:30 https://twitter.com/RT_Erdoğan).

The idealized martyr characters, as mentioned above, are also found in those TV series. The Nameless (*İsimsizler*), broadcasted in Kanal D, pro-AKP TV channel, is a good example, which is supervised by some of the pro-AKP veterans (Kanal D 2017). The setting of the Nameless is seemingly built upon the story of 'an ideal martyr' Muhammet Fatih Safitürk, a governor appointed as a trustee by the AKP who was later killed. The Nameless is produced by ES production, which also produced other pro-AKP Ottomanist TV series like Payitaht Abdülhamit or the Filinta. Unlike other above-stated TV series, The Nameless takes place in the Southeastern part of Anatolia between the Turkish special elite forces and the Kurdish 'terrorists' in real time. In the story, the protagonist character, Fatih, is a young and successful diplomat candidate, who was voluntarily selected to be appointed in place of former governor of 'Virankaya', martyred by the terrorists. As a patriotic and Muslim character, Fatih's aim with his staff is to fight and unmask the 'invisible enemies' and the 'puppets' in the region, who are being supported by 'external powers' indeed (Kanal D 2017). Fatih's prayer in the sixth episode swiftly became viral on social media. During the prayer, Fatih's team of police elite forces perform the *salaat* altogether just before their operation against the 'terrorists' and Fatih appeals to God which he ends in a prayer:

> Oh Lord...There are the ones wanting to silence Your adhan. They are using innocent people as human shields. Then, we have come here to offer our bodies as shields to those innocent people. We have loaded our guns with our faith, instead of bullets, in order not to let our homeland crushed under the feet of the villain, and in order to guard the heir of our ancestors, who shed blood on it. We effaced our names, identity disks and our ego. We accepted our names as Mehmet, Mehmetçik because of our Prophet. For the sake of Him, please help us... If we die, may our graves be gardens of heaven. We came together for the sake of Your love, then please hold our hands... Let us beat their plans, lies, and snakes. Those present in front of You will begin to attack soon in order to raise our flag and our adhan once more again. In order to raise your true name with the adhan [call to prayer] /Make them victorious, for this is the last army of Islam. The friends and foes know us like this. We are the army of Islam.

The above Islamist civilizational excerpt best illustrates how people are idealized shifting from human beings into a sort of military robotic clusters while erasing their names, identities, and souls in line with the political preferences of the current political regime of the AKP. In another episode, The Nameless draws a role model mother who lost his beloved son during the operations on the issue of how a martyrdom should be embraced, interpreted, and how it is a boastful ever on the earth for the family indeed. During one of the operations in the Eastern part of Turkey, one of Fatih's friends, Ersan, lost his life and he had already written a letter to be handed to his mother in case he lost his life. While the coffin of the 'martyr' standing wrapped with a Turkish flag in front of his mother, the letter is delivered, and mother begins to read in tears:

> Mom... Don't you tell me that I died. God says: do not call a martyr as a dead. Do not say that my Ersan is dead. Tell them that he went to sleep with his head on the lap of the Prophet. Tell them that he became a companion to [Prophet's grandson] Husayn. Tell them that he will meet with his grandfather who died in the Gallipoli campaign. But do not say that he died. Be proud of me, mom! Tell them that he coloured the crimson flag with his blood... Remember me whenever you see the flags! Do not cry after me!... Whenever you remember me, do not tell that wish he were alive now. Say long live my country mom!

Thereupon, the mother says loudly 'long live my country!' Meanwhile, as usual in the Turkish official funeral ceremony, Chopin's death march plays, a Kemalist secularist tradition that the Islamists have always resented. However, in the middle of the march, the friends of Ersan begin to call Islamic takbir, Allahu Aqbar, together, suppressing and silencing the official 'Western' death march. The letter of the martyr scene of The Nameless is meticulously thought and prepared for the civilizational populist necropolitical indoctrination and glorification of martyrdom, eulogized by the AKP government in today's Turkey.

There is another slogan from The Nameless, which went viral on social media as well as among the youth. It is the charismatic police elite force named Dayı's (Uncle) statement, 'We just point the gun, and Allah pulls the trigger'. In the series, the will of God and the will of the AKP government overlap with each other against the opposition, which is sketched as the civilizational threat, terrorists, traitors, or the puppets of the foreign hostile powers such as the Crusader Christian Western World. Beyond the TV series plot, this belief, identification of God's will with that of AKP's political will, has become a real motif in the police force and military. During the operations conducted in Syria and Eastern provinces, the official guards tied on their arms green bands on which was written a

Qur'anic verse: 'In fact, it was not you who killed them, it was Allah Who killed them', Al-Anfal 17. In her article, Tuğçe Madayanti from Birgün daily states that the Nameless has been solely planned to glorify death and make it attractive to the Turkish youth. She states that the facts and the fiction have been consciously mixed in the series and it directly aims to manipulate the followers' political and cultural behaviours (Madayanti 2017). For example, Madayanti states, by Virankaya, a fictitious place in the setting, reminds Viranşehir, Cizre, Sur, or Nusaybin, in which mostly pro-HDP Kurdish people live (Madayanti 2017). According to Madayanti, even the enemy names in the TV series connotate the names of the HDP deputies (Madayanti 2017).

There are also other TV dramas such as Teşkilat, the Organisation, which fully employs necropolitics (TRT 1 2022). Teskilat is subtitled as 'The story of those who died before they died', which has a canonical connotation: Muslims believe Prophet Muhammad to have said: 'die before you die'.

The high echelons of the AKP government, ministers, and Erdoğan himself visit the sets of the aforementioned TV series and pose with the actors and actresses to aggrandize the effect of these series on the AKP base. However, these TV series also affected the non-AKP voters as well. As stated above, Erdoğan strongly propagates these TV series in his rallies, and strongly advises in his speeches to the youth to watch these TV series to learn the truth and the history. Erdoğan points 'The Last Emperor' (*Payitaht: Abdulhamid*) (2017) TV series as an example, in which he is equated with the Pan-Islamist Caliphate-Sultan Abdulhamid II (r. 1876–1909) set by full of political analogies with that of moribund Ottoman Empire. Erdoğan says: 'Remember that we retreated from the homeland of 18,000 [sic] square kilometres to 780,000 square kilometres. Let's learn our history, learn what we used to be, and what we are like now. You are watching the Payitaht, aren't you?' (TRT Haber 2017).

Payitaht is a new addition to the pro-AKP historical-cum-contemporary dramas that aim to propagate the overlapping Erdoğanist narrative of historical and contemporary in-groups and out-groups (Çevik 2020, 177). It 'cultivates a mediated reality that builds on the AKP's version of history and therefore reinforces the illusionary idea that the fate of Turkey is similar to that of the Ottoman Empire' (Çevik 2020, 178). At the start of each episode, the drama declares that it is 'inspired by real historical events' (Erdemir and Kessler 2017). The series cultivates and propagates a worldview that connects the Ottoman past to contemporary politics and also 'feeds the existent divisions within Turkey by reinforcing the AKP's political discourse on key domestic and foreign policy issues' (Çevik 2020, 177).

Abdulhamid II is constructed in the series as the last Emperor to stand tall against the Crusader Western powers that constantly conspired against the Empire to destroy it, while still maintaining his status as a pious man. Erdoğan is presented in a similar light and this civilizational populist narrative construction 'creates an uninterrupted reality where two leaders of different eras are seen as mirror images of each other and as victims and saviours of the state' (Çevik 2020, 191). On the other hand, this series focuses 'on the fall of the Ottoman Empire and the role of domestic and foreign plots that conspired against the Ottomans' (Çevik 2019, 235). In an episode, when Abdulhamid discovers a British plot to sabotage his plans for a railway to Mecca, he says 'if they have a plan, God too has a plan' which 'just happens to be one of Erdoğan's signature lines appropriated from the Qur'an (Erdemir and Kessler 2017).

The villains in the series 'also bear a keen resemblance to Erdoğan's own bogeymen' (Erdemir and Kessler 2017). All the good things belong to Abdulhamid II 'and all the conspiracies and evil things are the business of secret organizations of Masons, Jews, and other plotters' (Erdemir and Kessler 2017). However, of all the villain characters, none are more sinister than the Jews. The series 'negatively portrays Jews as the jealous enemies of the Ottoman Empire' (Çevik 2020, 187). In an episode, a soldier opens his hand to find the coin is etched with a Star of David surrounding a squat cross in the style favoured by Crusaders and Freemasons. This is the signal to open fire on the royal carriage to assassinate Abdulhamid II (Erdemir and Kessler 2017).

'Resurrection' of a Hero

Multiple attempts were being made by the government broadcaster TRT to create a programme that can stand for and propagate the values that are espoused by the ruling AKP. It would be an understatement to say that one such attempt has become hugely popular among not only the local but also the global audiences. This attempt manifested itself in the form of a TV serial named Dirilis Ertuğrul or Resurrection Ertuğrul (as a Netflix adaptation). The twist in the story is that although it is a TV serial, it cannot be termed as mere entertainment. It has rather been employed by the AKP to blur the hitherto existing boundaries between two distinct categories of political history and entertainment. Although historical fiction is a genre that has existed for a long time, the extent to which this TV serial has fused the traditional boundaries is unprecedented. Also, it is important to note here that the history it draws on is the one that has been sanctioned by the state to fulfil political purposes. The following lines will explore the extent to which TRT's productions have been used for political ends. Also examined would be the fetishization of martyrdom that is evident in these serials.

In February 2017, TRT broadcasted an advertisement that ran for nearly four minutes. It contained a variety of leaders, termed 'Turkish' starting from Sultan Alparslan (credited as the founder of Turkish state in what was then known as Anatolia) and moving through the figure of Ataturk it reaches the current President Recep Tayyip Erdoğan. There is an explicit reference to the attempted coup against the current President in July 2016. The message of this advertisement is the depiction of President Erdoğan as a natural successor to the long line of leaders who braced difficult times and navigated their nation through them.

It is important to note the context in which this campaign was being run. It was preceding the constitutional referendum that was due to be held on 16th of April in 2017. The aim of the campaign was to instigate the voters by giving them obvious cues to encourage them in voting for a shift towards presidential form of government from the then prevalent parliamentary form. Among the numerous historical figures who were referenced in that commercial there was one named Ertuğrul Gazi. Some of the historical accounts suggest that he was the father of the founder of the Ottoman dynasty whose name was Osman Gazi.

As a highly Islamic title, Gazi refers to the ones who had joined the Islamic battles (jihads) and expeditions. Until recently, Ertuğrul was not an important, famous, political, or historical figure in the Turkish context for neither secularists nor the Islamists. Moreover, there is no historical record of Ertuğrul both in local and non-local libraries. The mainstream significant figures have been always Mehmet II, who conquered Constantinople, and Sultan Abdulhamid, who ended Ottoman parliament ruling the state in autocracy from 1876 until 1909 for the Islamist circles. Particularly, Abdulhamid was considered as the last restorationist Ottoman Sultan who tried hard to propagate Islam for his autocratic political aims to suppress opposition and intellectual elites within the country.

Ertuğrul's inclusion in the list containing famous historical figures, however, was not an isolated accident. He has become a household name thanks to the mega hit drama Dirilis Ertuğrul (TRT 2017) whose main lead, as the title of the drama suggests, is none other than Ertuğrul Gazi. This drama basically revolves around the story of a tribe who finds itself in an armed conflict with Knight Templars and Mongols and migrates towards the Roman region which contains modern-day Turkey. Although scant historical information is present about the actual figure who was the father of the founder of the Ottoman Empire, the character of the drama, however, is a beloved household name in Turkey and in many other countries of the world.

Overall, it might be claimed that Ertuğrul is a perfect exemplar and a carte blanche for building a myth and identification, an Islamic and nationalistic figure in a continuous jihadi context, who is always surrounded by the 'other' threats, struggling for life and death for his tribe and the God's command. The Resurrection is the story of the earlier foundations of the Ottoman state; the struggle of Ertuğrul with internal and external and enemies who are the Crusaders, Templars, Mongols, and the Byzantium Empire. The narrative is based on Manichaean binary oppositions and clear-cut distinctions between the good and the evil; the people and the enemies of the people; the Muslims and the Christians or others (Özçetin 2019b, 947). Ertuğrul is a flawless character (brave, pious, selfless, romantic, fearless, clever, etc.) and is presented as the charismatic leader and incarnation of the will of the nation but also the leader of the Muslim World (Özçetin 2019b, 947). The series 'teach' and insinuate the Turkish people's 'true' political realities behind the scenes without awakening the 'enemies.

One aspect of the investment in this series is financial and so is the effort to utilize this series for political purposes by making it a thing to be talked about as a dimension of the multifaceted efforts. It is interesting and perhaps important to note here that the efforts to exploit the series for political purposes were soon in offering after the show premiered. Take for instance the visit of the President of Azerbaijan Ilham Aliyev. Upon his visit, the theme played by the president's band was Diriliş theme song and the march itself was named as resurrection march. This has now become a major theme that is evident in almost all the government and party's events. Moreover, on the celebration of the 563rd anniversary of the famous conquest of Istanbul at the hands of 'Sultan Muhammad Fatih', theme chosen for the event was 'Resurrection Again, Rising Again'. Two of the main guests at that ceremony were certain actors from the show who had played the role of Ertuğrul Gazi's close confidants in the drama. One might question as to what were two thirteenth-century characters doing on the eve of the celebration of the event that took place in the fifteenth century but that goes perfectly along with the idea of a restorative response to the happenings of today.

Much of the content that is present in this serial can also be categorized as a political description of the current happenings in Turkey. An example would suffice to drive this point home. Most of the episodes in the second season of the serial are centred around the theme of a brother betraying or turning against his own blood due to the influence of external enemies.

All heroes in the serial are 'good orthodox Sunni Muslims' who have an unproblematic understanding of the ummah, embracing the idea of *gaza*. According to the series Ertuğrul is 'an imperial figure who is destined to lead the Islamic world and bring it together' (Özçetin 2019b, 947). Even before the formation of the Ottoman Empire, Ertuğrul's deeds are portrayed as conscious steps towards forming a huge imperial political power (Özçetin 2019b, 947).

Major ideological themes and the struggles of the AKP have consistently found their place in the Resurrection (Carney 2018: 97). It has been made very clear that the protagonist of the show, Ertuğrul, is in fact a historic representation of Erdoğan himself; while the AKP represents the resurrection of Turkish greatness, Erdoğan is Ertuğrul (Carney 2018, 100; Özçetin 2019b, 947).

The AKP promotes the Resurrection 'as "the show of the people", and as a cultural artefact belonging to the people. The show has been embraced as an alternative to morally degenerate cultural products of alienated Westernist/Kemalist cultural elites' (Özçetin 2019a, 942). A content analysis of the series showed that the Resurrection 'transfers Turkey's new political identity pointing to its new vision based on real policies and focusing on national unification' (Elitaş and Kır 2019, 41).

The Resurrection is about the civilizational struggle between Muslims represented by the Turks and Christians but parallels the current political tensions between Turkey and some European countries. In fact, the resurrection is 'intertwined with contemporary politics: specifically, the idea that the AKP represents the resurrection of Turkish greatness; that Erdoğan is Ertuğrul' (Carney 2018, 100). Senem Çevik (2019, 235) notes that 'there have been clear efforts to create a continuous historical interpretation between Ertuğrul and Erdoğan, thus instrumentalising popular culture in propagating government discourse'.

Glorifying Death, Beheading, Martyrdom, and Graves in a Jihadist Context

Through the Resurrection, the AKP not only seeks to glorify and idealize the past, but also claims ownership of it (Carney 2019, 101). What is more, 'the frequent and public use of both the term ("resurrection") and the serial (*Resurrection*) by the AKP regime is symptomatic of a broader necropolitics in Turkey: a fascination with and championing of death on behalf of the nation that has stark implications for everyday life, politics, and even the nature of democracy practiced there' (Carney 2018, 101).

It is interesting to note the significance of the title of Dirilis: Ertuğrul when it comes to the linkage between the season and the politics of death that surrounds it. There are multiple meanings that can be associated to this term 'Resurrection'. First and foremost, it indicates or refers to the arc of the character that is the primary focus of this serial. Although, only scant information is available that can shed proper historical light on the character of Ertuğrul, as noted above, the drama, however, involves the plot that sees the annihilation of the Kayi tribe at the hands of the invading Mongols on the one hand and at the hands of the 'infidel' Christian Byzantine military troops, and then it depicts the context in which the main character went on to assume the leadership position. There is not one but multiple resurrections that the lead character along with his tribe go through during the drama. The inclusion of this theme in the various government and party celebrations also indicates the desire to link the show with the contemporary politics of Turkey. It also aims to give the message that President Erdoğan in the garb of a modern-day Ertuğrul who will restore Turkey to great heights that it once enjoyed. Last but not least, Dirilis has a special annotation within the intellectual, political, and ideological mindset of the Turkish Islamism: taking back the state from the infidels and restoration of the caliphate. Here, Sezai Karakoç (d. 2021), one of the most renowned Islamist intellectuals in the Turkish context, and also the mentor of Erdoğan, holds a significant place in the making the word *dirilş* as a recurring theme and a mobilizational tool for the Turkish Islamism and a significant part of Islamist ideology. For this purpose, Karakoç published an Islamist newspaper, *Dirilş*, in 1960, and then established *Dirilş* publishing house in 1974, in which he published a series of *Dirilş* books such as *Dirilş Muştusu* (The Message of the Resurrection), *Dirilş Neslinin Amentusu* (The Faith of the Generation of the Resurrection), *Islamın Dirilişi* (The Resurrection of Islam), and

İnsanlığın Dirilişi (The Resurrection of the Humanity) together with a series of poems which contain '*diriliş*' as leitmotif.

In terms of necropolitics, the term 'resurrection' itself has a significant place both in the Islamist politics and the AKP series, and it is not a coincidentally picked word. The word resurrection itself is directly linked with the dead, necro indeed: In order to resurrect, you need to die first. Thus, the term along with the eponymous drama is an indication of the phenomena that for long has been what can be termed as an undercurrent in Turkish politics. The championing of death for the cause of the country or a nation or an imagined past or what can be termed as necropolitics has deep repercussions for the nature of political practices prevalent in the society. What this kind of serial entails is the normalization of death in living practices mainly by using and exploiting media for disseminating the requisite material for such purposes. In addition to glorification of death and martyrdom, the term itself inherently champions to kill the others as well. For instance, Suleiman Shah, the father of Ertuğrul, preaches to his son in the series: 'If the Bey is not seeking to drink the beverage of shahada (*şehadet şerbeti*) in front of his companions (alps), there is no benefit for anyone from that campaign son!'[2] In the age of empires, maybe this can be seen reasonable given the international/tribal system of the time, but in the series, we see that these themes are blended with the violent jihadism, seeking *shahada* (martyrdom) which means plunging into enemy knowing that you will die, like the suicide bombers.

The Erdoğanist dramas employed the Islamist and jihadi use of martyrdom and inserted it successfully within the nationalist and racial context, which have already been prevalent in the Turkish TVs. From time to time, we even witness those jihadi themes intertwined with the Kemalist references, in compliance with the AKP and the ultra-nationalist alliance after 2013. For instance, Ertuğrul's father Suleyman Sah gives a speech to his soldiers (*alp*s or *alperenler*) before a Christian castle raid stating that: 'thanks to the noble blood and the faith, we will collapse the Templers' castle on their heads'. Noble blood metaphor belongs to Mustafa Kemal here. Following Suleyman Sah's speech, the soldiers shout Allahu Akbar Allahu Akbar, swinging their swords.[3] Similarly, in another part of the drama, the Christian cardinal from the Templers disgraces his

---

[2] Date: 03 June 2015 / episode no 24 Episode name: Kutlu Fetih.

[3] Date: 03 June 2015 / episode no 24 Episode name: Kutlu Fetih.

own soldiers referring to a well-known Kemalist aphorism, when the castle raided by a few soldiers of Ertuğrul, the cardinal states that: 'Now I can see that one Turk is really worth the whole world'.[4] With these few references, of course, Erdoğan strengthens his cohabitation with some of the Kemalist wings.

Another impactful image that inoculates the jihadism to the viewers is uncensored beheading scenes, which are abundantly found in almost every episode. These scenes immediately become viral on social media, and the viewers share their pictures holding shotguns, rifles, axes, and swords wearing *alp* caps before their TVs. Beheaded enemies are sometimes Christian enemies, merchants, commanders, and sometimes the 'Muslim' enemies, who betrayed the Kayi community. The beheading ceremonies occur publicly and sometimes executed by Ertuğrul Bey himself accompanied by alps' Allahu Akbar shouting. In that respect, the scenes strikingly recall ISIS beheading scenes.[5] Though there is no beheading scene, the theme itself can be found also within the Payitaht Abdulhamid. For instance, in response to the pro-parliamentary (*Mesrutiyet*) opposing sides, including some groups of the 'minority' peoples, Abdulhamid orders in the drama to his grand vizier: 'Grant the rights who demand rights, behead those who disobey' which quickly has become one of the slogans by the AKP in the face of opposing political party rallies or social protests.[6]

Other scenes which recall jihadis are the carrying of the dead bodies of the alps to the burial place. Like the scenes which Turkish people remember from the HAMAS and Palestine, the martyrs are carried on a bunch of sticks sloppily on the shoulders of Ertuğrul and his companions among Allahu Akbar slogans, wrapped up with Kayi flag.[7] Sometimes, such burial scenes take up to 20 minutes, accompanied with Qur'an recitations, oaths for revenge, and glorification of martyrdom. During the ceremonies, the engaging in jihad is repetitively underscored. For instance, Suleyman Sah tells his people after the raid of Templers' Castle:

---

[4] Date: 03 June 2015 / episode no 24 Episode name: Kutlu Fetih.

[5] For beheading scenes see for example Date: 03 June 2015 / episode no 24 Episode name: Kutlu Fetih and 10 June 2015 episode no 24-episode name: A Nation's Resurrection.

[6] Payitaht episode 9.

[7] See for example 12 April 2017 episode no 84.

'Our duty is to walk on the path of God; our purpose is to disseminate God's religion. We have demolished the Templers' Castle [...] May God's mercy be upon our martyred soldiers who did not leave jihad[8] [people shout Allahu Akbar]'.[9] In another instance, the shaykh of the tribe, Ibn Arabi, prays to God after he sent off Ertuğrul Bey and his friends for the ambush of Christian troops saying: 'Oh Lord! Please help those who engage in jihad with their lives and their goods; we have bestowed your subjects to you who set out for shahadah'.[10] The shaykh then says that 'Muslim is a Muslim as long as he fights the infidels'.

It was in late February of the year 2015, that Turkish soldiers entered the Syrian territory to recover the artifacts located in the tomb of Suleyman Sah. One of the Turkish soldiers who was involved in the raid was killed during this military operation. This raid became a topic of controversy. It is also important to remember that it was also the time of election season in Turkey. The grave has been identified and celebrated as the grave of the Ottoman dynasty's founder's ancestor since the fifteenth century. It was during the reign of Islamist Sultan Abdulhamid II that a proper tomb was built over the grave. In the agreement that was reached between the Grand National Assembly of Ankara and France, it was agreed that:

> "The tomb of Suleiman Shah, the grandfather of the Sultan Osman, founder of the Ottoman Dynasty (the tomb known under the name of Turk Mezari), situated at Jaber-Kalesi shall remain, with its appurtenances, the property of Turkey, who may appoint guardians for it and may hoist the Turkish flag there."[11]

While the tomb had not featured much in the recently held mayoral elections, it had assumed a significant position in the electoral politics a year later. In the mayoral elections, the significant challenge posed to the AKP was emanating from its erstwhile ally known as the Gülen movement. There was also a corruption inquiry ongoing against the Erdoğan regime

---

[8] The word jihad is removed from the English subtitle version in the Netflix. See episode 72 in Netflix.

[9] 10 June 2015 episode no 24, episode name: A Nation's Resurrection.

[10] 12 April 2017 episode no 84.

[11] Franco-Turkish Agreement signed at Angora on 20 October 1921.

which the regime termed as a plot by the adherents of the Gülen movement in the bureaucracy. A large-scale crackdown on the police officials deemed closer to the movement put the investigation on hold. For that reason, in the parliamentary elections, the AKP was faced with a stiff challenge. It was in the February of 2015 that around 600 Turkish soldiers crossed the border into the Syrian territory and reached the tomb of Suleyman Sah. They recovered the artifacts located there and destroyed the remainder of the site to prevent its usage by the ISIS. It is interesting to note here that at the time of this operation, two months had gone by since the airing of the Resurrection and the character of Suleyman Sah had by that time became a popular name in the Turkish society. The government's focus on the burial site of a person who has just been popularized by a TV serial appears a well-coordinated effort to strike a conjunction between drama and the politics of the ruling party. Interest in a historical figure and his burial place is in keeping with the nationalist variants seen around the globe. What is striking, however, is the willingness to put at risk the lives of hundreds of soldiers to retrieve a person's alleged remains, someone who died many centuries ago and was not mummified. It attests to the fact that necropolitics or the politics of death is being indulged in with the help of media.

CONCLUSION

This chapter scrutinized the TV series that have been produced and funded by the AKP regime to analyse how the AKP is using the TV series by using Islamist civilizational narrative, necropolitical images and scenes of violence as an instrument of propaganda. The TV series have a significant role to convey the AKP's Islamist civilizational populist messages to its political base, seeing the total average time spent watching TV per day among the Turkish viewers is dramatically high. The common leitmotif of these TV series is that the Muslim World led by the Turkish nation is under a continuous threat, an imminent assault that would be staged by the inner and outer enemies, so we must rally around the flag, as boiled down the famous slogan of the AKP: one nation, one flag, one homeland, and one state. The nationalist and chauvinist senses, which have been already prevalent in the Turkish society thanks to Kemalists, are combined with the Islamist civilizational populism, the jihadi, violent

110   I. YILMAZ AND O. ERTURK

ornaments by the AKP regime, under the guise of the historical consciousness. It seems that the AKP regime has taken over what Kemalists created by successfully transforming them for their own ends.

REFERENCES

Abu-Lughod, L. 2005. *Dramas of Nationhood: The Politics of Television in Egypt.* Chicago, IL: University of Chicago Press.

Armstrong, William. 2017. 'What a TV Series Tells Us about Erdoğan's Turkey'. 14 May 2017. https://www.nytimes.com/2017/05/14/opinion/erdogan-tv-show-turkey.html.

Carney, Josh. 2014. The Prime Minister and the Sultan: Sacred History and Expression Collide in Turkey. In *The Turkish Touch: Neo-ottoman Hegemony and Turkish Television in the Middle East,* edited by J. Carney, L. Nocera, M.M. Kraidy, et al. Arab Media Report, 29–31. Milano: Reset.

Carney, Josh. 2018. 'Resur(e)recting a Spectacular Hero: Diriliş Ertuğrul, Necropolitics, and Popular Culture in Turkey.' *Review of Middle East Studies* 52 (1): 93–114.

Carney, Josh. 2019. 'ResurReaction: Competing Visions of Turkey's (proto) Ottoman Past in Magnificent Century and Resurrection Ertuğrul'. *Middle East Critique* 28 (2): 101–120.

Çevik, Senem B. 2019. 'Turkish Historical Television Series: Public Broadcasting of Neo-Ottoman Illusions'. *Southeast European and Black Sea Studies* 19 (2): 227–242.

Çevik, Senem B. 2020. 'The Empire Strikes Back: Propagating AKP's Ottoman Empire Narrative on Turkish Television'. *Middle East Critique* 29 (2): 177–197.

Coşar, Simten and Funda Gençoğlu Onbaşı. 2016. Moralism, Hegemony, and Political Islam in Turkey: Gendered Portrayals in a TV Series. *Journal of Mediterranean Studies* 25 (2): 217–234.

Davutoğlu, Ahmet. 2016. 'Başbakan Davutoğlu'nun Kut-Ül Amare Zaferinin 100. Yıl Programında Yaptığı Konuşmasının Tam Metni'. Akparti (blog), 29 April 2016. http://m.akparti.org.tr/site/haberler/basbakan-davutoglunun-kut-ul-amare-zaferinin-100.-yil-programinda-yaptigi-k/83812#1.

Elitaş, Türker, and Serpil Kır. 2019. Reading Turkey's New Vision Based Real Policies Through an Identity and their Presentation in Series as a Soft Power: A Study on the Series, Resurrection-Ertugrul. *Journal of Social Sciences* 8 (1): 41–62.

Emre-Çetin, Kumru Berfin. 2014. The 'Politicization' of Turkish Television Dramas. *International Journal of Communication* 8: 2462–2483.

Erdemir, Aykan, and Oren Kessler. 2017. 'A Turkish TV Blockbuster Reveals Erdoğan's Conspiratorial, Anti-Semitic Worldview. *The Washington Post*, 15

5 THE USE OF TV SERIES FOR CIVILIZATIONAL POPULIST ... 111

May. https://www.washingtonpost.com/news/democracy-post/wp/2017/05/15/a-turkish-tv-blockbuster-reveals-erdogans-conspiratorial-anti-semitic-worldview/

Erdoğan, R. Tayyip. 2017. Recep Tayyip Erdoğan Diriliş Ve Abdülhamid Yorumu, *Daily Motion*, www.dailymotion.com/video/x6ddp38www.youtube.com/watch?v=wUDgpNA5-38

Erdoğan, Recep Tayyip. 2018. '45. Muhtarlar Toplantısında Yaptıkları Konuşma', TCCB, 08 February 2018, https://www.tccb.gov.tr/konusmalar/353/89357/45-muhtarlar-toplantisinda-yaptiklari-konusma.html

Fields, Rona F. Fields. 'Cóilín Owens, Michael Berenbaum and Reuven Firestone'. *Martyrdom: The Psychology, Theology, and Politics of Self-sacrifice*. Westport: Praeger Publishers.

Hall, Stuart. 1980. 'Encoding/Decoding'. In *Culture, Media, Language*, ed. Stuart Hall et al., 128–138. New York: Routledge.

Harvey, D. 2005. *A Brief History of Neoliberalism*. Oxford: Oxford University Press.

Herman, E. S. and N. Chomsky. 1988. *Manufacturing Consent: The Political Economy of the Mass Media*. New York: Pantheon Books.

Hurriyet. 2017. www.hurriyet.com.tr/gundem/erdogandan-dirilis-ertugrul-aci klamasi-40383307.

İstanbul Bilgi Üniversitesi. 2018. 'Dimensions of Polarization in Turkey'. *Göç Çalışmaları - Uygulama ve Araştırma Merkezi*, 5 February 2018. https://goc.bilgi.edu.tr/en/news-and-events/182/launch-of-dimens ions-of-polarization-in-turkey/.

Kanal, D. 2017. 'Vatan İçin Kendinden Vazgeçenler!'. 12 December 2017. https://www.kanald.com.tr/isimsizler/haber/vatan-icin-kendinden-vazgec enler.

Madayanti, Tuğçe. 2017. 'İsimsizler: Gençlerden Elinizi Çekin!', 15 May 2017. https://www.birgun.net/haber/isimsizler-genclerden-elinizi-cekin-159566.

Matthews, Owen. 2002. '"The Minarets Are Our Bayonets" | The Spectator'. 23 November 2002. https://www.spectator.co.uk/article/-the-minarets-are-our-bayonets-.

Özçetin, Burak. 2019a. 'Religion on Air: The Birth and Transformation of Religious Broadcasting in Turkey'. *Middle East Journal of Culture and Communication* 12: 236–252.

Özçetin, Burak. 2019b. 'The Show of the People' Against the Cultural Elites: Populism, Media and Popular Culture in Turkey'. *European Journal of Cultural Studies* 22 (5–6): 942–957.

Porto, M. 2011. 'Telenovelas and Representations of National Identity in Brazil'. *Media, Culture & Society* 33 (1): 53–69.

112 I. YILMAZ AND O. ERTURK

RTÜK. 2018. *Televizyon İzleme Eğilimleri - 2018 Araştırması.* Ankara: RTÜK. https://www.rtuk.gov.tr/Media/FM/Birimler/strateji/raporlar/2018-rtukfa aliyetraporu_1000_(1).pdf

Sinanoğlu, Semuhi. 2017. 'Parti Ebed Müddet: Bir Siyaset Teknolojisi Olarak Yeni Osmanlıcı TRT Dizileri - Semuhi Sinanoğlu'. 30 March 2017. https://birikimdergisi.com/guncel/8236/parti-ebed-muddet-bir-siyaset-teknolojisi-olarak-yeni-osmanlici-trtdizileri.

Sozcu. 2016. www.sozcu.com.tr/2016/gundem/erdogan-tanitim-gecesinde-kon usuyor-1510563/, www.youtube.com/watch?v=rVJLBn8-dBI.

TRT Haber. 2017. 'Cumhurbaşkanı Recep Tayyip Erdoğan: Tarihi bilmek için Payitaht Abdülhamid'i izleyin'. 31 December 2017. https://www.trthaber. com/haber/gundem/cumhurbaskani-recep-tayyip-erdogan-tarihi-bilmek-icin-payitaht-abdulhamidi-izleyin-345026.html.

TRT. 2017. Yeni Dizi 'Mehmetçik Kûtulamâre' Fragmanı. *Youtube.* https://www.youtube.com/watch?v=_tKNv51EJ9s.

TRT. (2017). 'Diriliş "Ertuğrul."' https://www.trt1.com.tr/arsiv/dirilis-ert ugrul. Accessed 29 December 2022.

TRT. 2018. 'Mehmetçik Kut'ül Amare / Mehmetçik Kutlu Zafer', *TRT,* https://www.trtizle.com/diziler/mehmetcik-kutlu-zafer/ mehmetcik-kutulamare-1-bolum-129001

TRT 1. (2022). Teşkilat. https://www.trt1.com.tr//diziler/teskilat. Accessed 29 December 2022.

White, J. 2014. *Muslim Nationalism and the New Turks Updated Edition.* Princeton, NJ: Princeton University Press.

Yilmaz, Ihsan. 2021. *Creating the Desired Citizen: Ideology, State and Islam in Turkey.* Cambridge and New York: Cambridge University Press.

Yoshimi, S. 2003. 'Television and Nationalism: Historical Change in the National Domestic TV Formation of Postwar Japan'. *European Journal of Cultural Studies* 6 (4): 459–48.

CHAPTER 6

Targeting Children via Education for Populist Necropolitical Propaganda

INTRODUCTION

School education and textbooks are the significant and effective construction tools of nationhood used by the states (vom Hau 2009). New generations socialize through the educational parameters of the government, which manipulates people based on its ideological paradigms. Turkish governments are not exempt from such statements. All governments of Turkey, in one way or another, have utilized the education curriculum as an ideological tool to construct 'desired citizens' (Yilmaz 2021), favouring the dominant perspective of their time (Kaya 2016, 119). For instance, this was shown by Nahmiyaz's (2018) study that examines the Turkish national identity and images of the non-Muslim minorities living in Turkey such as Greeks and Armenians by focusing on Turkish history textbooks from the establishment of the Turkish Republic in 1923 until 2018. These textbooks delegitimize and dehumanize the 'other', while they present an elevated self-image of Turkishness characterized by heroism, endurance, courage, justness, and tolerance (Nahmiyaz 2018, 333). Kenan Çayır's (2009) analysis of social sciences textbooks after Turkey's curriculum reform of 2004–2005 found that even after the pro-EU reforms, the textbooks were 'still imbued with an exclusive and narrow definition of nationalism and citizenship, backed by the myth of origin, ethnocentrism and essentialism' (Çayır 2009, 39; 2014, 2015; see also Ince 2012).

© The Author(s), under exclusive license to Springer Nature Singapore Pte Ltd. 2023
I. Yilmaz and O. Erturk, *Populism, Authoritarianism and Necropolitics*,
https://doi.org/10.1007/978-981-19-8292-7_6

The use of textbooks and national curriculum by the government, which was already nationalist, gained both Islamist civilizational populist (Yilmaz 2018) and anti-Westernist outlook as the Justice and Development Party (Adalet ve Kalkınma Partisi, AKP) veered away from democracy as of the 2010s, returning to its Islamist roots (Erturk 2022). A recent report that focuses on textbooks written before and after the 2017 curriculum reform, analysed 16 textbooks with a focus on secularism and gender equality (Aratemur-Çimen and Bayhan 2018). The study found that both the 2016 and 2017 textbooks were written from a Turkish–Islamic Synthesis ideology but the 2017 textbooks were additionally 'based on political-Islamist discourse and issues related to women and gender equality have been almost totally removed' (Aratemur-Çimen and Bayhan 2018, 3). Although both 2016 and 2017 grade 9 religious culture and morality textbooks are Sunni-centred and deny other sects, beliefs, and worldviews, the 2017 textbook additionally has a predominant political-Islamist discourse (Aratemur-Çimen and Bayhan 2018).

The'pious citizen' paradigm created by the government of Erdoğan stands opposed to the desired secular citizen paradigm that has long stood at the core of the Turkish identity (see in detail Yilmaz 2021). AKP's strong grip over the minds of the modern Turkish generation allows them to pose themselves as a morally superior version of the previous ideal citizen model. It allows them to construct such a model of the ideal citizenry that aligns with the state's own ideology that everyone in the nation is expected to fit into. If one does not fit into this model, wherein their acts pose as anti-state behaviour, they are punished and stigmatized by the state (Lüküslü 2016). Erdoğan's post-2011 politics has been designed to influence the masses through subtle and subliminal messaging through media, civil society, security apparatuses, and education (Yilmaz 2018; Yilmaz and Erturk 2021a). The use of such tools took an even more aggressive and more direct approach after the failed mysterious coup attempt on 15 July 2016 that Erdoğan called 'a gift of God'.

The post-2016 coup period also saw a shift to the presidential form of government in which the AKP could reinforce their ideology with minimal checks and balances, under the authoritarian rule of the State of Emergency. The failure of the coup was used as legitimate reasoning by the education minister, İsmet Yılmaz, to restructure the new curriculum in 2017. This provided many new additions that later aided in the state's civilizational populist narrative and necropolitical propaganda, as well as together with a radical Islamist educational agenda that had been not able to find itself a place up until then, among the 'coup' fanfare. These included the removal of the theory of evolution the addition of a nationalist and more Islamized focus on a theological rather than scientific explanation for the formation of the world and, most particularly, the addition of 'jihad' as a key warfare concept in everyday religious life (Hurriyet 2017a, b; Birgun 2017).

The backdrop of the dynamic changes within the education system is the political struggle of the Justice and Development Party (AKP) surrounding the 2016 coup. It became the starting point of aggressive tactics to control the socio-political narrative of the country, dividing it into one that was pro-state and one that was posed as the enemy to the AKP government, which is identified now with the Turkish state itself. Such sort of antagonistic civilizationalist narrative had been already prevalent in the Islamist circles while they had been in the periphery of the Kemalist-dominated state since the foundation of Republican Turkey (Yilmaz 2016). However, the AKP's populist, Islamist, and authoritarian take on politics in the 2010s resulted in the severe polarization of Turkish society. It created a version of the pro-state citizen as those whose values are socio-politically aligned with nationalists in the outer, Islamist ideals in the core layers of its politics. National education channels are then utilized to train these 'pious generation' who are the true owners of the state to be responsible for punishing those who were not. Opposition towards the government was violently suppressed as the concept of jihad and nationalism were strongly correlated with the support of the national ruling party. It marked the beginning of the necropolitical 'Islamized identity' propagated within the youth of Turkey (Lüküslü 2016).

This chapter will deal with the question of how the AKP instrumentally has been using civilizational populist necropolitical use of nationalist and Islamic concepts, such as jihad, martyrdom love of homeland, sacrificing self for the religio-nationalist 'values' such as flag, call to prayer (*adhan*) and, mosques within the national curriculum and school textbooks, including some of the kids' magazines prepared for children's religious education by Turkey's Directorate of Religious Affairs (Diyanet İşleri Başkanlığı). The education reforms by the AKP throughout their rule will be examined to formulate the origins of the necropolitical propaganda and its inner machinations.

The Necropolitical National Curriculum from Kemalism to Erdoğanism

All governments of Turkey have utilized the education curriculum as an ideological tool to construct ideal citizens, favouring the dominant perspective of their time (Kaya 2016, 119).

A scientific analysis of social sciences textbooks after Turkey's curriculum reform of 2004–2005 found that even after the pro-EU reforms, the textbooks had continued to stay ultra-nationalist, which elevated ethnocentrism and essentialism surrounded with the notion of benevolent citizenship (Çayır 2009, 39). Nahmiyaz's (2018) study examines Turkish national identity and images of the 'other' by focusing on Turkish history textbooks from the establishment of the Turkish Republic in 1923 until 2018. The study shows that a negative framing of non-Muslim minorities existed in textbooks and that Greek and Armenian minorities in Turkey were constructed as 'significant others' that pose a threat to the nation's existence for the whole 95 years that were studied. The textbooks reflect an antagonistic binary world vision defined by friends on one side and enemies on the other, who pose external and internal threats to the Turkish nation. This not only delegitimizes and dehumanizes the other (non-Sunni Muslim and non-Turkish), but creates an elevated self-image characterized by heroism, endurance, courage, justness, and tolerance (Nahmiyaz 2018, 333). Another recent analysis of history textbooks found that the narrative that dominates these textbooks 'does not only alienate "other" groups but transforms them into "the enemies of the nation". The construction of these enemy images is done by juxtaposing the "others" to the perpetuated goodness and tolerance of Turks' (Akpınar et al. 2017, 28).

In the same vein, a recent report found that both the 2016 and 2017 textbooks were written from a Turkish Islamic Synthesis ideology but the 2017 textbooks were additionally 'based on political-Islamist discourse' (Aratemur-Çimen and Bayhan 2018, 3). Another report by the same authors examined new 26 textbooks written in 2017 and taught in primary (Grades 1–8) and secondary levels (Grades 9–12) across disciplines and found that these textbooks present a 'hostile conceptualization of non-Muslim minorities' (Aratemur-Çimen and Bayhan 2019, 38) and frame 'non-Muslim schools as tools of Western states seeking to dismantle the Ottoman Empire or to meddle in the internal affairs of the Empire' (Aratemur-Çimen and Bayhan 2019, 39).

Despite all these very significant continuities in relation to nationalism, insecurity, anxiety, fears, siege mentality, militarism, glorification of martyrdom and otherizations, the AKP has been gradually changing the legislation on education, the education system and national educational curriculum in line with the civilizational populist ideology especially since 2011 (see in detail Eroler 2018; Yilmaz 2022a, b).

The terms enemy, homeland, and martyrdom continue to pervade the narratives on the Turkish War of Independence and 'love of the homeland and its flag as a defining characteristic of Turkish society as well as the willingness to die during military service are emphasized and presented as the ideal attitudes expected from Turkish citizens' (Aratemur-Çimen and Bayhan 2019, 22–23). Poems such this one is used to support the argument:

> What makes a flag a flag is the *blood* that's on it
> What make a piece of land a homeland are those *willing to die* for it.

The books also attempt to mythicize the mysterious 15 July coup attempt in a way that implies it is Turkey's second War of Independence. 'Heroism', 'martyrdom', 'veteran status,' 'dying and shedding blood' for the homeland from the Kemalist times (Altinay 2006) have been expanded to the narratives of the 15 July and 'dying for the homeland' no longer entails only fighting against external enemies, but also against traitors and internal enemies (Aratemur-Çimen and Bayhan 2019, 24).

With the new curriculum, state-sponsored notions of *jihad* and other Islamist ideas have increasingly entered textbooks and public discourse. In universities, the concepts of *jihad* and *gaza* (two variations of a holy war) have entered the international studies and social studies textbooks, which are used to explain the notion of a holy war to protect and spread Islam against non-Muslims (Yanarocak 2016, 13).

The schools have become a necropolitical settings for the AKP, in which death and martyrdom images, stories, exhibition corners, and conferences are regularly displayed and organized. Children are exposed to such indoctrination so that they become pro-supportive for the regime. Some of the exemplary figures, such as 'martyred' governor Muhammed Safitürk's father Asim Safitürk have been invited to many educational conferences and events organized by the National Ministry in various cities around Turkey to address youth and teachers on the importance of martyrdom and the homeland, during the government's military operations against the Kurdish people both in Turkish eastern cities and Northern Syria (T.C. Hizan Kaymakamlığı n.d.; T.C. Geyve Kaymakamlığı 2017). To underscore the importance of the Olive Branch military operation in the Northern Syrian Kurdish provinces, for example, Safitürk, as an exemplar martyr father, resonated with the pro-AKP media, saying:

> We are sacrificing our children for the homeland. Not only our children, but also, we are ready to die, we are continuously ready to join to the front line. Owing to the fact that we sacrifice martyrs, we can easily perform our prayers [at mosques], we sleep at home, and walk in the downtown and the in the market. (AA 2018)

The significance of martyrdom for the children praised in every event organized by the AKP. In such events, the AKP echelons also divide 'our' ideal youth and 'their' youth, who are grown up in secular, or non-AKP supportive families. For instance, Erdoğan, comparing 'our youth' with 'their youth' says: 'Whose youth is nimbler and stronger? You shall explode those ballot boxes to the extent that they will be regretful for who they are' (Cumhuriyet 2018). While Erdoğan's speech is dominated with full of Islamist militarized lexicon such as terrorist, hell-fire, martyrs, ghazi, body corpse, tanks, fighter jets, and jihadi Qur'anic verses. Erdoğan, in his address, also wants pro-AKP pupils to carry *struggle* right into the hearts of schools, against the 'other students':

> The path of our youths means the path of our Turkey. If our faith is complete, if our belief is strong enough… then we can bring the great powers to heel. Today, it is time for struggle. You shall struggle at your schools, struggle at libraries, struggle at NGOs and at home. You shall struggle with your friends at your schools, especially in your friend circles through your ideas. In the same manner as you did on July 15, you shall struggle against the tanks, fighter jets, helicopters. As happening in the Euphrates Shield or Olive Branch [military] operations, you shall struggle with them, becoming their nightmare. (Cumhuriyet 2018)

Upon the inciting speech of Erdoğan, children begin to shout 'Reis! take us to Afrin', where the military operation was taking place in the north of Syria, Erdoğan suggests: 'God willing, we will go together' (Cumhuriyet 2018).

Similarly, Erdoğan's wife Emine Erdoğan explained that she feels happy as she witnesses the spirit of Manzikert, War of Independency, and the Gallipoli Campaign reincarnated by the pro-AKP youth and students during the coup attempt: 'the word of homeland has dwelled into the centre of our lives as it bled. The New generation knows what it means to give his life for the homeland' (T24 2017).

Jihad and Martyrdom as Necropolitical Instruments in Texts

While the institutional development pose as the backdrop of the state necropolitical propaganda, the use of Islamic education within the national curriculum is arguably its most evident tool deployed by the state to create a citizenry that follows the state's ideological perspective (Kaya 2016). The AKP has been gradually transforming the legislation on education, and national curriculum in line with its civilizational populist ideology (see in detail Eroler 2018; Yilmaz 2021). The curriculum now highlights *jihad*, martyrdom, and the state-constructed glorious history (Kandiyoti and Emanet 2017).

The National Educational Ministry has added some of the heavily politicized Islamist terminologies to the new 2017–2018 curricula de jure beginning from the sixth graders (Bilefsky 2017; Weise 2017; Evrensel 2017a). The new curriculum which was designed within the Islamist civilizational populist frame particularly includes necropolitical 'values' such as self-devotion, self-sacrifice, and martyrdom under the title of national and religious values (Çepni 2018). It is especially significant that in the new curriculum, jihad has been placed as one of the essential pillars of Islam along with prayer, fasting, etc. (BirGün 2017). With the statements of AKP deputy Ahmet Hamdi Çamlı, who is also a member of Parliament's national education commission:

> Jihad is Islam's most prior element...Jihad comes before prayer. When we look at Ottoman sultans, nearly all of them didn't even go to hajj in order not to abandon jihad. Our ministry made a very on-point decision. If prayers are the pillar of the religion, jihad is the tent. Without the pillars, the tent is useless. (Osborne 2017; The Independent 2017)

For the AKP, jihadi knowledge is so essential in education that it also precedes any other scientific subject, scientific education. For instance,

Çamlı also stated that 'there is no use in teaching math to a child who does not know the concept of jihad' (Spencer 2017). Çamlı implies that when the jihadi education is neglected, the country and the nation will be somehow invaded by the Westerners. He explains in his Twitter post what would happen in case of a lack of jihadi education: 'If there is no JIHAD in this nation's curriculum, WHITE MEN shall fill that breach and push [them] against us as a massacre machine' (Çamlı 2017). In addition to jihadism, other 'neglected' values like 'Kut'ül Amare spirit' has also been added to the new curriculum (Evrensel 2017a). The significance of Amare spirit is that it had been a local fight between the British forces and the Turkish forces in the Arab lands before World War I, which is used by the AKP to trigger the antiwesternism among the Turkish children. In the same sense, the minister of education İsmet Yılmaz explained that the concept of jihad must be introduced within the context of 'loving a nation' to school children. Yılmaz said: 'Jihad is an element in our religion. Our duty is to teach every concept deservedly and correct things that are wrongly perceived' (Altuntaş 2017).

The role of the Diyanet in collaboration with the efforts of the AKP is notable in that it was this joint effort that enabled the jihadi and pro-martyrdom narrative to be pushed onto the nation (Yilmaz and Erturk 2021a). Post-2016 saw an alliance between the two wherein jihad as a concept was embraced and taught as an honourable act that must be embraced as means for the protection of the homeland and Islam (Yilmaz and Erturk 2021b; Yilmaz and Erturk 2022). This narrative coincides with ones that glamorized Turkish history and the nation's success in the past. Indeed, this necropolitical use of jihad and martyrdom in education has begun with the cooperation between the Turkish national educational ministry and Diyanet in 2014–2015, under the guise of Ottoman-modelled *Sıbyan Mektebleri* (Infants School), in which children between 4 and 6 ages are educated by the short-term certificated tutors in the ministry's public education centres, selected by the local authorities (Cumhuriyet 2017). It is reported that in the Infants School, the children are being heavily invested in the 'beauties of the hereafter World', rather than the worldly life, and glorification of death. There are many cases reported that several families suffered from a heavy bombardment of necropolitical use of jihad and death by the regime apparatuses over their children.

There are also other ways of imposing civilizational populist necropolitical narratives on the school children. For instance, during the Turkish

6 TARGETING CHILDREN VIA EDUCATION FOR POPULIST … 121

military operations in the Eastern parts of the country and Syria, orchestrated by the AKP regime, the children and the parents in the schools have been informed that an activity called 'prayer chain' is set for the military forces, so that they kill and destroy all the enemies (Gökdemir 2016). Additionally, in some of the schools, children are charged with other activities such as '*hatim* (reciting the whole Qur'an) chain' by the schoolteachers or the officials from the Diyanet to rest the souls of the fallen. In the circles, some goals have been provided to the children and the parents like reciting specific Quranic verses repetitively during the given periods of the day (Gökdemir 2016).

These activities aim to implement the notion of martyrdom and jihad in education, and to shape children's mindsets in a necropolitical environment. Because of such heavy necropolitical investment and eulogization of death in education, some children began to see death as salvation in that they were told that they would become sinful as they become older (Öztürk 2017). It is also reported that some parents have complained that they began to receive questions from their children like 'this world is much boring, when will we die' (Cumhuriyet 2017). According to another report, the children, who were banned from drawing their mother, father, or sibling pictures by the tutors on the ground that they are un-Islamic, began to ask their parents if it is *haram* (prohibited in Islam) to live together with the family (Evrensel 2017b).

The intensity of the use of jihad and martyrdom within the necropolitical frame is much greater and more explicit in the İmam Hatips, since those children are already believed to come from a pious family and Islamic environments, so they are ready to embrace such ideological tunes. These necropolitical themes are combined with the Islamist ultimate idealism that is to establish an Islamic state in lieu of a republican one. Accordingly, for instance, in a pamphlet named *Imam Hatiplilik Şuuru* (Consciousness of being an Imam Hatip student) released by AKP-funded Ensar Foundation and written by renowned AKP mentor and theologian Hayrettin Karaman, it has been stated that a self-sacrificing population is required for the struggle of the Islamic State (Bulut 2017). This population, a constituent of Imam Hatip students is called 'Ensar generation' by Karaman, whose aim is to establish an Islamic state (Bulut 2017). In the pamphlet, distributed to the children in the schools, it has been demanded from the students to give out diligently, including their lives (Bulut 2017). In the pamphlet, according to Karaman, those teachers working in İmam Hatip schools are traitors if they neglect such Islamist principles to indoctrinate the students (Bulut 2017).

Similar to the 'prayer chain' or 'hatim chain', where the children become a significant part in the creation of such a necropolitical mission, fourth and fifth grade students were sporadically assigned to write letters to the 'martyred' soldiers in Gallipoli Campaign, to the civilians who lost their lives during the failed coup, or to the ones fighting in South-eastern Turkey, Kurdish majority parts of the country, or in the Olive Branch Operation in Syria in order to create organic and sensual links between the martyrs and them (BirGün 2018). In one of the letters, published on the official website of the National Education Information Network (EBA) as an ideal and exemplary student letter, a high school girl wrote:

> Oh, the Fallen Soldier for the Love of this Land,
>
> It is understood that the love of homeland inside of you is never-ending. At that night, I wish so much that I could have placed my body as a barrier before the traitors with you. I wish I had been right beside of you, one heart walking with the homeland-lovers [...] How on earth can arms, cannons, rifles and tanks stop the nation who is used to make history? If I am able to study carelessly in my school, if I am able to express my expressions freely now, it is just by means of you. May God bless your soul. Rest in peace. The homeland, the flag, democracy is entrusted to me. (EBA 2016)

The National Educational Ministry has added some of the heavily politicized Islamist terminologies like jihad, tawhid, wahdat (as a unitary Islamic nation), to the new 2017–2018 curricula de jure beginning from the sixth graders (Bilefsky 2017; Weise 2017; Evrensel 2017a, b). The new curriculum also includes other 'useful' values such as self-devotion, self-sacrifice, heroism, ummah and nation conscience, martyrdom, gathered under the title of national and religious values (Çepni 2018).

These necropolitical use of jihad, martyrdom, and death is double-edged and can shift according to the profiles of the target and the conditions as might be seen within the above examples. Through the official channels, these motives sometimes are curtailed with the term 'democracy' and 'human rights. For the Islamists, however, these civilizational populist necropolitical arguments are instruments on the path to creation of an Islamic state and Islamic ummah against the infidels while

Civilizational Populist Necropolitical Investment at the Schools

Within textbooks, the mysterious coup attempt itself is represented in a propagated manner wherein the martyrs are glamorized while anti-AKP individuals and groups are demonized within a religious backdrop. The textbooks present the dissident groups as enemies of the state. In this context, the political supporters are branded as being the real people and real Muslims while the others are stigmatized as existential threats to the national and religious cause. In doing so, the textbooks also create a clear correlation between Islamic religiosity and true citizenship, which also translates into non-Muslim citizens being categorised as the 'others'.

Erdoğan further elaborates on this by coinciding non-piety as going against the national mission.

> Do you want this generation to be a glue-sniffing (*tinerci*) youth? Do you want this generation to be a rebellious one against their elders? Do you want this youth to be torn apart from their national and moral values, to become a generation without a certain direction or any mission? (Ntvmsnbc 2012)

Interconnecting piety with national and moral values for the youth separated religious youth from those who don't agree with the ruling government's ideology and theology. Islamic identity was pragmatically merged with national identity, dividing the nations between believers (*mümin*); hypocrites (*münafik*) and infidels (*kafir*). The 'atheists' and 'glue-sniffers' who explicitly otherized within the narrative of the ideal Turkish youth. Within the national curriculum textbooks, the non-Muslims are described as being 'infidels'—'person who rejects—partially or as a whole—the principles of the religion that Prophet Muhammad brought from Allah' (Yanarocak 2022, 205; Açık et al. 2019). This separates Jews and Christians from the narrative of piety. Within the Muslim population, there remain various sects that are not given appropriate diverse attention within the curriculum. The heavy Sunni-influenced Islamic courses remain compulsory for minority Muslim groups including Shi'a, Alevis, Bahais, Yazidis and even Atheists (Yaşar 2020).

The national curriculum further moulds the narrative around violent discussions such as the topic of terrorism, which has become an umbrella term to define almost all opposing groups and parties. In terms of necropolitical use, the generic use of terror, and terrorism by the AKP government has become so extended that new definitions such as 'associated with terror' (*terör iltisaklı*) have entered into the literature. It is a necropolitical instrument of the government because 'terror' itself provides the government with a sort of right to exclude, outlaw, arrest, and forced disappearance as well as the right to kill. In connection with the 2016 coup, the Turkish textbooks denote the resistance groups against the AKP, such as the Gülen movement, as terrorists. The coup attempt was also used by the ruling elite as a scapegoat for many radical changes within the education system, including the destruction of 13,000 textbooks and the expungement of the rest on the charges of it pertaining 'terrorist content' (Kandiyoti and Emanet 2017). Regarding terrorism, Turkish books often discuss the Kurdish separatist group PKK (*Kürdistan İşçi Partisi*—Kurdistan Worker's Party) as well. The *Contemporary History* Book taught in Turkish schools mentioned the PKK in the context to terrorist organizations rather than placing their focus on global terrorist groups. Such narratives bring dangers of placing these minority groups in the 'otherized' category which are often targeted for violent jihadi nationalist motives in the line with the state's ideological necropolitical pursuits.

This struggle for the creation of the radical narrative has clearly become the official mainstream in the Turkish education system, as well as in the other parts of the state apparatuses, since the July 2015 failed coup attempt, which can be marked up as the starting of the Erdoğanist regime de jure with the help of State of Emergency. First, a decree was issued that the initial starting week of every academic year (if possible, the whole year) is fully devoted to the narration of the July 15 'Victory' (MEB 2016). The decree states: 'It is our common responsibility to raise our youth's awareness of martyrdom, state defence, national unity and solidarity' (MEB 2016).

The programme that was prepared by the Educational Ministry also proposes that the students, including their parents, should frequently commemorate and visit the martyrdom cemeteries and veterans, some activities such as writing letters or compositions for the martyrs, flag, love of country, country defence. On the last day of the programme, the students of the Imam Hatip schools are obliged to perform *hatim* prayers that are recited after the 'martyrs' killed during July 15. At every opportunity, the AKP government used their Islamist populist narrative to describe the coup as a western attempt to invade Turkey—a narrative that helped Erdoğan to mobilize masses within one night. On that night, 251 pro-state individuals lost their lives who, to this day, are commemorated as the 'martyrs' of that night (Yilmaz and Erturk 2021a; Yilmaz and Erturk 2022). Right after the coup, on 19 September 2016, eight-page booklets and in-class activities were organized in schools to teach children about the failed coup attempt. Constructing academic activities around 'July 15 Victory of Democracy and the Commemoration of Martyrs', 'Martyrdom of democracy' for the national cause was glorified as students were expected to listen to seminars, write letters and read poems to glorify those who had lost their lives in the struggle against government opposition (Aksam 2016). In this vein, Yilmaz and Erturk (2021b) argued that the AKP government utilized the political polarization around the 2016 coup attempt to create a concept of martyrdom that includes civilians through perpetuating the notions of 'sacrifice their lives for the leader's political cause' and justifying violence and revenge against anti-state behaviour. Such tactics were described as 'necropolitical acts'.

Contemporary Turkish and World History Book provided an in-depth explanation of the events of the coup, giving comprehensive information about the martyrs of the struggle. The religious text was cited alongside this to connect religious notes within the national struggle—quoting Surah Al Baqarah from the Quran (2:154):

> And do not say about those who are killed in the way of Allah, 'They are dead.' Rather, they are alive, but you perceive [it] not.

The textbooks are full of terms such as enemy, homeland, and martyrdom. Narratives on the Turkish War of Independence and 'love of the homeland and its flag as a defining characteristic of Turkish society as well as the willingness to die during military service are emphasized and presented as the ideal attitudes expected from Turkish citizens' (Aratemur-Çimen and Bayhan 2019, 22–23). The notion of death and blood are deeply engrained in the minds of the youth populous through adding such religious connotations within their curriculum and the reinforcement of it through national outlets. A prominent example of this is the mention is martyr's blood on Turkish soil being glorified within the national anthem.

Two stanzas within the full version of the national anthem written by Mehmet Akif Ersoy include, '*Turkish soil is unlike any other soil because Turks are sons of martyrs... and if one squeezes Turkish soil nothing but martyrs' blood would come out*' (a rough translation provided by Yanık and Hisarlıoğlu 2019). Such notions are further reinforced by the ruling elite to bring these ideals into the everyday lives of the Turkish youth. In his speeches, President Erdoğan often quotes two lines of Mithat Cemal Kuntay's poem, 'what makes a flag a flag is the blood on it; earth can only become a fatherland (*vatan*) when there are those willing to die for it'. A point to note in this necropolitical discourse is the importance of death placed on the propagators' side, where death for national cause and glory was amplified; killing and dying for the regime was the persisting narrative (Bakıner 2019). This provides a unique outlook on the general understanding of necropolitics.

The curriculum textbooks also quote one of Erdoğan's favourite poems, which he recites in public speeches that are broadcast live on almost all TV stations on Turkey. The poem by Arif Nihat Asya, entitled 'The Flag', is known for its militaristic language and glorification of martyrdom, while expressing respect for the Turkish flag:

> O the white and scarlet adornment of the blue skies,
> The bridal gown of my sister, *the shroud of our martyrs*,
> Radiating luminous lights, undulating gracefully!
> I read your epic and will write your legend.
> I will *dig a shallow grave* for those
> Who do not look at you the way I do.
> I will *ruin the nests of the birds*
> Who fly by without saluting you.
> (....)
> Just desire anywhere on earth!
> I will hoist you
> Wherever you wish! (Aratemur-Çimen and Bayhan 2019, 37, italics are ours).

In his speeches, Erdoğan frequently reiterates that he idealized a youth who is suing for their religion, chastity, piety, and grudge (Al-Monitor 2016).

'Heroism', 'martyrdom', 'veteran status,' 'dying and shedding blood' for the homeland from the Kemalist times (Altinay 2006) have been expanded to include the 15 July mysterious coup attempt discussions in the textbooks and 'dying for the homeland' no longer entails only fighting against external enemies, but also against traitors and internal enemies (Aratemur-Çimen and Bayhan 2019, 24). The books draw an analogy between Turkey's War of Independence and the 15th of July and use 'visuals that accompany stories of 15 July and texts of martyrdom, veteran status, heroism, commemorations, and monuments aim to mythicize the day and transmit it to new generations as a landmark historical event' (Aratemur-Çimen and Bayhan 2019, 25). This narrative presents 'decent citizens' as those who risk their lives in the fight against treacherous others who attack the homeland and are willing to sacrifice their lives for the homeland (Aratemur-Çimen and Bayhan 2019, 26).

Self-sacrifice and death have become an inseparable part of the AKP education in schools. In each school, especially after July 15 failed coup attempt, martyrs' corners were prepared and they were decorated with Islamic verses, hadiths, and visual pictures depicting martyrdom, in which pupils were indoctrinated with the glorification of death. Even in the kindergartens, commemorational activities were organized; therein children lie in front of the army tanks during the drama while the provincial directors of national education presented, in which bloody scenes like slaughtered bodies flattened here and there covered with Turkish flags (BirGün 2016).

Along with Quranic and Prophetic citations on the benefits of martyrdom and death, which have been politicized in favour of AKP government, Turkist and Nationalistic motives have been employed as a secondary path as well, to incite nationalistic senses of the people. This is also a result of AKP's coalition with the far nationalist party, the MHP. In such necropolitical propagation on the children, the families are also included. For instance, Mufti of Konya Meram province invites families and children to the organization *Who is Next for Sentry Duty*, with the quotes of non-Muslim Turkist ideologue Nihal Atsız, stating that:

A man grows within a cradle
So as to lie within a grave
And.... Heroes die
So as to keep the homeland alive.

The quote later has become viral after Erdoğan used it in one of his rallies in 2018, referring to the killed police officer Fethi Sekin (Yeni Şafak

2018). The poem partly contains erotic, androcentric, violent, and misogynistic metaphors such as the quote begins with 'God created girls/To be sold to the soldiers'.

The idealization of becoming a martyr is—even in the form of suicide attack—also propagated as an incentive action by State-run TRT one way or another. In one of the documentaries about the Syrian civil war, aired in November 2015, a Turkish interviewer asks one of the little Syrian refugee girls in Turkey 'What would you do if you had to fight?' Then the little girl replies 'I would blow myself up at a checkpoint' (Tremblay 2016).

Glorification of Martyrdom in Diyanet's Children's Magazines and Comics

In accordance with the AKP government's radical necropolitization of the education and curriculum, the Diyanet also unprecedently has begun to disseminate the radical Islamist values such as death, martyrdom, and jihad to the children in Qur'anic courses for children and publications for children. The Ministry of Education and the Diyanet have started to cooperate for this purpose. Significantly the Diyanet has entered the Educational Ministry's realm for the first time in Republican history, becoming the other pillar of student education. We witness this Diyanet's new role in the books it publishes and sells in Diyanet bookstores. It is possible to find out any radical, jihadi books in Diyanet bookstores as well as the necropolitical themes are replete in the books it publishes. For example, in the comics published in *Diyanet Çocuk Dergisi*, a magazine published by Diyanet for the children, in the April 2016 issue, martyrdom and death were glorified and presented something should be desired (Diyanet Cocuk 2016). In other cases, some of the comics begin with a hadith of the Prophet Muhammad, stating that 'A martyr would love to return to the world again in order to be martyred 10 times more after the honouring and prestige he/she receive in the heaven' (Diyanet Cocuk 2016, 4). In another comic, a father says to his son: 'How beautiful it is to be a martyr!'. The son asks, 'Can we really want to be martyred ever, dad?', the father replies 'Surely son. Who on earth does not want to gain the right to go to heaven!' (Diyanet Cocuk 2016, 4). The comics continue with another hadith regarding the importance of martyrdom. According to the hadith in the magazine, 'a martyr feels the pain when he/she was slaughtered as much as the one feels the pain when being pinched' (Diyanet Çocuk 2016, 4). The related comics are depicted between the father and his son again, during their visit to the martyrs' graveyard, ornamented with the Turkish flags, to urge the children that martyrs during the jihad is a sort of painless death:

> The son: Dad, who knows, how they suffered pain when they were being killed, didn't they?
> The father: Martyrs do not feel the pain as you think son!

In the comics, it is underscored that martyrdom is not only a manly Islamic duty. Hearing the conversation between the son and the dad, the little daughter, who is making a soldier salute to her mother, says: 'I wish I would be martyred'. The mother replies to her that if she desires to be martyred from heart, Allah will give its *sawap* (good deed) to her even if she is not martyred (Diyanet Cocuk 2016, 4). On the next page, another cartoon begins with another hadith, stating that 'God deletes all sins of a martyr except his/her debts'. In the cartoon, a father figure states showing the graves of martyrs that 'How beautiful, our martyrs resting purified from their sins'. Therefore, the daughter figure asks, 'Don't they have any sins?' The father replies: 'God forgives all the sins of the martyrs, my daughter' (Diyanet Cocuk 2016, 4). The last of the cartoons opens with another 'militarist' *hadith* as well: 'the hell-fire cannot touch to the eyes of the ones, whom had stood sentry' (Diyanet Cocuk 2016, 4).

CONCLUSION

This chapter addressed the use of both nationalist and Islamist civilizational populist necropolitical concepts, such as, jihad, martyrdom, sacrificing self for the religio-nationalist 'values' such within the national curriculum and school textbooks, including Diyanet's magazine for kids, *Diyanet Çocuk Dergisi*, which were redesigned by the AKP. The Turkish government had fashioned the national education curriculum into a mould that fits and reinforced their own civilizational populist ideological and political objectives. This was done through major curriculum changes such as rewriting historical events from a civilizational populist perspective, promoting Muslim scientists, favouring religious teachings over scientific ones, and increasing the number of religious courses. The new curriculum also includes other 'useful' values such as self-devotion, self-sacrifice, heroism, ummah and nation conscience, martyrdom, gathered under the title of national and religious values. Apart from that, school schedules were restructured to include time for students to perform their Friday prayers, encouraging and at times forcing students to pray every day; poems and events surrounding martyrdom and jihad became a notable element within school curriculum books. These changes present a drastic change in the Turkish education system as it became the site of political propaganda and social engineering to create the ideal pliant citizen. The Islamic religion is homogenized with Turkish identity, linking the two through state-sponsored pedagogy. In this vein, the Diyanet described this as 'God and fatherland' going hand in hand. The recent Turkish government of Erdoğan have slowly transformed the old Turkish-Islamic synthesis into an Islamist civilizational populist one, distancing themselves from Kemalist secularism. This process has radically accelerated after the mysterious coup attemp in July 2016.

Within these changes, the most prominent and pressing is the importance *jihad* has within school textbooks. Jihad, as a religious concept of sacrifice, is altered to be interpreted as a sacrifice for the state, *ummah* and religion, placing it as one of the essential pillars of Islam along with prayer, fasting, etc. Distancing themselves from the notion of peaceful jihad, the Turkish propaganda uses it to justify a narrative around the glory in giving up one's life for a cause—a cause that is manufactured to be one that reflects the AKP's own civilizational populist political and ideological values. National Education System is utilized as the most prominent and lasting tool for creating public compliance to such a change within society. Along with that, the Diyanet plays a crucial role in reinforcing this narrative by providing radical Islamist religious courses and teachers for the schools. Prayer rooms and mosques are built within every educational institute to further compel students to incorporate religion into their everyday lives. Sermons promoting martyrdom and sacrificing one's life for the protection of the nation, religion, *ummah* and God are perpetuated through Friday's call for prayers, and sermon promoted by the Diyanet, as part of the state's public education efforts.

The concepts of jihad and sacrifice for the nation is but an outcome of the national curriculum change. In essence, the education system is redesigned to reinforce the state's civilizational populist necropolitical propaganda through curating a religious image of the nation that blurs the lines between personal religion and national religious identity. Thousands of religious schools are made, replacing the previous secular institutes, to seep the state's propaganda within the Turkish youth and working alongside various other government institutions to ensure that the Turkish youth remain pious and pliant with the state religio-political ideology.

A Turkish psychologist, Professor Dr. Serdar Değirmencioğlu, points out that such publications and education for children, intertwined with religion which ultimately glorifies death and martyrdom are alarming in that it has the capacity to produce 'deadly terrorist attacks' elsewhere in the world (Koçer 2016; Haworth 2016). Değirmencioğlu also states that those comics are much more penetrating for 6–9 aged children for future ISIS-like suicide bombing, given the amount of rewards promised in the heaven (Koçer 2016). As a result of such a heavy necropolitical investment and death glorification, a family health official employed by AKP municipality in Istanbul noted: 'We witness children between the ages of 4 and 14 frequently in two categories: Either they are acting extremely bold and aggressive in ways that could physically hurt themselves and those around them or they are on the other side of the spectrum with a sincere phobia what we call death anxiety' (Tremblay 2016). Given the AKP has necropolitically started to indoctrinate education since 2010, this is a new phenomenon that appeared with the AKP government. The official reports several incidents noting that the situation is at an alarming rate, for example, some children were scared their parents would kill them so that they become martyrs (Tremblay 2016).

References

AA. 2018. 'Asım Safitürk: Şehidimizin Kanı Kimsenin Yanında Kalmamıştır'. *AA*, 4 February 2018. https://www.aa.com.tr/tr/turkiye/asim-safiturk-seh idimizin-kani-kimsenin-yaninda-kalmamistir/1053811.

Açık, Abdullah, Veli Karataş and Mustafa Yılmaz. 2019. *Ortaöğretim Temel Dini Bilgiler İslam Ders Kitabı*. Ankara: Milli Eğitim Bakanlığı Yayınları.

Açık et al. 2019. *Temel Dini Bilgiler* [Fundamental Religious Knowledge], 24–27. Milli Eğitim Bakanlığı.

Akpınar, Alişan, Sos Avetisyan, Hayk Balasanyan, Fırat Güllü, Işıl Kandolu, Maria Karapetyan, Nvard V. Manasian, Lilit Mkrtchyan, Elif Aköz Özkaya, Hasan Tahsin Özkaya, Garine Palandjian, Ararat Şekeryan, and Ömer Turan. 2017. *History Education in Schools in Turkey and Armenia A Critique and Alternatives*. Istanbul: History Foundation.

132   I. YILMAZ AND O. ERTURK

Akşam. 2016. *Dersimiz: 15 Temmuz şehitlerini anma* [Our Lesson: Commemorating the 15 July Martyrs]. September 19. http://www.aksam.com.tr/gun cel/dersimiz-15-temmuz-sehitlerinianma-c2/haber-550276.

Al-Monitor. 2016. https://www.al-monitor.com/tr/contents/articles/origin als/2016/06/turkey-education-erdogan-devout-generation-plan.html.

Altinay, Ayse Gül. 2006. *The Myth of the Military-Nation: Militarism, Gender, and Education in Turkey.* New York: Palgrave Macmillan.

Altuntaş, Öykü. 2017. 'Turkey's New School Year: Jihad in, Evolution Out', September 18, sec. Europe. https://www.bbc.com/news/world-europe-412 96714.

Aratemur-Çimen, C., and Sezen Bayhan. 2018. Secularism and Gender in Turkey's New Textbooks Research, Executive Summary. *Project: Ders Kitaplarında Sekülerizm ve Toplumsal Cinsiyet* (Secularism and Gender in Turkey's New Textbooks). https://www.researchgate.net/publication/328 413717_Secularism_and_Gender_in_Turkey\T1\textquoterights_NewTextbo oks_Research_Executive_Summary.

Aratemur-Çimen, C., and S. Bayhan. 2019. *Democratic Values and Democratic Citizenship in The Turkish Education System: Textbooks.* Lxelles: The European Liberal Forum.

Bakıner, O. 2019. 'These Are Ordinary Things': *Regulation of Death Under the AKP Regime.* Turkey's Necropolitical Laboratory: Democracy, Violence and Resistance, 25.

Bargu, B. 2019. Turkey's Necropolitical Laboratory.

Bilefsky, Dan. 2017. 'In Turkey's New Curriculum, Ataturk, Darwin and Jihad Get Face-Lifts'. *The New York Times.* September 18. https://www.nytimes. com/2017/09/18/world/europe/turkey-curriculum-darwin-jihad.html.

BirGün. 2016. 'Anaokulunda 15 temmuz tiyatrosu!' birgun.net. 22 December 2016. https://www.birgun.net/haber/anaokulunda-15-temmuz-tiyatrosu-140515.

———. 2017a. 'AKP'li Vekil: Cihat Bilmeyen Çocuğa Matematik Öğretmek Faydasız'. 22 July 2017. https://www.birgun.net/haber/akp-li-vekil-cihat-bil meyen-cocuga-matematik-ogretmek-faydasiz-171089.

———. 2017b. 'FETÖ, PKK, IŞİD ve cihat yeni müfredatta: '15 Temmuz cihattır'' [FETO, PKK, ISIS and Jihad are in the New Curriculum], Birgün, July 19, 2017a.

———. 2018. 'İlkokul çocuklarına Afrin mektubu!' birgun.net. February 7. https://www.birgun.net/haber/ilkokul-cocuklarina-afrin-mektubu-203338.

Bulut, Birkan. 2017. 'İmam hatiplerde cihat çağrısı!' Evrensel.net. November 8. https://www.evrensel.net/haber/337366/imam-hatiplerde-cihat-cagrisi.

Butler, Daren. 2018. 'Special Report: With More Islamic Schooling, Erdogan Aims to Reshape Turkey.' Reuters, January 25. www.reuters.com/article/us-turkey-erdogan-education/special-report.

6 TARGETING CHILDREN VIA EDUCATION FOR POPULIST ... 133

Camli, Ahmet Hamdi. 2017. @ahmethamdicamli, 03:31, July 19. https://twi tter.com/ahmethamdicamli.

Çayır, Kenan. 2009. Preparing Turkey for the European Union: Nationalism, National Identity and 'Otherness' in Turkey's New Textbooks, *Journal of Intercultural Studies* 30 (1): 39–55.

Çayır, Kenan. 2014. *Who Are We? Identity, Citizenship and Rights in Turkey's Textbooks*. Istanbul: History Foundation Publications.

Çayır, Kenan. 2015. Citizenship, Nationality and Minorities in Turkey's Textbooks: From Politics of Non-Recognition to 'difference multiculturalism'. *Comparative Education* 51 (4): 519–536.

Çepni (a), Ozan. 2017. 'Signed follow-up in Afyon: 'Let's go to the mosque' instead of homework.' Cumhuriyet, July 28. https://www.cumhuriyet.com. tr/haber/afyonda-imzali-takip-odev-yerine-haydi-camiye-666810.

Çepni (b), Ozan. 2018. 'Okula vaaz da girdi... 10 yaşındaki çocuklara "ümmet ve şehadet" anlatılacak'. January 9. https://www.cumhuriyet.com.tr/haber/ okula-vaaz-da-girdi-10-yasindaki-cocuklara-ummet-ve-sehadet-anlatilacak-901913. Accessed 26 Oct 2021.

Cornell, S.E., and M.K. Kaya (2015). The Naqshbandi-Khalidi Order and Political Islam in Turkey. *Current Trends in Islamist Ideology* 3.

Cranmer, F. 2008. 'Hasan and Eylem Zengin v Turkey.' *Law & Just. -Christian l. Rev.* 160: 53.

Cumhuriyet. 2015. 'Prayer Break at School,' April 10. https://www.cumhuriyet. com.tr/haber/okulda-namaz-molasi-251673.

———. 2017. 'Sıbyan Mektepleri Çocukları Böyle Zehirliyor... "Anne Ne Zaman Öleceğiz, Burası Çok Sıkıcı"'. October15. https://www.cumhuriyet.com.tr/ haber/sibyan-mektepleri-cocuklari-boyle-zehirliyor-anne-ne-zaman-olecegiz-burasi-cok-sikici-844971.

———. 2018. Recep Tayyip Erdoğan: 20 civarında 25 kadar şehidimiz var. February 1. https://www.cumhuriyet.com.tr/video/recep-tayyip-erdogan-20-civarinda-25-kadar-sehidimiz-var-917782. Accessed 30 Dec 2022.

Diyanet Cocuk. 2016. *Diyanet Cocuk*. April 2016 Issue. Ankara: Diyanet.

Doğan, N. 2020. 18. Yüzyılda Merkez-Taşra İlişkileri Çerçevesinde Kayseri Ayanları. Doctoral dissertation.

EBA. 2016. '15 Temmuz Şehitlerine Mektup'. Eğitim Bilişim Ağı (blog). July 23. http://www.eba.gov.tr/haber/1474532289.

Eroler, Elif Gençkal. 2018. *Dindar Nesil Yetiştirmek: Türkiye'nin Eğitim Politikalarında Ulus ve Vatandaş İnşası (2002–2016)*. Istanbul: İletişim.

Erturk, Omer F. 2022. 'Anatomy of Political Islam in Republican Turkey: The Milli Görüş Movement as a legacy of Naqshbandism.' *Contemporary Islam* 16 (2–3): 295–320. https://doi.org/10.1007/s11562-022-00500-x.

134 I. YILMAZ AND O. ERTURK

Evrensel. 2017a. '7. sınıftan itibaren çocuklara cihat kavramı anlatılacak'. January 15. https://www.evrensel.net/haber/304132/7-siniftan-itibaren-coc uklara-cihat-kavrami-anlatilacak.

———. 2017b. 'Sıbyan mektebinin "korkunç" dünyası!' Evrensel.net. October 15. https://www.evrensel.net/haber/335261/sibyan-mektebinin-korkunc-dunyasi.

Gercek Gundem. 2021. 'AKP's Nergis: It Feels Like Too Many Women Are Being Killed in Turkey.' March 9. https://www.gercekgundem.com/siyaset/ 257620/akpli-nergis-sanki-turkiyede-cok-fazla-kadin-olduruluyor-algisi-yarati liyor.

Gökdemir, Nurcan. 2016. 'Okul öncesi eğitime Osmanlı modeli: Sıbyan mektepleri'. birgun.net. May 24. https://www.birgun.net/haber/okul-oncesi-egi time-osmanli-modeli-sibyan-mektepleri-113296.

Gürcan, A.E. 2015. *The Problems of Religious Education in Turkey: Alevi Citizen Action and the Limits of ECTHR*. *IPC-Mercator Policy Brief*. Istanbul: Istanbul Policy Center.

Haberler. 2017. 'Investigation on a School in Şanlıurfa that Wears Headscarves for Female Students and Holds a Closing Party.' December 21. https://www. haberler.com/kiz-ogrencilerin-kapanma-partisine-sorusturma-10405495-hab eri/.

Haworth, Jessica. 2016. 'Turkish Government Publishes Cartoons "glorifying Martyrdom" to Children Which Compares Suicide Bombing to Feeling a Pinch'. April 4. https://www.mirror.co.uk/news/world-news/turkish-govern ment-publishes-cartoons-glorifying-7685101.

Hurriyet. 2012. 'We Will Raise Religious Youth." February 2. https://www.hur riyet.com.tr/gundem/dindar-genclik-yetistirecegiz-19825231.

———. 2017a. 'Evrim yok cihat dört başı mamur' [Evolution Is Removed, Jihad Is Flourishing]. Hürriyet, July 18. https://www.hurriyet.com.tr/gun dem/evrim-yok-cihat-dort-basi-mamur-40524324.

———. 2017b. 'Obligation of Ablution and Prayer Rooms for Schools.' June 25. https://www.hurriyet.com.tr/egitim/okullara-abdesthane-ve-mes cit-zorunlulugu-40500965.

Ince, Başak. 2012. Citizenship education in Turkey: inclusive or exclusive. *Oxford Review of Education* 38: 115–31. https://doi.org/10.1080/030 54985.2011.651314.

İpek, Hatice, and Fatih Yaşar. 2016. 'Peygamberimiz ve Küçük Ümmeti: Şehitlerimizden Allah Razı Olsun Kabirleri Nur İle Dolsun [Our Pophet and His Youngster Ummah: May God Bless Our Martyrs, May Their Graves Be Full of Holy Light]'. *Diyanet Çocuk Dergisi* [Diyanet Kids Magazine], April 2016.

Kandiyoti, D., and Z. Emanet. 2017. 'Education as Battleground: The Capture of Minds in Turkey.' *Globalizations* 14 (6): 869–876.

Kaplan, S. 2006. *The Pedagogical State: Education and Politics of National Culture in Post 1980 Turkey*. Stanford, CA: Stanford University Press.

Kaya, A. 2016. 'Ethno-Religious Narratives of Citizenship in Turkey: Fabricating Citizens Through National Education.' *Research and Policy on Turkey* 1 (2): 119–131.

Koçer, Zülal. 2016. 'Diyanet'ten çocuklara: Şehit olun'. Evrensel.net. March 28. https://www.evrensel.net/haber/276082/diyanetten-cocuklara-sehit-olun.

Letsch, Constanze. 2015. 'Turkish Parents Complain of Push Towards Religious Schools.' *The Guardian*, February 12. https://www.theguardian.com/world/2015/feb/12/turkish-parents-steered-religious-schools-secular-imam-hatip.

Lord, C. (2018). *Religious Politics in Turkey: From the Birth of the Republic to the AKP*, vol. 54. Cambridge University Press.

Lüküslü, D. 2016. 'Creating a Pious Generation: Youth and Education Policies of the AKP in Turkey.' *Southeast European and Black Sea Studies* 16 (4): 637–649.

Mbembe, A. 2006. 'Necropolitics.' *Raisons Politiques* 1: 29–60.

MEB. 2016. Okullar "15 Temmuz Demokrasi Zaferi ve Şehitleri Anma" etkinliğiyle açılacak. National Education Ministry (MEB), September 9. https://www.meb.gov.tr/okullar-15-temmuz-demokrasi-zaferi-ve-sehitleri-anma-etkinligiyle-acilacak/haber/11877/tr.

Meral, Z. 2015. *Compulsory Religious Education in Turkey: A Survey and Assessment of Textbooks*. US Commission on International Religious Freedom.

Nahmiyaz, Medi. 2018. Turkey: Greeks and Armenians in History Textbooks (1930–1910). In *Multiple Alterities: Views of others in textbooks of the Middle East*. London: Palgrave MacMillan.

Ntvmsnbc. 2012. Erdoğan: Gençlik tinerci mi olsun? February 6. http://www.ntvmsnbc.com/id/25319805. Accessed 19 Aug 2015.

Osborne, Samuel. 2017. 'Turkish MP Says, "no Use in Teaching Maths to a Child Who Doesn't Know Jihad".' *The Independent*, July 25. https://www.independent.co.uk/news/world/europe/turkish-mp-maths-teaching-jihad-child-muslim-islam-jihad-madrasa-secular-education-a7858451.html.

Öztürk, Nuray. 2017. 'Çok günah kazanmadan ölmem lazım anne!' Evrensel.net. October 31. https://www.evrensel.net/haber/336640/cok-gunah-kazanm adan-olmem-lazim-anne.

Ramazan, Altıntaş, and Vehbi Dereli. 2014. *Temel Dini Bilgiler - İslam 1: Öğretim Materyali* [Fundamental Religious Knowledge—Islam 1: Learning Material], 130–132. Milli Eğitim Bakanlığı.

Spencer, Robert. 2017. 'Turkish MP: "There Is No Use in Teaching Math to a Child Who Does Not Know the Concept of Jihad".' July 23. https://www.jihadwatch.org/2017/07/turkish-mp-there-is-no-use-in-teaching-math-to-a-child-who-does-not-know-the-concept-of-jihad.

136 I. YILMAZ AND O. ERTURK

T24. 2017. *Emine Erdoğan: Yeni nesil, vatan için candan vazgeçmeyi çok iyi biliyor*, June 8. https://t24.com.tr/haber/emine-erdogan-yeni-nesil-vatan-icin-candan-vazgecmeyi-cok-iyi-biliyor,407888. Accessed 30 Dec 2022.

T.C. Geyve Kaymakamlığı. 2017. 'GEDEP Projesi Kapsamında Asım Safitürk Hocamız Konferans Verdi'. *T.C. Geyve Kaymakamlığı*, 20 December 2017. http://geyve.gov.tr/gedep-projesi-kapsaminda-asim-safiturk-hocamiz-konferans-verdi.

T.C. Hizan Kaymakamlığı. n.d. 'Asım Safitürk İlçemizde Konferans Verdi.' *T.C. Hizan Kaymakamlığı.* http://www.hizan.gov.tr/asim-safiturk-ilcemizde-konferans-verdi.

The Independent. 2017. www.independent.co.uk/news/world/europe/turkish-mp-maths-teaching-jihad-child-muslim-islam-jihad-madrasa-secular-education-a7858451.html.

Tremblay, Pinar. 2016. 'How Glorification of Martyrdom Produces Child Suicide Bombers in Turkey–Al-Monitor: The Pulse of the Middle East'. August 28. https://www.al-monitor.com/originals/2016/08/turkey-gazian tep-attack-child-suicide-bomber.html.

Üstel, Füsun. 2011. 'Makbul Vatandaş'ın Peşinde: II. Meşrutiyet'ten Bugüne Türkiye'de Vatandaş Eğitimi'. 5. baskı. İstanbul: İletişim.

vom Hau, M. 2009. Unpacking the School: Textbooks, Teachers, and the Construction of Nationhood in Mexico, Argentina, and Peru. *Latin American Research Review* 44: 127–154.

Weise, Zia. 2017. 'Turkey's New Curriculum: More Erdoğan, More Islam'. February 13. https://www.politico.eu/article/erdogan-turkey-educat ion-news-coup-analysis-curriculum-history-istanbul/.

Yanarocak, Hay Eytan Cohen. 2016. *Turkey's Curriculum Under Erdoğan, The Evolution of Turkish Identity: An Interim Report.* Jerusalem: Hebrew University of Jerusalem.

Yanarocak, Hay Eytan Cohen. 2022. *The Evolution of the Turkish School Textbooks from Atatürk to Erdogan.* Lanham, Maryland: Lexington Books.

Yanık, L.K., and F. Hisarlıoğlu. (2019). *'They Wrote History with Their Bodies': Necrogeopolitics, Necropolitical Spaces and the Everyday Spatial Politics of Death in Turkey*, 46–70. Turkey's Necropolitical Laboratory: Democracy, Violence and Resistance.

Yaşar, A. 2020. 'Reform in Islamic Education and the AKP's Pious Youth in Turkey.' *Religion & Education* 47 (4): 106–120.

Yeni, Şafak. 2018. Cumhurbaşkanı Erdoğan: Kahramanlar can verir yurdu yaşatmak için, *Yeni Şafak*. https://www.yenisafak.com/video-galeri/gun dem/cumhurbaskani-erdogan-kahramanlar-can-verir-yurdu-yasatmak-icin-216 6981.

Yilmaz, Ihsan. 2016. *Muslim Laws, Politics and Society in Modern Nation States: Dynamic Legal Pluralisms in England, Turkey and Pakistan*. Reprint. London and New York: Routledge.

Yilmaz, I. (2018). 'Islamic Populism and Creating Desirable Citizens in Erdogan's New Turkey.' *Mediterranean Quarterly* 29 (4): 52–76. Chicago.

Yilmaz, Ihsan. 2021. *Creating the Desired Citizens: State, Islam and Ideology in Turkey*. Cambridge and New York: Cambridge University Press.

Yilmaz, Ihsan. 2022a. *Authoritarianism, Informal Law, and Legal Hybridity: The Islamisation of the State in Turkey*. Singapore: Palgrave Macmillan.

Yilmaz, Ihsan. 2022b. 'Islamist Populist Nation-Building: Gradual, Ad Hoc Islamisation of the Secular Education System in Turkey.' *Religions* 13 (9): 814. https://doi.org/10.3390/rel13090814.

Yilmaz, Ihsan, and Omer F. Erturk. 2021a. 'Populism, Violence and Authoritarian Stability: Necropolitics in Turkey.' *Third World Quarterly* 42 (7): 1524–1543. https://doi.org/10.1080/01436597.2021.1896965.

Yilmaz, Ihsan, and Omer F. Erturk. 2021b. 'Pro-Violence Sermons of a Secular State: Turkey's Diyanet on Islamist Militarism.' *Jihadism and Glorification of Martyrdom*. *Religions* 12 (8): 659. https://doi.org/10.3390/rel12080659.

Yilmaz, Ihsan, and Omer Erturk. 2022. 'Authoritarianism and necropolitical creation of martyr icons by Kemalists and Erdoganists in Turkey.' *Turkish Studies*, 23 (2): 243–260. https://doi.org/10.1080/14683849.2021.194 3662.

PART II

Necropolitics in Authoritarian Action

CHAPTER 7

Necropolitics and AKP's Blame Avoidance

INTRODUCTION

Politicians resort to blame avoidance when they fear being held guilty for political failures. It is a vital issue for policymakers because research finds that voters are much more inclined to remember the losses and sufferings than gains (See Weaver 1986, 373). Thus, for officeholders, blame can lead to political bankruptcy, the destruction of personal reputation, and following these things, a loss of power (Hansson 2015). Due to voters' 'negativity bias' (Psychologists revealed that the human mind is more inclined to remember unpleasant, harmful, and traumatic events than positive ones, and this is called negativity bias) (Rozin and Royzman 2001; Kanouse and Hanson 1987), politicians, government bureaucrats, and policymakers primarily seek to avoid blame when they are criticized or held responsible for the electorally risky issues such as social policy reforms, government expenditures, scandals, policy gaffes, or mismanagement of disasters and fiascos which can be attributed to their government (Weaver 1986; Vis 2016; Pierson 2007; Hood 2011, 9–14; Boin et al. 2010).

As we will see in this chapter, the AKP's responses to the incidents that resulted in deaths is a text-book case of blame avoidance. The AKP has chosen to get away with these deaths without any accountability or blame by using the concept of martyrdom, which appeals to both the

© The Author(s), under exclusive license to Springer Nature Singapore Pte Ltd. 2023
I. Yilmaz and O. Erturk, *Populism, Authoritarianism and Necropolitics*, https://doi.org/10.1007/978-981-19-8292-7_7

141

religious and nationalistic senses of Turkish people. Thus we will be investigating how the AKP, an authoritarian and Islamist civilizational populist party, tries to avoid blame by spinning, manipulating, and bending the arguments and the perceptions of the public via necropolitics and by restricting opposition voices and media, while trying to turn blame into credit or justification for its political survival (Hood 2011, 18).

The chapter first examines the AKP's use of martyrdom and as part of its *presentational strategies* in blame-generating issues that resulted in deaths. Then, we focus on how offering 'rewards' as a strategy of blame avoidance and bargaining over the martyrdom produce co-optation and cooperation between the parts (office holders, victim families, public). In this part, we will show that how the AKP elites have benefitted *bargaining* via *rewards* as a supporting strategy for martyrdom. In this part, we will scrutinize with empirical evidence that how *carrots*—financial aids, promises, privileges, social status, and significantly a promise of a house—as a reward by the government officials for the victim families played significant role in addition to martyrdom, to deflect blame and avoid policymakers' responsibilities in disasters and fiascos. When some victim families resist cooperation, the AKP regime employs *sticks*. Thus, this part looks at *what happens when the officials do not keep their promises subsequently*, and *what happens when the families hold responsible the policymakers and they insist on putting the blame on the government*, by focusing on the subsequent accounts of the victim families by asking.

BLAME AVOIDANCE TACTICS

Political leaders generally require three ways of coping with blame avoidance: *stonewalling versus cooperating, denying versus acknowledging, and persevere versus resign*. Boin et al. explain these three attempts as:

> Leaders can stonewall fact-finding efforts by keeping tabs on files, people, and other sources of information. They can also pretend to co-operate and flood their inquisitors with truckloads of mostly tangential records. [...] Leaders may attempt to conserve their legitimacy either by accepting responsibility or by denying it and blaming force majeure or other actors for damages, glitches and errors.[...] They can deploy several tactics to defuse criticism and maintain their legitimacy: arguing that continuity is vital in a time of crisis; setting up an (other) Inquiry to 'buy time'; sacking

or sanctioning lower-level officials; announcing sweeping reforms to show they have got the message. (Boin et al. 2010, 708–710)

Weaver has shown that there are eight blame-avoiding strategies that policymakers can apply: (Weaver 1986, 384–390) *agenda limitation, redefine the issue, throw good money after bad, pass the buck, find a scapegoat, jump on the bandwagon, circle the wagons,* and '*stop me before I kill again*' (see Weaver 1986). Policymakers' effort to keep the blame-generating issue off the agenda is *agenda limitation strategy*. If they fail to succeed a blame-generating issue off the agenda, 'they may be able to reshape' and *redefine the issue*, such as 'developing new policy options which diffuse or obfuscate losses' (Weaver 1986, 385–386). *Throw good money after bad*, Weaver's third strategy, is usually employed by the office holders under the circumstances of negative-sum games; when there is no way left to prevent losses, or other strategies failed, the policymakers may be able to prevent or obstruct by providing extra resources 'to shore up the status quo' thus can avoid suffering losses. *Pass the buck*, as a fourth strategy, is explained by Weaver as such: 'if a blame-generating decision has to be made, policymakers are likely to try to delegate that decision to someone else' (Weaver 1986, 386). During the times that the political leaders fail to *pass the buck*, they are likely pass the blame on others, and this is called *find a scapegoat*, the fifth strategy (Weaver 1986, 387–388).

Weaver's *pass the buck* and *find a scapegoat* have been expanded by Hood and Ellis as *agency strategies,* and *lightning rods*. Hood writes that *agency strategies* 'deal mainly with the perceived agency dimension of blame' and it is the 'issue of who or what can be held responsible for what can be held responsible for someone sees as avoidable harm' (Hood 2011, 17), while Ellis showed the use of *lightning rods* in blame avoidance by examining its use by the U.S. presidents. He states that the US presidents tactically throw their policy advisors and other officers from the government as baits in response to public anger so that public blame those officers instead of the incumbent president in case of crises and thus, he/she receives no harm for their popularity (Ellis 1994). Baekkeskov and Rubin showed that, in two different cases, 2003 SARS and 2009 H1N1 epidemics, the authoritarian Chinese government widely used Ellis', and Hood's strategies in responding blame avoidance (Baekkeskov and Rubin 2017).

As a sixth strategy, *jump on the wagon*, Weaver states that political leaders may jump on the wagon and avoid blame if there is any other working popular alternative, and when their other strategies do not work. Weaver notes that this is also related to the 'desire to turn blame into credit' (Weaver 1986, 388). If other strategies are not viable in deflecting blame, the officeholder can adopt the seventh strategy, *circle the wagons*. According to this strategy, a political leader diffuses the blame-generating issue 'by spreading it among as many policymakers as possible' for fear that he/she will take the lead in blame (Weaver 1986, 385, 388–389). Finally, the eighth strategy, in which political leaders 'know that they are doing is wrong, but they can't help themselves' is defined as *stop me before I kill again* (Weaver 1986, 389).

In his book, *The Blame Game*, Christopher Hood denotes that *presentational strategy*, which might also be named as 'spinocracy', 'involve[s] various ways of trying to avoid blame by spin, stage management, and argument' (Hood 2011, 17). It also 'denotes attempts to affect the harm perception [...] and various forms of persuasion' by proposing persuasive justifications and manipulating or diverting the public attention off the subject (Hood 2011, 47–49). In authoritarian regimes, *presentational strategy* includes secrecy, that is restricting flow of information, and strict surveillance of media outlets, while it occurs priming the media in democratic ones (Baekkeskov and Rubin 2017, 428). This is related to 'the rhetorical dimension of politics and management, the dynamics of public attitudes and opinion' (Hood 2011, 17). Hood continues:

> The presentational strategist aims to work on the loss or harm perception dimension of blame, for example by accentuating the positive to counter negativity bias, and focuses primarily on what information to offer, when and how. Presentational strategists aim to find ways of showing that what might be perceived as a blameworthy problem is in fact a blessing in disguise, for instance as short-term pain that will produce long-term gain. (Hood 2011, 17)

Redefine, Reshape, Spin, and Manipulate the Blame

Generally speaking, *presentational strategies* are the ways in which policymakers try to (1) redefine, reshape, spin, and manipulate the issues so as to divert public attention from the subject. The main aim here is to persuade society that such crises are normal and can happen anywhere, anytime. The presentational strategy also includes (2) restricting flow of information by imposing restrictions on opposing voices in the media other than the government's narration (Baekkeskov and Rubin 2017, 428), together with the fabrication and spread of persuasive pro-government narratives, (3) efforts to turn blame into credit or justification (Hood 2011, 47–49; Weaver 1986, 385–386). Here, we analyse how the AKP, for its political survival and reinforcement of the status quo, tries to deflect blame by using presentational strategies in the incidents that resulted in death.

Within the context of necropolitics, Bakiner is one of the few scholars that broadly dealt with what strategies the AKP developed regarding the management of death, how the death became 'an area of patronage' and hegemony of the incumbent party, as it moved towards authoritarianism. The loss of life, work accidents, military conflict, natural disasters etc., are one of the most important events that can reduce the political support of the governments and can lead the personal reputation of the officeholders. We argue in this chapter that when such crises occur, the AKP government has both employed blame avoidance strategies and improved itself on this issue. Bakıner identified four strategies used by the AKP to regulate death. These are (1) the *expansion of martyrdom* 'used as a religious justification for military casualties, into the civilian sphere, and the increasing distribution of material benefits through formal laws and informal government discretion regulating civilian and military conceptions of martyrdom'; (2) the *normalization of death* 'as an inherent feature of some citizens' occupational, socioeconomic and in some cases, gender position'; (3) the *depoliticization of death* 'to eliminate the risk of dissident mobilization after deadly incidents'; (4) *controlling the narrative* 'around the news of death to maintain discursive hegemony' (Bakıner 2019, 26).

The initial response of the AKP to the failures that resulted in the loss of life is to absorb its earlier impact on the society and disorient and stun public opinion by redefining the cases as normal. For instance, Erdoğan explained that 'there is a concept known as work accidents in the literature' adding that such explosions happen all the time in mines, by giving various examples from world history, to the Soma mine disaster, the deadliest labour catastrophe ever in Turkish history occurred in Manisa on 13 May 2014, in which 301 miners died (Cumhuriyet 2014). Erdoğan also defined the issue as 'nature of the business' (Daloglu 2014). The same strategy is followed in the incident, known as Aladağ boarding girls'

Qur'anic school tragedy, in which eleven female students and a teacher were burned to death in 2016. The incident is defined as 'an act of fate' and was not fully inspected since the dormitory was being run by a pro-AKP religious community, as in the case of Soma (Shafak 2016).

As examples of other presentational strategies that the AKP skilfully employed, we can examine the two separate incidents that resulted in the loss of Turkish soldiers. In 2018, two Turkish soldiers froze to death in the eastern province of Tunceli due to inadequate equipment such as sleeping bags, camouflage, and boots. The event became a big issue in the media and among the opposition parties. Main opposition party CHP leader Kemal Kılıçdaroğlu said that policymakers have to be held responsible for this failure (Milliyet n.d.), while some others filed a criminal complaint against President Tayyip Erdoğan, Minister of national defence Hulusi Akar, minister of interior Süleyman Soylu, and Gendarmerie general commander Arif Çetin on charges of 'neglect of duty' (Odatv 2018). Similar to his other accounts, to minimize failures, Erdoğan stated that 'in martyrdom, there exists bullets, as well as freezing' (Evrensel 2018), and stated that his grandfather also froze to death and become martyr during the World War I in order to normalize soldier's death of hypothermia (Hürriyet 2018).

In addition to reshaping the issue by claiming normalization of the death, the AKP gets to benefit from other elements of presentational strategy, spinning, manipulating, and diverting the public attention off the blame. The AKP carries the agenda into other stages such as Islamic religion. Erdoğan tries to ward off the blame that was asked by Kılıçdaroğlu, the head of the main opposition secularist party by telling the public that Kılıçdaroğlu does not possess belief in martyrdom, implying that he is not even a Muslim (for Erdoğan's excommunicative discourse in politics, see Erturk 2022). Erdoğan vociferously said: 'you have no right to depreciate this nation and this country. You have already no belief of martyrdom. But the families [of the dead soldiers] had believed in martyrdom. But you have no such sense' (BBC 2018). By doing this, Erdoğan does not only use martyrdom to avoid the blame but he also attempts to de-legitimise the criticism by alleging that it is raised by a political actor who is a civilizational other who is hostile the people's civilization, i.e. Islam.

The case of captured and then killed soldiers by the militants of the ISIS is another example of how the AKP tried to manage public perception by manipulating and spinning. In this case, the AKP used its media and the social media trolls to resonate and propagate the narrations that were fabricated by the officeholders in blame avoidance. In 2016, two Turkish soldiers were captured and then burnt to death by the ISIS jihadists in Syria. Having the ISIS streamed the burning video of the soldiers on social media, the government immediately restricted access to social media and related news and soon the AKP ministerial cabinet proclaimed that the footage was fabricated indeed (Sputnik 2016; Hurtas 2017).

What is more, in order to appease the anger and possible protests, the AKP deputy Şamil Tayyar officially announced that the captive soldiers were already members of the ISIS indeed, and they voluntarily joined ISIS during the operations (Sputnik 2016). The burnt soldiers and their mournful families were tarnished by the pro-AKP national and social media and trolls for months in that they consciously tried to bother AKP government and personally Erdoğan with their explanations. However, the soldier's silenced father stated that both the government and Turkish Armed Forces did not answer any of their petitions and questions about the fate of his son, so they are in perish because of their son's footage in which he seemed to be burnt death with another soldier (Yeşilçınar 2017). However, almost a year later, after the incident was off the popular agenda, the father was later informed by the government officials that the family members would be rewarded with martyrdom privileges, his son would be officially bestowed with martyrdom status and therefore his file would be closed soon (Yeşilçınar 2017).

Impose Restrictions on Access to Opposing Voices and Media

As a part of the *presentational strategy*, the government immediately imposes bans on the media for the news that may have the capacity to turn into massive protests, and restricts flowing of related news including the viewers' comments. The news on soldiers burnt by the ISIS and girl students died in the fire were banned, 'on the grounds that they may turn into acts and protests that can lead to disrupt the peace, safety, and public order throughout the country' (BBC Türkçe 2016).

Another example is the death of high-ranked Turkish Army officers, including two of the intelligence officers who were killed in Libya. Normally, when the blame could easily be put on the Gülenists, or other demonized groups such as radical leftists or Kurdish nationalists, the AKP government makes sure to organize official funeral ceremony with fanfare, as in the other cases such as Safitürk, 15 July victims etc., and the high echelons attend the ceremony, give a speech in front of the coffin in front of live TV cameras and try to turn the funeral into a credit. These events are mostly streamed on TV live. However, in this case, since it was impossible to blame the 'internal enemies' or Western powers, Erdoğan passed on the event by saying 'We have a few martyrs [in Libya]'. Then, he added, in order to normalize the event: 'My brothers and sisters, we will never forget that the martyrs' hill will not be empty' (Euronews 2020a). The dead bodies of the officers were buried without official funeral, secretly, off the eyes. When the death news has appeared in the media, complaints questioning the Turkish soldiers' existence in Libya rose among the society. Additionally, Erdoğan's use of the quantifier 'a few' for the 'martyrs' has led to anger and circulated on social media. Immediately, the journalists who reported the case were arrested the following day, and their houses were stormed by the police early in the morning hours, and access to the news restricted (BBC Türkçe 2020). The news reporting has been defined as a 'betrayal' by the regime media (Sabah 2020). We see the same tactic followed on the issues that the government seized that it would be totally unreasonable to shift the blame. For instance, as mentioned before, it chose defamation of the family instead of accusing ISIS, though the burnt soldiers' videos streamed on social media.

Turn Blame into Credit

Seeking efforts to turn blame into credit is one of the other available tactics in *presentational strategies*, employed by the power holders. The Eren Bülbül case is a good example of this use. On August 2017, a local 15-year-old boy was killed by the outlawed Kurdish separatist PKK (Kurdistan Workers Party) fighters while Turkish military officers wanted to get help from him as an informant and guide in their military operation in Trabzon countryside. The boy's mother held the prime minister, ministers, and the authorities responsible (Gazete Duvar 2017). It is known that Erdoğan frequently underscores the importance of having more than three children and identifies womanhood over motherhood. Thus, in this case, Erdoğan praised the mother of Bülbül in front of the masses stating that she has thirteen children: 'You have fulfilled the order of Allah and His messenger, what a beautiful mother you are'. Then, he told the mother that she is great because thanks to 'martyr' Eren, 'you have guaranteed heaven together with your 13 children' (Beyazgazete 2017). Here Erdoğan obviously is trying to turn blame into credit by ornamenting the incident with religious themes and martyrdom. Additionally, as mostly seen in other similar cases, by rewarding martyrdom as a religious rank and official status, the AKP urges the victims' families and voters that they are advantageous side out of this 'loss.' For instance, as Erdoğan underscored 'guaranteed' heaven for the entire family of the 'martyred' boy, Diyanet mufti of Ankara preached that a martyr can bring 70 of his relatives into heaven (Hızlı 2015). In the same sense, Erdoğan told a soldier's mother, who was captured and then killed during the Turkish Army's rescue operation, that 'not every mother can catch such an honour but you got this honour now as a neighbour of the Prophet and the martyrs in hereafter' (Sözcü 2021). These are mere examples in which the Erdoğanist regime wanted to turn blame into credit, martyrdom here, an advantageous tool for its political survival.

Unlike other examples, the way the AKP has used martyrdom of the 15 July incident in turning the blame into credit is undisputedly a unique example in its kind. It is different from other cases in that Erdoğan turned death into a 'gift from God' for his political survival thus could suppress the opposition violently in this incident while he is trying the ward off the blame in others. Additionally, the media has not been restricted in this case, on the contrary, the martyrs' stories have been released and circulated by the AKP for years. Also, while Erdoğan saw martyrdom as normal and privileged in other examples by deflecting responsibilities, his main argument, in this case, was that 'they will pay the price of our 251 martyrs!', seeking and 'hunting' responsible ones.

However, the opposition parties' criticisms of the government's neglectful attitude before the failed mysterious military coup of 15 July, which is named by the opposition as the 'controlled coup' attempt, appeared. According to the opposition parties, the AKP elites together with Erdoğan and some other confidantes in intelligence and Turkish Army knowingly allowed the coup attempt, and they blatantly allowed civilians to die that night (Taş 2018). Thus, the AKP avoids any blame via echoing civilian martyrs around 251, who died that night. Those martyrs and their relatives were announced as civil martyrs and heroes publicly.

Bargaining via Rewards

The AKP supports and strengthens *presentational strategy* by allocating *carrots*—privileges and promising rewards to the victim families. Financial aid, promises, privileges, social status, and significantly a promise of a house as a reward by the government officials for the victim families played a significant role in addition to martyrdom, to deflect blame and avoid policymakers' responsibilities in disasters and fiascos.

The prime reward that is granted by the AKP to the victim families is the status of martyrdom. This includes the civilian loss in line with the size, 'fatality', and the capacity of the incident (if it causes popular criticism, electoral punishment, etc.) that resulted in massive deaths.

In the Turkish legal system, there has been neither a legal definition of 'martyrdom' (*şehitlik*), nor a legal attribution for whom would be titled as a 'martyr' (*şehit*). Turkish Anti-Terror Law Nr. 3713 only includes the procedures and principles about the 'employment of the martyred relatives and the disabled ones' who got wounded or lost (either military or civil servants) their lives due to terror acts. It might be asserted that 'martyrdom' or titling somebody as a 'martyr' is 'tacitly' under the tutelage of the Turkish Armed Forces or Turkish Judiciary, without leaning on any specific legal base (Şen 2015). During the AKP rule, this authority seems wholly and arbitrarily to be customized by the AKP for its own political end. In 2012, the AKP government changed the regulations of martyrdom to deem the civilians who lost their lives because of terrorist attacks martyrs. This change was geared to ease the pressure on the AKP government in the face of increasing civilian tolls in the clashes with the PKK. Moreover, the broadened definition of martyrdom also includes victims of natural disasters, large scale incidents and even pandemics.

In the case of Soma mine disaster in 2014 when 301 miners were killed in the worst mining disaster in the country and the government was under immense pressure. While visiting Soma, Erdoğan was protested and he chased after a protestor, calling him an Israeli offspring. One of his advisors was seen kicking a protesting miner who was lying flat on the ground while Erdoğan's bodyguards apprehended him. The opposition media was stronger and relatively more independent at that time which was before the coup attempt in 2016. Thus, many TVs were able to show the footage of both incidents. Fearing that these might cost the AKP some votes, there was an urgent need for the AKP to deflect the blame. Accordingly, it was announced immediately that those who lost their lives were called as 'civil martyrs' or 'martyrs of the mine', and their relatives were granted the 'advantages' of Terror Law Nr. 3713: salary, employment, and scholarships (Güzel 2014). The status of martyrdom for the casualties in mining was granted for the first time in Turkish history. The same procedure was followed in the Ermenek mine disaster, in which 18 miners lost their lives in October 2014. After the incident, the Minister of Family and Social Services Ayşenur İslam said: 'All martyrs will be given both death pensions and death income [...] 1 person from the family will be employed' (Al Jazeera 2014).

The enactment of the law of civil martyrdom by the AKP has another role in addition to blame avoidance. We have learnt from the accounts of Sedat Peker, a Turkish mob boss who was sponsored by the AKP elites and had him organize a series of propaganda meetings and some the dirty operations to spread fear to opposition between 2015 and 2020, that the law on civil martyrdom was enacted by the AKP regime to mobilize civilians in case of political protests of the government and possible internal clashes. Having become a confessor upon a conflict of interest, Peker claimed that he drafted himself the law 'civil martyrdom' proposed and submitted it to the AKP government himself. He states that he was inspired by Nazi propaganda minister Goebbels's *totalerKrieg* (total war) (Reis Sedat Peker 2021), which meant calling and including people in the war. Peker states that this is important to mobilize civilians in a state of war because people will not be afraid of what will happen to their families when they die if they know that the state will grant them martyrdom pension (Reis Sedat Peker 2021). In order to terrorize the opposition parties and the media, for instance, Peker confessed that he was asked by AKP elites to organize the well-attended violent protests and assaults on Hurriyet media centre, some journalists and deputies (Gazetesi 2021; BBC Türkçe 2021). This is best seen on the night of July 15 when some civilian and pro-AKP mob groups, including Peker's group, were invited and were provided with heavy guns organized by the AKP, to occupy the Bosporus Bridge, airports, military bases, and TV stations, and clash with the so-called coup stagers. In his confessional videos, Peker also 'claimed that the minister of interior distributed unregistered weapons to civilians during and after the coup attempt on July 15, 2016' (Bianet 2021).

The regulations and financial aids are mostly determined and distributed through the Ministry of Family, Labour, and Social Services. Reminding that the Presidency of Relatives of Martyrs and Veterans is elevated to the statute of General Directorate during the AKP period, the minister Zehra Zümrüt Selçuk stated that they employed 39,550 relatives in the civil service as of September 2018, and this number was only 6315 before the AKP rule (Karadağ 2018). Minister Selçuk's statement is rather helpful to understand what AKP hopes from the new regulations which she defined a 'New Vision' in employment politics of martyr and veteran relatives: 'Because we know that they are not separate, those who died while working in the mines for our country and those who struggle in the fronts. Because sweat, shed from the forehead, and the blood, shed for the homeland is equally sacred' (Karadağ 2018; T.C. Devlet Personel Başkanlığı 2017). These attempts show that the martyrdom discourse in blame avoidance is supported by funds, rewards, and some privileged status, which can take the remaining family members to an economically, socially and religiously elevated and reputable rank within society. As a result, martyrdom becomes an excuse for the family to absorb the blame and the possible responsibility deficits of the incumbent government.

If martyrdom were solely about religious attribution, not endorsed by official guarantees, the families would not buy it alone. Thus, the policymakers strengthen martyrdom with the rewarding strategy by providing the victim's family members with extra resources to satisfy them, make them loyal to the authority, and prevent them from voicing their grievances to the opposition media outlets, or to politicians from the opposition. Such bargaining usually happens in front of the public, open to media and live TV streams, thus aiming to eliminate public blame and criticizing. For instance, Erdoğan publicly announced that the annual income of the newly opened Eurasia tunnel would be transferred to the families of the martyrs (CNN Türk 2016). Later, it was revealed that he did not do so. The ideal family response that government expects here that expressions such as 'fatherland first'. Here, financial aid, the promise of rewards, and significantly a promise of a house as a reward by the government officials for the victim families play a special role. Along with the legal martyrdom rewards, such as pensions, social services, etc., policymakers promise free home as a reward in one of the most helpful blame avoidance acts after the martyrdom. In this bargaining, it is revealed that some documents and petitions were signed by the veterans and the victim families in return for rewards, so that they would not file compenzation cases against the government (Halktv 2020). By doing so, the officeholders also protect themselves from the courts in return for rewards.

Sometimes, family members directly ask for financial help from the policymakers in return for their losses. Victim Eren Bülbül's brother-in-law, for instance, called the authorities to help Eren's family, underscoring that the family's financial situation is rather poor. As noted above, this usually happens by granting or building a house for the family on the basis of martrydom (Habertürk 2017). In this instance, Eren Bülbül's poor family's house was replaced with a triplex, luxury one. The key to the house was given to the hand of mother by President Erdoğan in a meeting organized by the AKP (Hürriyet 2018). The same is true for the Soma and Ermenek 'martyrs of the mine'. While the government explained that the Housing Development Administration (TOKİ) would provide each victims' families with houses in Soma, the number of house promise was doubled for Ermenek victim families. For instance, in Ermenek, minister İslam said that 'each martyr family will be given a home' (Al Jazeera 2014), while AKP minister Lütfi Elvan states that the martyr families will be given one more home, and the rental income that families will obtain from these second houses will contribute to their budgets (Türkiye Odalar ve Borsalar Birliği 2015).

To what extent could Erdoğan become successfull in his rewarding tactic? From the election results that were held in the following year we see that the government strategy of martyrdom and throw good money became successful in blame management. In both districts, the AKP became the most popular party, and even increased its share of the vote in Ermenek (Hürriyet 2015).

However, as understood from the later accounts of the families of the victims', it is revealed that the policymakers do not always fulfil what they promised. When the initial impact of the incident passes, when it drops off the agenda, politicians' interest disappears simultaneously. For instance, it is understood from the late complaints of the Soma families that many of those rewards and promises, including civil martyrdom, have not been met, and the promises were just used as a tool for blame avoidance when the issue was still hot. A mine worker, who lost his nephew in the disaster, defined those promises of rewards as '*suspayı*' (hush money) (Milliyet 2015). Ahmet Cata, who lost his two sons during the Soma disaster also said: 'We get 1,000 lira (£230; $370) a month as our sons' pensions, [...] nobody from the government has visited us, nobody has come to see how we are. I feel betrayed. I used to vote for the [governing] AK Party but never again' (Lowen 2015). Ergul Yuksel, a widow who lost her husband in Soma, claims that 'the government is protecting those responsible, shifting the blame' (Lowen 2015). The same is true for some of the Ermenek victims. For instance, a widow Şadiye Çoksöyler, who lost her husband in the Ermenek mine disaster, stated after six years passed: 'After the mining disaster, many officials came here. At that time, they told me that my husband would be given the title of martyr. 6 years have passed since the incident, but still the title of martyrdom has not been given. [...] After the accident, we were promised that all our rights would be given to us, but we still have not been paid our compensation. They even saw too much for us to pay the price of our lives' (Sözcü 2020b).

More examples can be given. For instance, a veteran who was injured and survived bombed attack on December 2016 initially explained: 'Thanks God for that. May my life be sacrificed for the homeland' (Sözcü 2016). However, the policymakers did not fulfil their promises of rewards and failed to employ the veteran later. Thus, the veteran's father exclaimed: When my son was first wounded, everyone came and made promises. However, no one is asking how we are now' (Cumhuriyet 2017). The most striking example is the protests of '15 July martyrs' families and 'veterans' after four years in 2020, in front of the AKP headquarter and Ministry of Family, Labour, and Social Services, where the government built its authoritarian discourse over them. The angry protesters claimed that the authorities have not fulfilled their promises, they still have not benefited from Law Nr. 3713 and wanted the AKP government to distribute the donation money that was collected from the people, which is about 300 million TL (400,000 USD) (Euronews 2020b). In the press release, veterans and victim families stated: 'In the public opinion, they [policymakers] created the perception that "they [victims] receive 3200 salary and each veteran has been given a house" but this does not reflect the truth' (Sözcü 2020a). Another'15 July veteran' Rıfat Kayran, who stated that his name and photo were shown as a propaganda in the billboards for months after the incident, said:

> On July 15, upon the message that was sent me from my party [AKP] and upon the order of our president, I left my three children and my wife and set off to go to occupy Atatürk Airport. I jumped over the barriers en route and injured my right arm and leg when a tank drove onto me. Because of my patriotism, thus, I became the guest honour of our president as a veteran and our prime minister sent a letter of gratitude to my home. [...] I have been invited many organizations [organized by the AKP] as a

veteran. For that reason, some amount of money sent to my bank account from the Ministry of Family. But Esenler district governorship does not give me my veteran status [...] They said, "Don't say anything to anyone, we will give you your status". They jerked me over for months but still didn't give it. They played with my honour two times. (Damga Gazetesi 2019)

The *sticks* used by the AKP regime in case of resistance in cooperation and co-optation are lynching, social defamation, dismissal from the job, loss of social status and privileges, and police intervention. These are some of the strategies that the authorities employed in such cases. When the protests became massive, the authorities did not hesitate to use force. For instance, during the 15 July victim and veteran protests in 2020, many protesters were taken into custody and the police used force to disperse the groups. Many protesters were injured (Euronews 2020b).

The government starts black propaganda, social lynch, and defamation, when the victim families continue holding the authority culpable and insist their blame. This mostly happens when the families contact the opposition media outlets or the politicians from the opposition. As seen in the case of the captured two Turkish soldiers by the ISIS, to deflect the blame, the AKP deputy Şamil Tayyar alleged without a shred of evidence that the captured soldiers voluntarily became ISIS member. The burnt soldiers and their mournful families were tarnished by the pro-AKP media and social media and trolls for months.

Similarly, the same strategy is followed in the case of Gendarmerie captain Ali Alkan, who died after the attack by the PKK in Şırnak province in August 2015. During the funeral ceremony, Ali's brother Mehmet, who is also a member of the Armed Forces in the lieutenant colonel rank, screamed in grief and shouted that his brother was just 32-year-old and could not live his life yet: 'Who is his murderer? Who caused this?' (Girit 2015). Hugging his younger brother's coffin in tears, Mehmet yelled: 'How come those who have been speaking about peace now speak only of war?' (Girit 2015). Criticizing AKP high echelons' discourse on martyrdom, especially targeting Minister Taner Yıldız's previous statement about his personal 'desire' for martyrdom, Mehmet publicly condemned: 'There is nothing like sitting in a palace surrounded by bodyguards or riding in an armoured car and declaring I want to be a martyr (*şehid*). If you want to be a *şehid*, go and be a *şehid*' (Bar'el 2015). As a response to this spontaneous protest, two people whom took part in the funeral were arrested 'for "insulting the president" at the ceremony—a crime now punishable by up to four years' imprisonment' (Ahval 2017). Also, a social lynch campaign led by the AKP trolls on social media started to spread disinformation that Mehmet and his family were from the heteredox Alevi sect of Islam, the demonized minority religious sect by the orthodox Sunni Islam, and that's why, it was alleged, he had intentionally acted so in order to debilitate the leader of the Sunni Muslim World and civilization, the AKP's power (Cumhuriyet, n.d.). Later, with the AKP's massive purges in 2016, lt. col. Alkan was also sacked from his job and has been publicly announced as a terrorist (Ahval 2017). Having been purged, Alkan joined the opposition People's Republican Party (CHP). Pro-AKP media outlets proclaimed this news with the titles 'Former Lt. Col., fully supported by the PKK and FETO is (now) in the CHP' (Ahaber 2017).

The previously discussed case of Muhammed Safitürk, an appointed trustee governor by the AKP in place of HDP's elected mayor municipality is another example to see what happens when the family members insist on inquiring about the policymakers' responsibility and blame. On November 2016, pro-AKP media and the policymakers claimed that Safitürk was killed in PKK bombing in Mardin (Yilmaz and Erturk 2021). Erdoğan himself attended the funeral and gave a speech on the importance of martyrdom, leaning his hand onto the coffin of the victim. Safitürk's father has also been invited to many AKP events, educational conferences and events organized by the Ministry of National Education in various cities around Turkey to address youth and teachers on the importance of martyrdom and the homeland (T.C. Hizan Kaymakamlığı n.d.) However, two years later, as trials proceeded and the testimonies and claims revealed, some controversial questions emerged in both opposition media and the Safitürk family members' statements. The 'martyrdom' case turned into a total fiasco, in which the city governor, police chiefs, and some other AKP intelligence became involved. Thus, the family raised their objections and began to assign blame to the government. For example, brother Ali Haydar Safitürk has said that he has serious suspicions that the police tampered with forensic evidence, casting doubt on the official narrative (Öztekin 2018). He said that half an hour later, the police chief had washed, wiped, and cleaned the Safitürk's office without a crime scene investigation arrived, where the bomb exploded, and thus deleted all the materials in the district governor's office (Yeni Şafak 2021). He also explained that after the bombing, his brother was knowingly and forcefully left to die under the control of the policy-makers by transferring to the wrong hospital department and then to a hospital in Gaziantep from Mardin under the command of the city governor after he was initially transferred to a hospital in Mardin, though the doctors rejected the city governor's insistence on the transfer (Milli Gazete 2020). Additionally, Safitürk's brother lodged a complaint against the city governor and chief of police, who investigated the case that he obfuscated the evidence. Brother Ali Haydar Safitürk later explained that he was 'threatened' with the loss of his family's privileges and reputation by removing officially Safitürk's status of martyrdom unless he dropped his complaints (Evrensel 2020). Later it was also revealed that journalists following the case were threatened and told to stop reporting on the trial (Gazete Karinca 2018).

Nihal Olçok case is another impactful example of what happens when the family insists on blaming and holding the government culpable. On the night of 15 July, Olçok's ex-husband Erol and his 16-year-old son were shot dead on Bosporus Bridge. Erol Olçok was a prominent ally and a spin doctor of Erdoğan. He was known as 'one of the architects of Erdoğan's rise to power' (Levin 2016). Soon, he became one of the exemplary civilian martyrs that widely propagandized in favour of the regime following the event. His name and photo were everywhere on billboards, parks, etc. However, not for long, as Mrs. Olçok followed the cases in the courts, she broke official narration by asking some controversial questions regarding the death of her ex-spouse and her son that night. For instance, similar to Safitürk's case, Mrs. Olçok argued that when she arrived at the bridge that morning, the roads were washed by the AKP municipality and thus the evidence had vanished. Olçok added that they were told that bridge surveillance cameras were not working, no gun shells were found, and gunshot residue testing was not done; thus she said that she was not able to file a case against the people who shot her ex-spouse and son (DW Türkçe 2019). She explained that pro-AKP propaganda banners referring to the failed coup had been already prepared before the coup had occurred, implying that the regime organized the coup because it derived most of the benefit from it (Artı Tv 2021). She confronted a series of difficulties in response to her explanations to the opposition media. For example, she said that she was no longer mentioned as the mother and wife of a martyr since she questioned the official July 15 narrative (Halktv 2020). She explained that she felt unsafe in Turkey and went abroad (DW

Türkçe 2019), and the parental rights of her other children were given to their uncle (Sputnik 2019).

Subsequent complaints from victim's families challenge the AKP's martyrdom strategy for dealing with death and disaster. Therefore, we can surmise that martyrdom alone in blame management does not work if government promises to families remain unfulfilled. Martyrdom, when supported with rewards as a blame management strategy, appears to have worked well for the regime. In such cases, martyrdom supported with family rewards is often perceived as a win–win situation. This tactic has become common, and it may be that Turkish people, who are essentially third-world citizens, now believe that they will become privileged and compensated when they are visited during a disaster or crises by high-ranked government officers. We find, therefore, that when the martyrdom and throwing good money after bad strategies are combined the AKP is able to successfully practice blame avoidance.

People are aware of the AKP's necropolitics and respond accordingly. A subcontracted woman worker's speech in the pulpit before Mr. and Mrs. Erdoğan on March 8 International Women's Day organization, organized by the AKP, is a good example. The woman said that: 'Oh my Lord! Let our president complete his duties. Oh, my Lord! Because our country, humanity and the whole Islamic community need him. If his life will not be long enough for this, oh my Lord, please take my life and give it to him! May my life be *halal* (Islamically permissible) for you as your mother's breast milk!' (Habertürk 2016). As a result, the audience, including president Erdoğan, cried. However, this sacrifice of life offer was made for a reward. The last part of the speech, which is absent in the pro-government media, reads: 'As subcontracted workers, we have a dream, we have a hope, the most importantly we have desire to become full-time ongoing payrolled employees' (Habertürk 2016).

Conclusion

The AKP regime has mainly used two blame avoidance strategies, *presentational strategies* and *bargaining* via *rewards*, in managing blame avoidance and coping with crises that resulted in the deaths of workers, soldiers, or civilians. The empirical findings have shown that in the first strategy, presentational strategy, the AKP has used three subcategories as a tactical response to deadly failures (loss of lives in workplace accidents, armed clashes, or socio-political events): (a) redefined, spun, and manipulated the public perception so as to avoid blame; (b) restricted access to opposing voices and media; (c) tried to turn blame into credit by using martyrdom in an Islamist and nationalist context. The use of martyrdom, in particular, has proven irresistible to the AKP on many occasions when attempting to manipulate public perception of a disastrous event or to turn blame into credit. The AKP's use of martyrdom helped the party re-frame the freezing to death of poorly equipped Turkish soldiers as yet more cases in which young Turkish men willingly martyred themselves defending the nation. While this effort may appear transparent, it may well have proven successful in at least directing attention away from the cause of the soldiers' deaths (the lack of equipment) and towards more abstract questions of whether martyrdom is an appropriate concept for the government to invoke at any time. Indeed, Erdoğan himself used the subsequent discussion of the appropriateness of martyrdom as a concept to lecture his political enemies on its importance not merely to the state but to the families of the dead.

Equally, Erdoğan's skilful re-framing of the death of Eren Bülbül from its initial perception as a failure of the government to protect its citizens, to a case where a young Turkish person was martyred by the nation's Kurdish enemies, shows how adept he is at turning blame into credit. Erdoğan weaves together an Islamist and nationalist martyrdom narrative in which the death of Bülbül becomes something positive, and he praises the boy's mother as if she was not herself another victim of the Turkish government's inability to solve the Kurdish problem, but was rather a willing participant in the conflict, who sent her son to be martyred in the name of Islam and the AKP. By re-framing the events to transform the dead child into a martyr, and his mother into a proud mother of a martyr, Erdoğan successfully transformed blame into credit, a technique made possible by his use of the potent martyrdom narrative.

In *bargaining* via *rewards*, the second strategy, the AKP officeholders have widely used carrot tactics, promises of financial aids such as extension and regulation of (civil) martyrdom, buying a house for the victim families, allocating social privileges. Here, in response to financial and social privileges, the victim's families have mostly cooperated and co-opted with the regime and bought into the martyrdom discourse. As this chapter has revealed, it is clear that martyrdom as a concept has become a password that signifies a win–win situation for both parties: officeholders ward off blame while victim's families receive satisfying rewards, made up of financial aids, legal assurances, and social privileges. However, as might be inferred from the subsequent accounts and complaints of the victim families, it appears that martyrdom on its own does not work when the rewarding promises are not fulfilled by authorities. The evidence shows that AKP elites have not always fulfilled their promises. The purpose of the *bargaining* via *rewards* strategy was to create a propaganda and persuasion tool so as to soften the initial impact of the crises, appease social anger, and thus avoid blame that may have the capacity to debilitate its political power. In the cases where the rewarding strategy failed, for example, when the victim families refused to serve the AKP's agenda by allowing their relative to be turned into a martyr and instead sought to hold the government responsible for their death, the Erdoğanists have threatened the families with punishment, defamation, social lynch, suing, stigmatization, and dismissal from employment, sometimes following through on their threats.

Thus, the AKP is able to destroy the lives of the families who refuse to allow their loved ones to be transformed into martyrs who died for the AKP and its various political and social agendas, and in doing so can stifle the voices of people who wish to confront the party with its own failings. However, it appears that the party's first and preferred option, when dealing with the families of soldiers or other people who have died due to government negligence, is to bargain via positive rewards rather than coerce them with threats of punishment.

REFERENCES

Ahaber. 2017. 'FETÖ ve PKK'nın tam destek verdiği Yarbay Mehmet Alkan CHP'de'. Ahaber. November 7. https://www.ahaber.com.tr/gundem/2017/11/07/feto-ve-pkknin-tam-destek-verdigi-yarbay-mehmet-alkan-chpde.

Ahval. 2017. 'Can Any Turkish Opposition Escape the Terrorist Label?' November 11. https://ahvalnews.com/freedoms/can-any-turkish-opposition-escape-terrorist-label.

Al Jazeera. 2014. 'Ermenekli Madenci Ailelerine Ev ve Maaş Sözü'. December 8. http://www.aljazeera.com.tr/haber/ermenekli-madenci-ailelerine-ev-ve-maas-sozu.

Artı Tv. 2021. Nihal Olçok: 15 Temmuz'da Darbe Başarılı Oldu | Erk Acarer Ile Haber Peşinde. https://www.youtube.com/watch?v=bb_JC-jAIz0.

Baekkeskov, Erik, and Olivier Rubin. 2017. 'Information Dilemmas and Blame-Avoidance Strategies: From Secrecy to Lightning Rods in Chinese Health Crises.' *Governance* 30 (3): 425–443. https://doi.org/10.1111/gove.12244.

7 NECROPOLITICS AND AKP'S BLAME AVOIDANCE 161

Bakıner, Onur. 2019. "'These Are Ordinary Things": Regulation of Death Under the AKP Regime'. In *Turkey's Necropolitical Laboratory*, ed. Banu Bargu, 25–45. Edinburgh University Press. https://doi.org/10.3366/j.ctvs32r1g.6.

Bar'el, Zvi. 2015. 'The Criminal Offense of Criticizing Erdoğan'. September 1. https://www.haaretz.com/.premium-turkeys-Erdoğan-goes-on-the-offensive-1.5393503.

BBC. 2018. 'Tunceli'de Iki Askerin Donarak Hayatlarını Kaybetmesi: Erdoğan "Askeri Teçhizatlar En Modern Teçhizattır" Dedi'. October 30, sec. Türkiye. https://www.bbc.com/turkce/haberler-turkiye-46034639.

BBC Türkçe. 2016. 'Adana'da öğrenci yurdunda yangın'. *BBC News Türkçe*, November 30. https://www.bbc.com/turkce/haberler-turkiye-38154528.

———. 2020. 'Gazeteciler Barış Terkoğlu ve Hülya Kılınç tutuklandı, İçişleri Bakanı Soylu "Devlet sırrı denilen birşey vardır" dedi'. *BBC News Türkçe*, March 4. https://www.bbc.com/turkce/haberler-dunya-51731672.

———. 2021. 'Metin Külünk: Sedat Peker'in "çanta çanta" para gönderdiğini iddia ettiği AKP'li siyasetçi'. *BBC News Türkçe*, June 6. https://www.bbc.com/turkce/haberler-dunya-57374500.

Beyazgazete. 2017. 'Erdoğan, Eren Bülbül'ün annesiyle yaptığı görüşmeyia çıkladı | Şehit, Cumhurbaşkanı, Recep Tayyip Erdoğan, Antalya'. Beyaz Gazete. August 13. https://beyazgazete.com/video/webtv/siyaset-3/Erdoğan-eren-bulbul-un-annesiyle-yaptigi-gorusmeyi-acikladi-463172.html.

Bianet. 2021. 'Sedat Peker Claims Interior Minister Armed Civilians After 2016 Coup Attempt'. *Bianet*, 9 July 2021. https://bianet.org/english/politics/247014-sedat-peker-claims-interior-minister-armed-civilians-after-2016-coup-attempt.

Boin, Arjen, Paul 'T Hart, Allan McConnell, and Thomas Preston. 2010. 'Leadership Style, Crisis Response and Blame Management: The Case of Hurricane Katrina.' *Public Administration* 88 (3): 706–723.

Hürriyet. 2018. CHP leader criticizes gov't over death of two soldiers. Hürriyet Daily News, October 30. Accessed 16 March 2019. http://www.hurriyetdailynews.com/chp-leader-criticizes-govt-over-death-of-two-soldiers-138419.

CNN Türk. 2016. 'AvrasyaTüneliaçıldı'. CNN Türk. December 20. https://www.cnnturk.com/turkiye/avrasya-tuneli-acildi.

Cumhuriyet. 2014. '1800'lü yıllardaki maden kazalarıyla kıyasladı'. May 14. https://www.cumhuriyet.com.tr/haber/1800lu-yillardaki-maden-kazalariyla-kiyasladi-71957.

———. 2017. 'Kayseri gazisinin babası: Oğlum yaralandığında herkes vaatlerde bulundu, şu an halimizi soran yok'. December 20. https://www.cumhuriyet.com.tr/haber/kayseri-gazisinin-babasi-oglum-yaralandiginda-herkes-vaatlerde-bulundu-su-an-halimizi-soran-yok-889724.

162   I. YILMAZ AND O. ERTURK

————. n.d. 'Yarbay Mehmet Alkan'ın Ailesi: Mezheplere Saygısızlık Yapılıyor'. Accessed 29 June 2021. https://www.cumhuriyet.com.tr/haber/yarbay-meh met-alkanin-ailesi-mezheplere-saygisizlik-yapiliyor-351584.

Daloglu, Tulin. 2014. 'Erdoğan Says Mining Accidents "Nature of the Business"'. Al-Monitor. May 14. https://www.al-monitor.com/pulse/originals/2014/05/turkey-soma-mine-Erdoğan-accident-investigation.html.

DW Türkçe. 2019. Nihal Olçok: AK Parti Yanlış Yapmadı Biz Onu Şımarttık. https://www.youtube.com/watch?v=05XobRk1a1w.

Ellis, Richard J. 1994. Presidential Lightning Rods: The Politics of Blame Avoidance. *University Press of Kansas*. https://doi.org/10.2307/j.ctv1p2gjtd.

Erturk, Omer. 2022. Anatomy of political Islam in Republican Turkey: The Milli Görüş Movement as a legacy of Naqshbandism. *Contemporary Islam* 16: 295–320. https://doi.org/10.1007/s11562-022-00500-x.

Evrensel. 2018. Erdoğan: Şehadetin içinde kurşun da var, donmak da var. Evrensel.net, October 30. Accessed 16 March 2019. https://www.evrensel.net/haber/364718/erdogan-sehadetin-icinde-kursun-da-var-donmak-da-var.

Euronews. 2020a. 'Erdoğan: Libya'da bir kaç tane şehidimiz var'. *Euro News*. February 22. https://tr.euronews.com/2020a/02/22/Erdoğan-libya-da-bir kac-tane-sehidimiz-var-sehitler-tepesi-bos-kalmayacak.

————. 2020b. '15 Temmuz Gazileri AK Parti Önünde EylemYaptı, 2 Gazi Yaralandı'. June 16. https://tr.euronews.com/2020b/06/16/15-temmuz-gazileri-ak-parti-onunde-eylem-yapt-2-gazi-yaralandi.

Evrensel. 2020. 'Kaymakam Fatih Safitürk'ün ağabeyi tehdit edildiğini açıkladı.' *EvrenselGazetesi*, October 6, available at https://www.evrensel.net/haber/417322/kaymakam-fatih-safiturkun-agabeyi-tehdit-edildigini-acikladi.

GazeteDuvar. 2017. 'AnnedenTepki: Eren'in Oraya Götürülmesi Binde Bin Ihmaldir'. August 14. https://www.gazeteduvar.com.tr/gundem/2017/08/14/anneden-tepki-erenin-oraya-goturulmesi-binde-1000-ihmaldir.

Damga Gazetesi. 2019. 'Gazilik unvanını çok gördüler!' https://www.gazete damga.com.tr/. *Damga Gazetesi*, February 21. https://www.gazetedamga.com.tr/yerel-haberler/gazilik-unvanini-cok-gorduler-h14899.html.

Gazetesi, Evrensel. 2021. 'Sedat Peker: Milletvekili istedi, Hürriyet gazetesi baskınını ben yaptırdım'. Evrensel.net. May 20. https://www.evrensel.net/haber/433321/sedat-peker-milletvekili-istedi-hurriyet-gazetesi-baskinini-ben-yaptirdim.

Gazete Karınca. 2018. 'Safitürk davasını haberleştiren gazeteci Nalin Öztekin tehdit edildi.' Gazzete Karinca, October 23.

Girit, Selin. 2015. 'Turkey PKK Conflict: Turks Question Explosion in Tensions.' *BBC News*, September 2, sec. Europe. https://www.bbc.com/news/world-europe-34116818.

7 NECROPOLITICS AND AKP'S BLAME AVOIDANCE 163

Güzel, Şerife. 2014. 'Başbakan Erdoğan'dan Soma'da Yaşanan Maden Faciasında Ölen Maden İşçileri İçin "sivil Şehit" Talimatı.' Habertürk, May 18. https://www.haberturk.com/gundem/haber/949279-somada-olen-301-madenci-sivil-sehit-sayilacak.

Habertürk. 2016. 'Cumhurbaşkanı'nı Ağlattı Mektup: Benim Ömrümden al Ona Ver.' March 7. https://www.haberturk.com/gundem/haber/1206124-kadin-iscinin-mektubu-cumhurbaskanini-aglatti.

———. 2017. 'Eren Bülbül'ün Eniştesinden Yardım Çağrısı.' August 24. https://www.haberturk.com/gundem/haber/1609368-eren-bulbul-un-enistesinden-yardim-cagrisi.

Halktv. 2020. Nihal Olçok: Şehit Oğlumun Doğum Gününde Yetimhanede Uyudum. https://www.youtube.com/watch?v=B4P2bErCwIo.

Hansson, Sten. 2015. 'Discursive Strategies of Blame Avoidance in Government: A Framework for Analysis.' *Discourse & Society* 26 (3): 297–322. https://doi.org/10.1177/0957926514564736.

Hızlı, Mefail. 2015. 'Kıskanılacak Şehitler'. September 29. https://ankara.diy anet.gov.tr/Sayfalar/contentdetail.aspx?MenuCategory=Kurumsal&conten tid=157.

Hood, Christopher. 2011. *The Blame Game: Spin, Bureaucracy, and Self-Preservation in Government*. Princeton: Princeton University Press.

Hürriyet. 2015. 'Soma ve Ermenek'te kim ne kadar oy aldı?' June 8. https://www.hurriyet.com.tr/gundem/soma-ve-ermenek-te-kim-ne-kadar-oy-aldi-29227206.

———. 2018. 'Anahtarı Erdoğan Verdi! İşte Şehit Eren Bülbül'ün Ailesine Hediye Edilen Ev.' June 13. https://www.hurriyet.com.tr/galeri-anahtari-Erd oğan-verdi-iste-sehit-eren-bulbulun-ailesine-hediye-edilen-ev-40866800.

Hurtas, Sibel. 2017. 'Turkey Finally Acknowledges Soldier Executed by IS.' Al-Monitor. October 20. https://www.al-monitor.com/pulse/originals/2017/10/turkey-syria-ankara-accepts-soldiers-executed-by-isis.html.

Kanouse, David E., and L. Reid Hanson Jr. 1987. 'Negativity in Evaluations'. In *Attribution: Perceiving the Causes of Behavior*, 47–62. Hillsdale, NJ, US: Lawrence Erlbaum Associates, Inc.

Karadağ, Kemal. 2018. '580 şehit yakını, gazi ve gazi yakınlarının atamasıyapıldı'. *Hürriyet*. http://www.hurriyet.com.tr/ekonomi/580-sehit-yakini-gazi-ve-gazi-yakinlarinin-atamasi-yapildi-40956175.

Levin, Ned. 2016. 'Erdoğan Ally Died in Bosporus Bridge Confrontation.' *Wall Street Journal*, July 19, sec. World. https://www.wsj.com/articles/Erdoğan-ally-died-in-bosporus-bridge-confrontation-1468949276.

Lowen, Mark. 2015. 'Turkey Mine Disaster: Raw Anger in Soma a Year On.' *BBC News*, May 13. https://www.bbc.com/news/world-europe-32709431.

164   I. YILMAZ AND O. ERTURK

Milli Gazete. 2020. 'Şehit Kaymakamın ağabeyinden flaş iddialar: İyileşecekti, vali...' Milli Gazete, October 6. https://www.milligazete.com.tr/haber/557 5603/sehit-kaymakamin-agabeyinden-flas-iddialar-iyilesecekti-vali.

Milliyet. 2015. 'Soma Faciasından Bir Yıl Sonra–Verilen 15 Vaatten Sadece 5'i Tutuldu.' May 14. https://www.milliyet.com.tr/gundem/soma-faciasindan-bir-yil-sonra-verilen-15-vaatten-sadece-5-i-tutuldu-2058725.

———. n.d. 'Donan Askerlerin HesabıVerilmeli.' *Milliyet*, Accessed 29 June 2021. https://www.milliyet.com.tr/siyaset/donan-askerlerin-hesabi-verilmeli-2769338.

Odatv. 2018. 'Savcı Donarak Ölen Askerler Için Hulusi Akar'ı Ifadeye Çağıracak Mı.' November 1. https://odatv4.com/savci-donarak-olen-askerler-icin-hul usi-akari-ifadeye-cagiracak-mi-01111856.html.

Öztekin, Nalin. 2018. 'Kaymakam Safitürk suikastinde önemli iddialar.' Arti Gerçek, October 15. http://artigercek.com/haberler/kaymakam-safiturk-sui kastinde-onemli-iddialar.

Pierson, Paul. 2007. *Dismantling the Welfare State? Reagan, Thatcher, and the Politics of Retrenchment*, 8th ed. Cambridge: Cambridge Univ. Press.

Reis Sedat Peker. 2021. (8.BÖLÜM) Fırtınalarla Büyüyen Fidanlar Rüzgarlarla Yıkılmazlar. https://www.youtube.com/watch?v=sYvs-m5hFso.

Rozin, Paul, and Edward B. Royzman. 2001. 'Negativity Bias, Negativity Dominance, and Contagion.' *Personality and Social Psychology Review* 5 (4): 296–320. https://doi.org/10.1207/S15327957PSPR0504_2.

Sabah. 2020. '4 dakika ara ile ihanet! MİT şehitlerimizi böyle deşifre etmişler.' Sabah, May 7. https://www.sabah.com.tr/gundem/2020/05/07/4-dakika-ara-ile-ihanet-mit-sehitlerimizi-boyle-desifre-etmisler.

T.C. Devlet Personel Başkanlığı. (2017, December 12). Şehit Yakını, Gazi Ve Gazi Yakınlarına İlişkin Düzenlemelerin Yapıldığı 7061 Sayılı Kanun Resmî Gazete'de Yayımlanarak Yürürlüğe Girdi. T.C. Devlet Personel Başkanlığı. http://www.dpb.gov.tr/tr-tr/duyuru/sehit-yakini-gazi-ve-gazi-yakinlarina-ili skin-duzenlemelerin-yapildigi-7061-sayili-kanun-resmi-gazetede-yayimlanarak-yururluge-girdi. Accessed 2 April 2019

Şen, Ersan. 2015. '"Şehit" kime denir?' *Haber7*. http://www.haber7.com/yaz arlar/prof-dr-ersan-sen/1620770-sehit-kime-denir.

Shafak, Elif. 2016. 'After Turkey's Failed Coup, a Sense of Fatalism Has Set in.' *The Guardian*, December 21, sec. World news. https://www.theguardian. com/world/2016/dec/21/turkey-failed-coup-fatalism-president-Erdoğan-crackdown-liberals-secularists.

Sözcü. 2016. 'Kayseri'de yaralanan er Recep Güney "Vatana canım feda.' Sözcü TV, December 21. https://tv.sozcu.com.tr/2016/haber/video/kayseride-yar alanan-er-recep-guney-vatana-canim-feda.

———. 2020a. 'AKP Önünde "Toplanan Paralar Nerede" Diyen 15 Temmuz Gazilerine Polis Müdahalesi.' June 16. https://www.sozcu.com.tr/2020a/gundem/akp-onunde-toplanan-paralar-nerede-diyen-15-temmuz-gazilerine-polis-mudahalesi-5876429/.

———. 2020b. 'Ermenek'te Hayatını Kaybeden Madencinin Eşi: Canımızın Bedelini Ödemeyi Bile Çok Gördüler.' October 28. https://www.sozcu.com.tr/2020b/gundem/ermenekte-hayatini-kaybeden-madencinin-esi-canimizin-bedelini-odemeyi-bile-cok-gorduler-6101980/.

———. 2021. 'Gara Şehidinin Annesini Telefonla AKP Kongresine Bağladılar.' February 15. https://www.sozcu.com.tr/2021/gundem/gara-sehidinin-ann esini-telefonla-akp-kongresine-bagladilar-6261774/.

Sputnik. 2016. '"Bakanlar Kurulu toplantısından: IŞİD'in Türk askerleri videosu montaj".' December 30. https://tr.sputniknews.com/turkiye/201612301 026556751-bakanlar-kurulu-isid-goruntu/.

———. 2019. 'Nihal Olçok: Her yalnız kadın gibi evlatlarımla aynı soyadını taşıyıp onların koruması altına girmek istedim.' July 12. https://tr.sputni knews.com/turkiye/201912071040784825-nihal-olcok-her-yalniz-kadin-gibi-evlatlarimla-ayni-soyadini-tasiyip-onlarin-korumasi-altina-girmek/.

Taş, Hakkı. 2018. 'The 15 July Abortive Coup and Post-Truth Politics in Turkey.' *Southeast European and Black Sea Studies* 18 (1): 1–19. https://doi.org/10.1080/14683857.2018.1452374.

T.C. Hizan Kaymakamlığı. n.d. 'Asım Safitürk İlçemizde Konferans Verdi.' Accessed 6 November 2020. http://www.hizan.gov.tr/asim-safiturk-ilcemi zde-konferans-verdi.

Türkiye Odalar ve Borsalar Birliği. 2015. 'Ermenek'te Maden Kazasında Hayatını Kaybeden Madencilerin Ailelerine Evleri Teslim Edildi.' February 28. https://www.tobb.org.tr/Sayfalar/Detay.php?rid=20136&lst=MansetListesi.

Vis, Barbara. 2016. 'Taking Stock of the Comparative Literature on the Role of Blame Avoidance Strategies in Social Policy Reform.' *Journal of Comparative Policy Analysis: Research and Practice* 18 (2): 122–137. https://doi.org/10.1080/13876988.2015.1005955.

Weaver, R. Kent. 1986. 'The Politics of Blame Avoidance.' *Journal of Public Policy* 6 (4): 371–398. https://doi.org/10.1017/S0143814X00004219.

Yeni Şafak. 2021. 'Şehit Kaymakam Muhammed Safitürk'ün ağabeyinden çarpıcı iddialar.' Text. Yeni Şafak. January 14. https://www.yenisafak.com/gun dem/sehit-kaymakam-muhammed-safiturkun-agabeyinden-carpici-iddialar-3594436.

Yeşilçınar, Fırat. 2017. 'IŞİD'in yakıldığı iddia edilen askerin babası dava açtı.' *Journo* (blog), October 5. https://journo.com.tr/isid-tarafindan-yakildigi-iddia-edilen-asker.

Yilmaz, Ihsan, and Omer Erturk. 2021. 'Authoritarianism and Necropolitical Creation of Martyr Icons by Kemalists and Erdoğanists in Turkey.' *Turkish Studies*, June, 1–18. https://doi.org/10.1080/14683849.2021.1943662.

CHAPTER 8

Necropolitics and Martyrdom in AKP's Authoritarian Stability

INTRODUCTION

Similar to the Kemalists, the Erdoğanist AKP regime have been utilizing necropolitical martyrdom narratives for legitimation, repression and mobilization (Yilmaz and Erturk 2021a; 2021b; 2022). This chapter argues that civilizational populist necropolitics has a pro-violence dimension centred around blood, death, and martyrdom narratives, and is used by authoritarian regimes to establish and perpetuate their rule. Our discussion of civilizational populist necropolitics in this chapter describes the politicization of death and the construction and political instrumentalization of narratives about blood, death, and martyrdom in everyday political use in Turkey. We show how AKP and Erdoğan construct these necropolitical narratives, which claim that the nation, homeland, Ummah and Islam are facing existential threats that can only be tackled by sacrificing lives. They also simultaneously use these and previously sacrificed lives to rally people around the flag, to legitimate actions of the AKP and Erdoğan, to justify repression and revengeful violence against the opposition, and to co-opt some oppositional groups. Thus, necropolitical mobilization becomes a matter of 'life and death' and dying for the salvation of the people, religion and the Muslim World against the evil enemies at home and abroad and martyrdom becomes an absolute necessity to save the nation and its people. Thus, these civilizational populist necropolitical narratives thus help the Erdoğanist regime to maintain authoritarian

© The Author(s), under exclusive license to Springer Nature Singapore Pte Ltd. 2023
I. Yilmaz and O. Erturk, *Populism, Authoritarianism and Necropolitics,*
https://doi.org/10.1007/978-981-19-8292-7_8

167

stability (Gerschewski 2013) as it uses violent rhetoric (in this case, necropolitics based on populist narratives of martyrdom, blood, and death) for repression, legitimation, and co-optation (Yilmaz and Erturk 2021a).

The chapter focuses on the three pillars of authoritarian stability: repression, legitimation, and co-optation. These three sections show how Erdoğan and the AKP have used the civilizational populist necropolitical narrative of martyrdom for repression, legitimation, and co-optation, respectively.

NECROPOLITICS AND REPRESSION

AKP and Erdoğan have used an Islamist civilizational populist necropolitical narrative to securitize and criminalize political opposition in Turkey. When infamously describing the failed coup attempt of July 2016 as a 'gift of God', Erdoğan was underlining this opportunity for securitization and thus repression. He often framed the coup attempt as a foreign (i.e. Western) conspiracy that used its traitor pawns inside Turkey but has emphasized that thanks to the martyrs, the conspirators could not achieve their aims (Erdoğan 2016; Yilmaz 2021).

He openly and publicly promised that he will continue to 'behead' the traitors, implying there were external powers behind them. According to Erdoğan: 'Without crushing out the pawns, we cannot beat the rooks, bishops, knights, queen, and the king. For that reason, we will [firstly] decapitate these traitors' (AA 2017; Bilginsoy and Fraser 2017).

In the post-2015 period, political discourse and media production have been constructed on the basis of Erdoğan's old radical Islamist ideology, Milli Görüş Movement, and Naqshbandi roots (see Erturk 2022; 2020) and converged on imagining Turkey as a martyr nation, and public declarations of wanting to kill and die for the regime have permeated the public sphere (Bakıner 2019, 33–34). Here, death does not belong only 'to the "Other", as is the case with a more traditional understanding of necropolitics. Rather death becomes the one and only condition to become "oneself", shifting our understanding of necropolitical boundary-making' (Yanık and Hisarlıoğlu 2019, 63).

During and in the aftermath of the coup attempt, martyrdom and risk of life were used by Erdoğan: 'We will continue this struggle with our nation at the expense of our lives if needed …. There is nothing can stop the nation who is not afraid of death' (Erdoğan 2016). To mobilize the crowds against his 'enemies', he insinuated that there would have been serious consequences if people had not sacrificed their lives at that night (Erdoğan 2016). He argued that '250 martyrs are our sun because, in return for them, we saved our future' (Sabah Daily 2017). Ever since the coup attempt, the AKP has been trying to convince its supporters that it is possible to write history with their own bodies, to reach democracy and to express the national will at the same time (Yanık and Hisarlıoğlu 2019, 63).

After the coup attempt, a considerable portion of the civil and military bureaucracy, including approximately 50% of all admirals and generals in the Turkish military, about 4000 judges and prosecutors, more than 9000 police officers, more than 8000 academics, 28,000 teachers, and more than 150,000 public servants, were purged (OHCHR 2018). About 150,000 people were detained and more than half a million people have been prosecuted on terrorism charges. Many universities, thousands of private schools, more than a thousand civil society institutions, and 130 media outlets, including TV stations, newspapers, news agencies, radio stations, and publishers were disbanded or liquidated without any judicial proceedings (BBC 2016b). Since the coup, the AKP has constantly argued that 'opposition to the Government is an insult to the "democracy martyrs" [those killed on 15 July]' (Houston 2018, 537). Erdoğan consistently justified the purges with a populist necropolitical narrative and promised the crowds that he could not stop wiping out the 'virus' which has spread throughout the state like a 'cancer' (Al Jazeera Turk 2017; Cumhuriyet 2018). He also said that 'we can't slow down ... this isn't a twelve-hour-operation' (Al Jazeera Turk 2017).

Amidst and through civilizational populist necropolitical siege mentality narratives, Erdoğan has eliminated any criticism in which he is accused of arbitrary and illegitimate acts. For instance, following the coup attempt, purged state officials have been denied judicial process and domestic remedies, and they demanded justice. However, these demands were tarnished publicly by Erdoğan with a necropolitical justification: 'people died what are you talking about huh!?' (Al Jazeera 2016). In response to the criticism of the opposition parties regarding the extrajudicial acts and excessive measures, and when these purged people applied to the courts to be reinstated, Erdoğan used the same necropolitical narrative to legitimate why he 'intervened' in the judicial process and asked the judiciary to proceed with the purges: 'Some of the [purged] people apply [to the courts] claiming that they were exposed to unjust treatment. What on earth are you talking about? Who will pay my 251 martyrs' families' ransom?' (Al Jazeera 2016).

Erdoğan frequently reiterated this decisive repressive attitude towards over 500,000 indicted people after the coup attempt: 'Sorry! Our judiciary is doing what is needed …. Otherwise, how do we give account to our 251 martyrs, 2 thousand 193 ghazis?' (CNN Türk 2019). After the imprisonment of a lawmaker from the main opposition party, the Republican People's Party (CHP), the CHP organized a protest march (Justice March). Erdoğan responded to this with a similar narrative: 'You will not be able to survive …. There is justice in this country thus you will not succeed to escape from the claws of the justice …. The justice we are looking for is the blood of our 250 martyrs' (AA 2017). Erdoğan's same necropolitical narrative is seen in his remarks when he decided to imprison many of the Kurdish legislators and mayors of the Peoples' Democracy Party, HDP, including their party leader Selahaddin Demirtaş. Erdoğan said: 'We can't release them [from the prisons]. If we let them be released, our martyrs hold us responsible in the eternal world' (Euronews 2019).

Erdoğan's necropolitical narrative has been employed also by the other AKP politicians to silence the opposition. For instance, in reaction to the CHP leader Kemal Kılıçdaroğlu's criticism of the mass detentions, purges and imprisonments following the coup attempt, an AKP minister, Mehmet Özhaseki, stated that 'there is nothing to take seriously in his remarks …. We have 250 martyrs' (Gündoğmuş 2017). When another lawmaker criticized the purges, an AKP lawmaker, Julide İskenderoğlu, who was also the AKP's chair of the women's branch, claimed that the opposition lawmaker should pay the price as he 'has no right to harm the souls and the families of the 250 martyrs' (İskenderoğlu 2018).

From time to time, Erdoğan has added to this necropolitical narrative a threat of capital punishment to spread fear. He publicly underscored that he was ready to reinstate the death penalty as the president 'if the people demand it' (BBC 2016a). In another incident, Erdoğan declared at a local election rally held on 19 March 2019: 'We have made a mistake by abolishing the death penalty [in 2004]. Why mistake? I cannot bear feeding those who martyred my 251 citizens, my soldiers, my policemen, in the prisons' (BirGün 2019).

The AKP has systematically heightened the necropolitical narrative during elections since the coup to curb opposition. In popular and local elections held between 2015 and 2019 (seven in total), martyrdom had been consistently used to create a sense of righteousness and legitimacy for the high-intensity state terror and political repression. Seeing that the necropolitical narrative was useful in earlier election campaigns, Erdoğan has continued to use it in attempts to increase the AKP's vote and secure longevity for his autocracy. To give an example, in the Constitutional Referendum campaign held on 16 April 2017, which was to replace the parliamentary system with a Turkish-style presidential system without checks and balances, he declared that more lives and blood would need to be sacrificed: 'Oh my brothers! We will have more orphans to be caressed. We have much more bloods [sacrifices] to be shed for our motherland, independency, future' (T24 2017).

As these examples show, the AKP has used necropolitical narrative as an instrument of repression to suppress and intimidate the opposition, to justify its unlawful judiciary intervention, and to signal that other punitive actions, such as civil war or reinstatement of the death penalty, are also at their disposal. Similarly, necropolitics has been used for legitimation by the AKP and Erdoğan.

NECROPOLITICS AND LEGITIMATION FOR AUTHORITARIANISM

Civilizational populist necropolitical narrative has also been a useful tool for claiming legitimacy for Erdoğan and the AKP. As seen in the statements of Erdoğan and his colleagues discussed in the previous section, this narrative not only legitimates and justifies repression, but also lends legitimacy to the continuation of their authoritarianism while simultaneously delegitimizing and 'securitizing' (Yilmaz and Shipoli 2022) the opposition.

Since 'particularly strong solidarity ties are established during periods of violent struggle such as war and liberation movements which are often used as powerful legitimation narratives' (von Soest and Grauvogel 2017, 290), the Erdoğan regime has been trying to turn the 15 July coup attempt and 'the Democracy Martyrs who saved the nation, its will, the fatherland and Islam' into a new 'foundational myth' (See von Soest and Grauvogel 2017, 290) of the Turkish nation. This necropolitical siege mentality narrative helped the AKP to construct itself in the leading role of the modern liberation movement of 2016 according to this novel foundational myth (Taş 2018, 14–15).

The 'martyrs' of the 15 July incident have been used by the AKP to play a legitimating role for the regime by building identity, mass mobilization, and collective memory. The democracy martyrs have been enshrined in textbooks, official commemorations, statues, and murals. By keeping martyrdom visible and alive in the politics, media, movies, TV serials, schools, mosques, commemorations, and everyday social life of the Turkish people, the AKP elite have sacralized and thus legitimized their political discourse, ideology, and actions.

The failed coup, and stories of 250 Democracy Martyrs, have now taken prominent places in the textbooks of the current era, framing Erdoğan and the AKP as defenders of the national will and Islam who did not hesitate to sacrifice their lives for the survival of their nation, state, country, and religion against internal and external enemies. This necropolitical foundational myth of the AKP regime that has sacralized Erdoğan's rule thanks to the martyrdom narrative has resonated with the MHP especially, as we will see in the next section on co-optation.

NECROPOLITICS AND CO-OPTATION

Co-optation by necropolitics is an expected potential outcome of legitimation by necropolitics. Legitimating narratives and constructs have helped the AKP to successfully co-opt the opposition far-right nationalist party, the MHP (Yilmaz, Shipoli and Demir 2021).

As mentioned above, the necropolitical narrative of the AKP is not new, and its equivalent is deeply embedded in the Turkish militarist culture and Turkish nation-building project. The most prominent and staunch advocate of this narrative has always been the far-right MHP. The MHP is the embodiment of far-right Turkish nationalism in the parliament (Celep 2010). It has based its political outlook on a relentless opposition to the HDP and Kurdish minority's rights and also on the martyrs whose lives were lost as a result of the pro-Kurdish outlawed Kurdistan Workers Party (PKK)'s attacks.

Until mid-2015, the MHP accused the AKP of treason, and accused Erdoğan of being a leader who sold out the nation and its martyrs by serving the separatist PKK and its foreign (i.e. Western) sponsors, Turkey's eternal enemies (Celep 2010; Selçuk et al. 2019). Three weeks before the 7 June 2015 elections, the MHP leader Devlet Bahçeli said that these elections were the most important in Turkish history and implied that the AKP was working for the USA conspiracists that aimed to divide and rule the Middle East (Bahçeli 2015). However, this tension eased following the AKP's loss of majority in the parliament in the elections, after the AKP failed to co-opt the pro-Kurdish HDP. Thus, Erdoğan changed his pro-Kurdish rights policies and demonized the HDP. This move enabled Erdoğan and the AKP to move closer to the MHP's narrative and policies on Kurds and facilitated a co-optation of the MHP (Yeni Şafak 2020).

Even though the U-turn on the Kurdish rights, AKP's move towards Turkish nationalism, the vilification of the HDP, and the usual co-optation incentives such material benefits, power-sharing, and letting the MHP pack the bureaucracy with its militants have been the most decisive factors in the AKP's co-optation of the MHP, it is plausible that the necropolitical narrative of the AKP that simply parroted the previous MHP lines has also been an additional enabling factor. The use of martyrdom as a foundational myth has played a key role in the 'rally around the flag' effect (Pevehouse and Goldstein 2017, 121), which not only legitimizes the sovereign's coming acts but also facilitates its co-optation of other actors that espouse the same foundational necropolitical myth repertoire.

The AKP has also used martyrs and attendance of martyr funeral ceremonies by the elites to minimize the differences between different groups in society and to gather them under the same interests, which were designed by the AKP. By allowing key players from various political parties to attend while denying permission for certain others to attend, the AKP sends a message to its and MHP's supporters that the AKP and MHP are in conformity, at least temporarily, and not enemies for the time being (Habertürk 2015).

The martyrdom narrative is so powerful and irresistible in the Turkish political culture that by employing this narrative, the AKP has forced other political parties, not just the MHP, to side with it against the pro-Kurdish HDP on different occasions.

CONCLUSION

This chapter has shown how the AKP has used civilizational populist necropolitical martyrdom narratives to repress political opposition, legitimize its rule and actions, and at times co-opt other political parties and organizations and draw them into its sphere of influence. Like all other authoritarian regimes, the AKP seeks to repress its enemies (the opposition, dissidents, human rights advocates, undesired minorities, journalists and academics) To do this it uses—among other things—a necropolitical martyrdom narrative, through which it demonizes, securitizes and ultimately criminalizes political opposition in Turkey. The AKP frames its political enemies as an existential threat to the people of Turkey, Islam and the Muslim World, and therefore praises the martyrs who have died to save these 'sacred' things in the face of the existential threats. Kemalists, other secularists, Gülenists, Kurdish activists, and other 'enemies' of the AKP are represented in the party's civilizational populist necropolitical narrative as criminal murderers responsible for the deaths of innocent martyrs. At the same time, the AKP's martyr-icons are held up as praiseworthy individuals because they died fighting the regime's enemies, and thus the enemies of the Turkish people. Therefore, to give the martyr-victims justice, and to protect the people of Turkey from their enemies, the AKP claim it is necessary to repress 'threatening' political opposition figures and groups. Erdoğan's mass arrests and purges of political opposition following the failed 2016 coup are thus framed as a form of justice by the AKP, and a tribute to the martyrs who willingly laid down their lives for the regime and the Turkish people while fighting their enemies.

The AKP thus also uses a necropolitical martyrdom narrative to legitimize its rule and in particular its use of violence against 'enemies'. For example, the party has sought to turn the July 15 failed coup into a new foundational narrative (presented even to children in schoolbooks), in which brave citizens gave their lives to save the nation from 'evil' Gülenists and secularists, and God Himself intervened to save the people. By portraying all political opposition as accessories to the failed coup attempt Erdoğan is able to frame himself as a national saviour and protector of the people, further legitimizing his position as leader. At the same time, the necropolitical martyrdom narrative allows the AKP to frame all its actions—including mass arrests and the intimidation of political opposition—as necessary to protect the causes that the martyrs' died protecting.

The martyrdom narrative aids the AKP in its co-optation of other political parties, and more broadly assists the party in gaining greater control over the nation. The most significant co-optation occurred when the AKP used—in part—its necropolitical martyrdom narrative to end its enmity with the MHP and draw them into a coalition. The partnership between the two parties, which assures a parliamentary majority and the retention of Erdoğan as president, has helped the AKP extend its political control and ultimately reshape Turkish national identity. When the AKP switched from supporting Kurdish rights, to condemning Kurdish activists as anti-Turkish, they were able to draw support for the previously hostile MHP. Furthermore, by portraying the coupists as enemies of the nation and its people, and portraying people killed by the coupists as national heroes, the AKP was able to create a narrative irresistible to the ultra-nationalist MHP. Equally, by controlling the state funerals of alleged martyrs, the AKP has been able to invite, ignore, or disinvite attendees, alternatively drawing some politicians close, while excluding others and portraying them as enemies of the martyrs.

While not arguing that necropolitical narrative has been the most decisive tool of the authoritarian toolbox for authoritarian regime stability and longevity, this chapter has argued how the necropolitical narrative is used alongside other better known and more widely used authoritarian stability instruments. The rich literature on martyrdom shows that it has always been used for nationalist political mobilization and authoritarian legitimation. It is therefore not surprising that the AKP, an authoritarian regime with a history of strong militarist and martyrdom memory culture, has consistently resorted to using narratives of 'authoritarian necropolitics' and martyrdom to legitimize its rule, and to repress and to co-opt the opposition and the elite.

The Erdoğanists possess an Islamist civilizational populist worldview and vision for Turkey that is significantly different to that of their Kemalist predecessors. The Kemalists sought to fashion the then new Republic of Turkey as a secular nation, breaking sharply from the Ottoman past by ending the Caliphate and bringing religion under the control of the secular state. The Erdoğanists, however, have increasingly sought to empower pro-AKP religious authorities, encourage Turkish people to feel nostalgic towards the Ottoman era and desire to be the protector and leader of the Muslim World.

References

AA. 2017. 'Cumhurbaşkanı Erdoğan: Bizim Aradığımız Adalet, 250 Şehidimizin Kanıdır,' June 20. https://www.aa.com.tr/tr/gunun-basliklari/cumhurbas kani-Erdoğan-bizim-aradigimiz-adalet-250-sehidimizin-kanidir/845777.

Al Jazeera. 2016. 'Erdoğan: Acırsanız acınacak hale gelirsiniz,' October 22. http://www.aljazeera.com.tr/haber/Erdoğan-acirsaniz-acinacak-hale-gel irsiniz.

176   I. YILMAZ AND O. ERTURK

Al Jazeera Turk. 2017. 'Erdoğan: Bu iş 12 saatlik bir iş değil,' July 17. http://www.aljazeera.com.tr/haber/Erdoğan-bu-12-saatlik-bir-degil.

Bahçeli, Devlet. 2015. 'Milliyetçi Hareket Partisi Genel Başkanı Sayın Devlet BAHÇELİ'nin, 'Aksaray Mitingi'nde Yapmış Oldukları Konuşma. 12 Mayıs 2015.' http://88.255.31.62/htmldocs/genel_baskan/konusma/3825/index.html.

Bakıner, Onur. 2019. '"These Are Ordinary Things": Regulation of Death under the AKP Regime.' In *Turkey's Necropolitical Laboratory*, edited by Banu Bargu, 25–45. Edinburgh University Press. http://www.jstor.org/stable/10.3366/j.ctvs32r1g.6.

BBC. 2016a. 'Turkey Coup Attempt: Erdoğan Signals Death Penalty Return.' *BBC News*, July 19, sec. Europe. https://www.bbc.com/news/world-europe-36832071.

———. 2016b. 'Turkey Shuts More than 130 Media Outlets,' July 28, sec. Europe. https://www.bbc.com/news/world-europe-36910556.

Bilginsoy, Zeynep, and Suzan Fraser. 2017. 'Erdoğan Vows to Behead "traitors" on Anniversary of Failed Turkey Coup.' *The Independent*, July 15. https://www.independent.co.uk/news/world/europe/turkey-Erdoğan-vows-behead-traitors-anniversary-coup-rally-speech-president-a7843321.html.

BirGün. 2019. 'Erdoğan: Yeni Zelanda saldırgandan hesap sormazsa biz sorarız.' *BirGün Gazetesi*, March 19. https://www.birgun.net/haber-detay/Erdoğan-nolur-oylarimizi-boldurmeyelim.html.

Celep, Ödül. 2010. 'Turkey's Radical Right and the Kurdish Issue: The MHP's Reaction to the "Democratic Opening".' *Insight Turkey* 12 (2): 125–142.

CNN Türk. 2019. 'Cumhurbaşkanı Erdoğan: Şu anda cezaevlerinde 30 bin 559 FETÖ'cü bulunuyor.' CNN Türk, April 10. https://www.cnnturk.com/turkiye/cumhurbaskani-Erdoğandan-onemli-aciklamalar-1004.

Cumhuriyet. 2018. 'Erdoğan: Bu Virüs Kanser Gibi,' March 19. https://www.cumhuriyet.com.tr/video/Erdoğan-bu-virus-kanser-gibi-945216.

Erdoğan, R. Tayyip. 2016. '"Ölümden Korkmayan Bir Milleti Durduracak Hiçbir Güç Yoktur".' T.C. Cumhurbaşkanlığı. November 22. https://www.tccb.gov.tr/haberler/410/61088/olumden-korkmayan-bir-milleti-durduracak-hicbir-guc-yoktur.html.

Erturk, Omer. 2020. 'The Myth of Turkish Islam: the influence of Naqshbandi-Gümüşhanevi thought in Turkish Islamic orthodoxy.' *British Journal of Middle Eastern Studies*, 49:2, 223-247. https://doi.org/10.1080/13530194.2020.1782727

Erturk, Omer. 2022. 'Anatomy of political Islam in Republican Turkey: the Milli Görüş Movement as a legacy of Naqshbandism.' *Contemporary Islam* 16(2-3) 295–320. https://doi.org/10.1007/s11562-022-00500-x

Euronews. 2019. 'Demirtaş Kararı Sonrası Erdoğan: Bunları Bırakamayız, Eğer Bırakırsak Şehitlerimiz Bize HesapSorar | Euronews,' September

8 NECROPOLITICS AND MARTYRDOM IN AKP'S ... 177

21. https://tr.euronews.com/2019/09/21/demirtas-karari-Erdoğan-bunlar-birakamayiz-birakirsak-sehitlerimiz-bize-hesap-sorar.
Gerschewski, Johannes. 2013. 'The Three Pillars of Stability: Legitimation, Repression, and Co-Optation in Autocratic Regimes.' *Democratization* 20 (1): 13–38. https://doi.org/10.1080/13510347.2013.738860.
Gündoğmuş, Yıldız Nevin. 2017. 'Çevreve Şehircilik Bakanı Özhaseki: İnsan Hayatı Üzerinde Plan Yapılmaz.' AA, April 4. https://www.aa.com.tr/tr/politika/cevre-ve-sehircilik-bakani-ozhaseki-insan-hayati-uzerinde-plan-yap ilmaz/788913.
Habertürk. 2015. 'Dağlıca şehidi Okan Taşan son yolculuğuna uğurlandı.' September 10. https://www.haberturk.com/gundem/haber/1126814-dag lica-sehidi-okan-tasan-son-yolculuguna-ugurlandi.
Houston, Christopher. 2018. 'Plotters and Martyrs: The Justice and Development Party's (AKP) Constituting of Political Actors in the 15 July Coup Event.' *Politics, Religion & Ideology* 19 (4): 531–545.
İskenderoğlu, Jülide. 2018T04:50. '250 Şehidimizin ruhunu ve onların ailelerinin yüreklerini incitmeye kimsenin hakkı yoktur. #MilleteHesapVerCihangir pic.twitter.com/ghzG7rykZ8.' Tweet. *@jiskenderoglu* (blog). 2018T04:50. https://twitter.com/jiskenderoglu/status/1058325492783345664.
OHCHR. 2018. 'Report on the Impact of the State of Emergency on Human Rights in Turkey, Including an Update on the South-East: January–December 2017.'
Pevehouse, Jon C. W., and Joshua S. Goldstein. 2017. *International Relations.* Eleventh Edition. Boston: Pearson.
Sabah. 2017. '250 şehidimizbizimgüneşlerimiz.' Sabah, July 16. https://www.sabah.com.tr/gundem/2017/07/16/sehidimiz-bizim-guneslerimiz.
Selçuk, Orçun, Dilara Hekimci, and OnurErpul. 2019. 'The Erdoğanization of Turkish Politics and the Role of the Opposition.' *Southeast European and Black Sea Studies* 19 (4): 541–564. https://doi.org/10.1080/14683857.2019.1689902.
Soest, Christian von, and Julia Grauvogel. 2017. 'Identity, Procedures and Performance: How Authoritarian Regimes Legitimize Their Rule.' *Contemporary Politics* 23 (3): 287–305.
T24. 2017. 'Erdoğan: Vatan için, istikbal için akıtılacak çok kanımız var; 16 Nisan bunun için çok önemli.' T24, March 23. https://t24.com.tr/haber/Erdoğan-vatan-icin-istikbal-icin-akitilacak-cok-kanimiz-var-16-nisan-bunun-icin-cok-onemli,395248.
Taş, Hakkı. 2018. 'The 15 July Abortive Coup and Post-Truth Politics in Turkey.' *Southeast European and Black Sea Studies* 18 (1): 1–19. https://doi.org/10.1080/14683857.2018.1452374.
Yanık, Lerna K., and Fulya Hisarlıoğlu. 2019. 'They Wrote History with Their Bodies': Necrogeopolitics, Necropolitical Spaces and the Everyday Spatial

Politics of Death in Turkey.' In *Turkey's Necropolitical Laboratory: Democracy, Violence and Resistance*, edited by Banu Bargu, 46–70. Edinburgh University Press.

Yeni Şafak. 2020. 'Cumhurbaşkanı Erdoğan: Omuzların üzerinde baş kalmayacak.' Yeni Şafak, March 2. https://www.yenisafak.com/gundem/cumhurbas kani-Erdoğan-konusuyor-3527852.

Yilmaz, Ihsan. 2021. *Creating the Desired Citizen: Ideology, State and Islam in Turkey*. 1st ed. Cambridge University Press. https://doi.org/10.1017/978 1108961295.

Yilmaz, Ihsan and Omer Erturk. 2021a. 'Populism, Violence and Authoritarian Stability: Necropolitics in Turkey.' *Third World Quarterly* 42(7), 1524–1543. https://doi.org/10.1080/01436597.2021.1896965.

Yilmaz, Ihsan and Omer Erturk. 2021b. 'Pro-Violence Sermons of a Secular State: Turkey's Diyanet on Islamist Militarism, Jihadism and Glorification of Martyrdom.' *Religions*. https://doi.org/10.3390/rel12080659.

Yilmaz, Ihsan and Erdoan Shipoli. 2022. 'Use of Past Collective Traumas, Fear and Conspiracy Theories for Securitisation and Repression of the Opposition: The Turkish Case.' *Democratization* 29(2), 320-336. https://doi.org/ 10.1080/13510347.2021.1953992.

Yilmaz, Ihsan and Omer Erturk. 2022. 'Authoritarianism and necropolitical creation of martyr icons by Kemalists and Erdoğanists in Turkey.' *Turkish Studies*, 23:2, 243–260. https://doi.org/10.1080/14683849.2021.1943662

Yilmaz, Ihsan, Erdoan Shipoli, and Mustafa Demir. 2021. 'Authoritarian Resilience through Securitisation: An Islamist Populist Party's Co-optation of A Secularist Far-Right Party.' *Democratization* 28(6), 1115–1132. https:// doi.org/10.1080/13510347.2021.1891412.

PART III

Necropolitics and Turkish Society

CHAPTER 9

Necropolitics and Turkish Society

INTRODUCTION

Turkey is nearing 100 years since its inception as a republic. Uncertainty approaches along with the centennial and surrounds its future when it comes to the country's democratic dispensation. One particular aspect of the growing authoritarian tendencies of the political regime is what Banu Bargu describes as a 'necropolitical undercurrent' that silently flows under the surface of the political dispensation (Bargu 2019). What this undercurrent reveals is an intricate connection between democracy and violence. As discussed in the previous chapters, it has been established that the civilizational populist narrative churned out by AKP under the leadership of Erdoğan is necro political in nature.

In these chapters, we undertook an analysis of the civilizational populist necropolitical use of martyrdom and martyr icons in the context of religion, TV series, school textbooks, blame management, and authoritarian stability. Moving on, this chapter will be devoted to a brief analysis of how the AKP's systematic fetishisation (Carney 2018) and continuous propagation of death and violence (Yilmaz and Erturk 2021) has been received and resonated within the social realms and how it has influenced the attitudes of its ordinary supporters and voters, including rank and file AKP politicians, bureaucrats, and pro-AKP journalists. Our data are derived from the incidents that occurred after 2015, when the AKP signalled full authoritarianism by manipulating the election results

© The Author(s), under exclusive license to Springer Nature
Singapore Pte Ltd. 2023
I. Yilmaz and O. Erturk, *Populism, Authoritarianism and Necropolitics*,
https://doi.org/10.1007/978-981-19-8292-7_9

181

sabotaging the rules of parliamentarian democracy when the HDP, the Kurdish political party passed the electoral threshold, which meant for the AKP that it would have the sufficient majority in the parliament to form the government no more (Yilmaz et al. 2021). Until that time, an occasional objection from the 'martyr' families had been heard, criticizing Erdoğan's policies in those clashes and deaths. But the time when the AKP regained a parliamentary majority in the November elections held in 2015, those sporadic objections were fully eliminated by authoritarian measures.

'TELL US TO KILL, WE WILL KILL; TELL US TO DIE, WE WILL DIE'

When the authoritarian leadership begins to glorify sacrifice, martyrdom, and violence publicly in its speeches, some impressionable followers respond in a similar and reciprocatively manner to show their allegiance in the *da'wa* (cause), party politics. Moreover, these followers compete with each other to show how they are ready to fulfil leader's or party's demands when the need arises. This is shown not merely through their slogans, but also via their abilities and arms that are provided and approved within a political inner network by the authority itself. Such organizational capabilities and tactics are mostly seen in almost each Middle Eastern dictatorship, in which masses feel themselves to show their support publicly in return for gains, or just solely for the sake of the da'wa (the religio-political cause) For instance, the motto or the slogan *bil rooh, bil dam, nafdeek ya* Saddam/Bashar/Nasser (with our lives, with our blood, we sacrifice ourselves for you), which have become the leitmotif of the Islamist politics for decades has been the most common slogan in Arab-speaking regimes in the Middle East anyone can hear in Syria, Iraq, Egypt, or Lebanon etc. In addition to the slogans, they organize convoys in which attendants expose and fire their arms. Taking this phenomenon one step further, some vigilantes among the groups are wearing white shrouds to prove that they are serious and not joking, and ready for self sacrifice on the path of their leader. For instance, having taken the control of Kabul, which ran into the day that Afghanistan freed from the British, the Taliban fighters marched through Kandahar in white shrouds uniforms (Sky News 2021). During the protests and upsurge against the Shah, pro-Khomeini demonstrators had worn white shrouds as well in order to display how they were willing to embrace death, remaining indifferent to curfews, etc.

(Fischer 1980, 204, 214). Such wearing shrouds can be also seen in Palestinian Hamas and Iraqi protests against Israel and the USA (Curtius and Miller 2000; Coles 2020).

In the Turkish case, because of the Islamist (Yilmaz and Bashirov 2018; Yilmaz 2021) aspect of the AKP regime and its ideological ties to radical Turkish Islamism (Erturk 2022a; 2022b), there are strong similarities in the use of necropolitical tools with that of the other Muslim majority countries and their Islamist groups. The counterpart of the slogan which begins with *bil rooh* is that 'tell us to die we will die, tell us to kill we will kill', while the image of a white shroud as a sign of intimidation and violence is common image in all the Islamist regimes. Along with its Islamic façade, martyrdom, self-sacrifice, and praise for violence in the AKP context coined with the hector persona of Erdoğan. By the same token, as we have widely discussed in the previous chapter, it turned out to be an act of intimidation and fear against the opposition political parties and sides like the Republican People's Party (CHP), Peoples' Democratic Party (HDP), Alevis, secularist, and other opposing Islamic groups such as Gülenists or Furkanists. In support of the AKP's martyrdom narrative, during the AKP political rallies, the crowds frequently interrupt Erdoğan's speech with the slogans, 'Tell us to kill, we will kill. Tell us to die, we will die; Erdoğan, Erdoğan, Erdoğan' (Fox 2017) to show their willingness for a possible violent task produced by the AKP. Skipping Kemalists' 'We are Mustafa Kemal's soldiers', such slogans that praise violence over the opposition had not been familiar in Turkish politics before as suggested above that they are mostly common in Muslim majority dictatorships. As analysed previously, this terrorizing and fear is also fully propagandized through TV series and a team of Twitter trolls on social media, financed by the AKP government itself.

Reminiscent of the scenes usually seen in some of the Middle Eastern Islamist regimes, AKP supporters in 'white shrouds' have special significance in the AKP rallies as of 2013. This phenomenon is also new in the Turkish politics and was introduced by the AKP after the 2010s. In such an introduction, without doubt, the AKP's ideological ties stretching back to Iran Islamic revolution in the 1980s, and Muslim Brotherhood have a special place. Though Kemalists and nationalists have frequently addressed the Turkish flag as a primary necropolitical tool in the official ceremonies and school dramas, such scenes with white shrouds have not been witnessed before in Turkish political history. This was a mere imitation of the way people do in Islamist regimes such as Hamas in

Palestine or Iran. For instance, during the protests and upsurge against the Shah, pro Khomeini demonstrators and paramilitary groups in Iran were usually wearing white shrouds in order to display how they were ready and willing to embrace death (Fischer 1980). This might be taken as the initiation point for the militarization of the AKP followers in the Turkish case, especially the youth. It simply means that those groups are willing to embrace death for the love of Islamist Erdoğan regime.

Together with the slogans, wrapping up with white shrouds have become a common sign of AKP support, significantly when referendums or elections approach to intimidate the opposition parties. This is the mere use of necropolitical tool in the Turkish context, as will be seen in the following examples. The visibility of pro-AKP white shrouds is also beyond the rallies. For example, about two thousand party members in Şanlıurfa province marched arms in arms, with the slogans and banners 'Worn their shrouds, AK guards are coming' (Haber7 2014). In another incident seen in Trabzon airport, AK party province youth branch welcomed Erdoğan in white shrouds, with the banners written 'Came with the shrouds, together with you to death' (Cumhuriyet 2013). An AKP alderman from Kocaeli municipality attended the provincial advisory council in a white shroud stating that he wore the shroud as an answer to those whom wished to disparage Erdoğan's political authority: 'I am ready to die, ready to wear a shroud, ready to bestow all my assets for my prime minister' (Yarar 2013). Shroud rhetoric is also found in Erdoğan's narratives. For example, he addresses the media after Istanbul bombings in 2016 which resulted in thirty-eight casualties and 155 injuries, that 'we have already accepted the rank of martyrdom as the greatest of the ranks...We have set out to this road wearing our shrouds. We are the members of a religion, of a faith, which granted martyrdom as the greatest honour of all' (BirGün 2016). Similarly, the minister of foreign affairs Mevlüt Çavuşoğlu stated that they, from the outset, began this 'holy journey' with their leader Erdoğan in their shrouds (AA 2016). Erdoğan's cult as an Islamist personality is a key point in triggering such necropolitical behaviour, as will be discussed below.

Sacrificing Life for Erdoğan and His Religious Cause (da'wa)

As seen in the cults of the personality of the communist party leaders (Popan 2015), in the Turkish case, the ranks and file have begun to employ the acts at every opportunity to prove their commitment to the leader under the guise of da'wa, in the sense of sycophancy, mostly waiting for being rewarded either physically or spiritually for their acts. These shows of commitments not surprisingly are dominated by necropolitical use of speech revolving around self-sacrifice, martyrdom, kill, and pillage. The letter of a subcontracted woman worker, which she recited before Erdoğan on March 8 International Women Day organization is the best example. In the organization, the workwoman is announced to the pulpit to recite her letter while Mr and Mrs Erdoğan were taking a seat. The woman stated that:

> Oh, my Lord! Let our president complete his duties. Oh, my Lord! Because our country, humanity and all Islamic community need him. If his life will not be long enough for this, oh my Lord, please take mine and render it to him! *May my life be halal* (Islamically permissible) *for you* as your mother's breast milk! [Erdoğan cries while Mrs Erdoğan nods] I have two kids. Everyone can easily mother for my kids. But no one can serve to my beautiful country, to humanity and to Islam as you do. (Habertürk 2016)

Yet, there are other examples, mostly propagated by the so-called pro-Erdoğan media outlets, in which families 'joyfully' granted when they learned their sons, or brothers were martyred. These examples are sketched as a normative way of Islamic way of embracing death, blended with nationalistic sentiments. A district governor Muhammed Safitürk, a police officer Ahmet Alp Taşdemir, a civilian Erkan Yiğit, and twin police officers Ahmet and Mehmet Oruç are some of the 'ideal' and 'palatable' examples chosen and propagated by the regime for months, showing that how martyrdom is a privileged institution and should be embraced readily and happily by the families. These examples are also vital to understand how pro-AKP people receive and to what extent do political discourse of glorification of martyrdom along with other fictional statements, post truth news, conspiracy theories and siege mentality paradigm succeed within the minds and social lives in Turkish citizens. Here, the Erdoğan cult plays major role in each case as well. For instance, during his son's funeral ceremony in 2016, father Safitürk in front of his son's corpse glorified Erdoğan and the da'wa implying that his son's death was of major importance vis a vis Islamic da'wa, represented by Erdoğan, stating as follows:

May Allah grant triumph to our president, who is the source of the whole ummah's pride, to his supporters, prime minister, ministers, our deputies, and their [AKP's] all the followers and sympathizers; may Allah be pleased with them.... May Allah save them from any harm in this world, and I hope we will be together in the heaven. He [Erdoğan] is like my brother. No, not indeed, I am not able to even express my affection with the words.... His majesty frequently stated in his speeches that 'what makes flags is the blood on them/ the soil is a country if someone dies for it' [...] (Milliyet 2016).

In return, Erdoğan reminded the importance of martyrdom in Islam, with the Quranic verses he recited. He also underscored the pre-eminence of Shari'a rule in such events, in that it enables execution, blaming the Western norms of rule as a hindrance. Erdoğan's following speech shows how he skilfully builds his necropolitical narrative as an ideal pattern, as a guide for those who would like to employ a similar outline, a sort of common language, in support of his religious da'wa. Additionally, as will be seen in the following example, this is a whole sample in that it best suits Mbembe's (2003) definition of necropolitics that the sovereign determines who has the right to live or die, in that while Erdoğan is fully content with the 'martyred' ones on his path, which is a controversial issue as discussed before, he points his political opponents as a target who deserves to be killed, 'executed' when his people demand arguing that such demand is fully compatible with the demand of God, Shari'a. Erdoğan said in the Safitürk's funeral while it was streamed live on the TV channels:

Oh, my brothers!... As recited in the Quranic verses, in the name of Allah, *kullu nafsin dhaiqatul mawt, thumma ilayna turjaoon* (29:57), meaning we will return to God Himself. You know, martyrdom is the greatest of the ranks after the Prophethood. And we believe that our brother Muhammet Fatih is one of those, reached to that rank.... My dear brothers, I would like to clearly state that these soils are not ordinary soils. Martyrs have always gushed out from these soils...This people have given many martyrs for these lands. With the help of God, we will eradicate them all...if we unite, if we become bigger, if we become more alive...We say that Muhammet Fatihs do not end. In this country, there are also a lot of Muhammet Fatihs. We will raise many, God willing! Do not forget that *bismillahirrahmanirraheem* (in the name of Allah), as our God ordained to us, as long as we behave decisively in this path [fight], we will reach out the victory that he promised to us...I already said, I will approve the death penalty when it is adopted by the parliament. It is not the West to decide, it is only us! What George or Hans say does not concern us. What concerns us is what Allah revealed. (Milliyet 2016)

In response to Erdoğan's heavy use of necropolitics, the statement of Safitürk's spouse is a good example of how such discourse resonated and was interpreted by the family members. During the funeral ceremony, Safitürk's spouse states in tears standing by the coffin: 'martyrdom has suited you well my darling! A district governor was going to be martyred and yes, it would have been you my love' (Milliyet 2016).

Such incidents and necropolitical discourse were heavily maintained to reverberate by the high echelons of the AKP through AKP media channels, and social media users for months. This is a process showing how an ideal and model Islamic family members should embrace the death. Later, father Safitürk has been invited to many educational conferences and organizations organized by the National Ministry in various cities to preach the importance of martyrdom, the homeland to the students and the teachers in which named as the 'Values of my Nation'. In the political struggle of Erdoğan vs Kurdish movement, Safitürk became the ideal leverage and myth maker in building necropolitical models. To underscore the importance of the suppression of Kurdish politicians at home and the Armed Forces' Olive Branch Operation led by the 'chief commander' Erdoğan, Safitürk, as a model and a palatable martyr parent propagated by the AKP media, says: 'We are sacrificing our children for the homeland. Not only our children, but we are also ready to die, we are continuously ready to join the front line. We sacrifice martyrs, thereby easily performing our prayers, sleeping at home, and walking in the downtown and the market' (AA 2018a).

Another good example of the role of the Erdoğan cult and necropolitics is the case of Ahmet Alp Taşdemir, a member of the Police Elite Special Operations unit died during the PKK attack in Diyarbakır province in November 2017. Soon, Taşdemir has become viral in both social and national pool media as an idealized martyr. As in the case of Safitürk, Taşdemir's father was an imam. As we have seen on the TVs, Father Tasdemir, having stepped out of the mosque where he was working, heard for the first time his son was martyred, and his initial statements before the cameras:

Our ancestors have glorified the adhan [call to prayer], the flag and the crescent for hundreds of years. The crescent, the adhan, the flag will continue to rise on the shoulders of this noble nation god willing. Thank God, my son has reached to the rank of martyrdom, which is adjacent of the Prophets... our God has glorified us with his [the son] martyrdom. I have submitted to the ordinance of my God. I have no compliance. May God grant long life to our ummah, our nation and our homeland. May God protect this nation. My son has been martyred while he is engaging jihad against the Zionists, idolatries, Crusaders. I feel honoured for this. I am thankful to God for He granted us such a rank. (Yeni Şafak 2017)

There are also other examples. Sergeant Ömer Bilal Akpınar, killed during the Olive Branch operation in Syria states in his letter that 'this is the fight between the Cross and the Crescent, faith and disbelief, Righteousness and Falsehood, idolatry and Tawhid' (Diktepe 2018).

The fact that the whole process was recorded, and the previous arrangements were done by the AKP-run channels and newsagents, chiefly the Anadolu agency and Yeni Şafak, before the father heard his son's death is a good point showing how such necropolitical events planned for political ends and propaganda by the regime. In order to increase the impact of the propaganda, later, this video was broadcasted for months with a touching theme by the pro-AKP media outlets with the photographs and footage titled as 'He learned his son's martyrdom in the mosque where he is working' or 'my son has been martyred while engaging jihad' (Yeni Şafak 2017).

The pro-AKP Yeni Şafak also released specially cropped videos of 'martyrs', selected from former years whose stories are epic and palatable. In another video released by Yeni Şafak daily website, titled 'a martyr who does not fit into his coffin Selçuk Paker' the social messages of the slaughtered soldier are shown accompanying a highly epic music behind. The video opens with that Paker died in Diyarbakır Sur province in 2015. The highlighted messages of Paker in the videos are: 'I made a wish for God to engage in jihad', 'Firman (the Edict) belongs to State, "Sur" belongs to us!', 'Heroes love sound of sword clashes', 'Campaign from us, Victory from God', and 'Oh Lord! Help us against the unbelievers, Qur'an 1:286 translation'. In the lyrics of background music, it is said that Paker's chain of 'shahadah' began with Hamza fallen in the Battle of Uhud, uncle of Prophet Muhammad, and continued with Halisdemir, sending greetings

9 NECROPOLITICS AND TURKISH SOCIETY   189

all the other martyrs. Yeni Şafak says that they yearningly commemorate the second death anniversary of the martyr (Yeni Şafak 2018). The Prophet Muhammad's uncle Hamza is deemed the father of all martyrs.

There is another example showing how Erdoğan's cult of personality worked for self-sacrifice for some of the people, who controversially died during the bombings in front of Erdoğan's residence in Ankara on 15 July, the failed coup attempt. In a video, a young man Erkan Yiğit, a member of a group just arrived from Adana in order to stop the coup attempt reads a quartet reportedly written by himself for Erdoğan by raising Rabia sign to the camera: 'Let there be violence all around the world / Let the happiness be postponed for different springs / Now that the death will come once in a life / Why it would not be for Reis [Erdoğan]?' (TRT Avaz 2016). This is modified from a jihadist radical Islamist nasheed, 'when the blood fell into the soil' sung by Grup Genç. In original, why it would not be for Allah? The last two lines of the stanza belong to al-Qaida founder Abdallah Azzam (Oliver and Steinberg 2005, 100). This example also proves that Erdoğanist propaganda achieved identification of Islamic cause with the persona of Erdoğan in general among the radicals.

Like Safitürk's spouse embrace of death, Yiğit's spouse remarks after his husband's death is also significant to understand how Erdoğanist cult of personality and necropolitics successfully intertwined each other in the Turkish case. The woman says: 'He could have died all the way; he could have died in a traffic accident as well. At least, he died for a cause. I am proud of being his wife, I am happy. I will raise my children, God willing, lest they would not become traitors for this nation, for this homeland' (TRT Avaz 2016). In most of the cases, Erdoğan's cult of personality is blended with a father figure. Father image is a really strong and authoritarian image in the Turkish culture, which must be submitted to any case whatever the result is. As the time moves through 2018, in line with consciously escalated tensions that precede heavy security questions hyped up by AKP government through media, we are witnessing that the other footages are released by the state-run AA, or other pro-AKP media outlets in which families display their 'sincere' intimacy and dedication to the cult of Erdoğan. The telephone conversation footage between reportedly a newly widowed woman and Erdoğan, or a mother's telephone conversation with Erdoğan, who has just lost her son during the military operation show the climax point for the palatable martyrdom on the persona of Erdoğan. In these conversations, we see that martyrdom on the path of

Islam, ummah, nation and the homeland have been gathered under the sole formula, which is Erdoğan himself. In the first example, the woman says: 'without hesitation, I have four daughters and three sons more, and may they be sacrificed to you! May all of them be sacrificed to you! My blood, my soul, and my veins are praying for you. May Allah be with you' (AA 2018b). The conversation in the latter example is as follows:

Erdoğan: We will take revenge of our martyrs' blood God willing.
Mother: You are our father, destroy those buggers my dad!... Destroy those terrorists so that nothing has left from them [...] We have our God with us, we have our father Tayyip with us!... One more thing, destroy those terrorist-lovers so that no one be hurt anymore. Efface them! Efface their roots!
Erdoğan: Erdoğan: God willing, we will do it together. (AA 2018c)

Similarly, another example showing an ideal family member for death for the love of Erdoğan reveals the extent to which Necro politics has marked the psyche of the populace. Similar to above-mentioned propaganda organizations of the Erdoğanist regime, the AKP organized a programme named the July 15 Martyrs' Relatives and Veterans, in which Mr. and Mrs. Erdoğan were also present. In the programme, the members of the martyred families are invited successively to the theatre stage and let them express their 'feeling' on how valuable thing to die for the love of some values, in front of Erdoğan and the AKP high echelons. Such invitation creates a sense of being chosen, gifted on the screens, a sort of enviable thing, while it is streamed online on TV channels. As an ideal example, we will take the speech of a father of a twin police officer, who died during the bombings in a coup attempt in 2016. In his speech, the father constantly eulogizes Erdoğan and his da'wa and expresses his gratitude to him and how he is lucky for being the chosen one:

> Dear my president, I sacrificed my two sons for the homeland at that night...but when I see you are at the head of eighty million even at the expense of death, our hearts turned into spring and seriously alleviated the grief of losing our children [...] Dear my president, never be sad! Eighty million sons are ready to sacrifice themselves for this homeland, never walk alone, my dear president! Those traitors will be drowned in the blood they

shed and if you let them breathe anymore, then our breaths are haram from now on! (TRT Avaz 2017)

In such a chamber of propagation, it is most likely that the texts that the family members read in those organizations are written by Erdoğan's text writers as a part of the necropolitical use of martyrdom and its fuse with Erdoğan's cult of personality. The above examples are clear proof of how necropolitics has become the routine of Turkish politics and society, because of diligent propaganda planning and the use of media by the AKP.

Conclusion

This chapter primarily dealt with the prevalence and acceptance of civilizational populist necro politics among the AKP's grassroots supporters. The data gathered from the incidents that occurred after 2015, shows that the necropolitical narrative of the AKP has been readily embraced, disseminated, and accelerated by the AKP grassroots. Furthermore, it has become the normative language between the voters and the AKP, becoming a sort of political allegiance manifestation that must be presented to show how they are supportive of the regime.

References

AA. 2016. 'Dışişleri Bakanı Çavuşoğlu: Biz Bu Yola En Başından Kefenimizle Çıktık,' July 23. https://www.aa.com.tr/tr/15-temmuz-darbe-girisimi/disisl eri-bakani-cavusoglu-biz-bu-yola-en-basindan-kefenimizle-ciktik/613914.

———. 2018a. 'Asım Safitürk: Şehidimizin Kanı Kimsenin Yanında Kalmamıştır,' February 4. https://www.aa.com.tr/tr/turkiye/asim-safiturk-sehidimizin-kani-kimsenin-yaninda-kalmamistir/1053811.

———. 2018b. @anadoluajansı, 05:05, February 7. https://twitter.com/anadol uajansi/status/961224283748933632.

———. 2018c. 'Cumhurbaşkanı Erdoğan'dan Şehit Annesine Taziye Telefonu,' February 7. https://www.aa.com.tr/tr/turkiye/cumhurbaskani-erdogandan-sehit-annesine-taziye-telefonu/1057250.

Bargu, Banu, ed. 2019. *Turkey's Necropolitical Laboratory: Democracy, Violence and Resistance*. Edinburgh University Press. http://www.jstor.org/stable/10. 3366/j.ctvs32r1g.

BirGün. 2016. 'Erdoğan: Biz Bu Yola Kefen Giyerek Çıktık,' December 11. https://www.birgun.net/haber/erdogan-biz-bu-yola-kefen-giyerek-ciktik-139124.

192   I. YILMAZ AND O. ERTURK

Carney, Josh. 2018. 'Resur(e)recting a Spectacular Hero: Diriliş Ertuğrul, Necropolitics, and Popular Culture in Turkey.' *Review of Middle East Studies* 52 (1): 93–114.

Coles, Isabel. 2020. 'Tens of Thousands March in Baghdad Against U.S. Troops in Iraq.' *WSJ*, 24 January. https://www.wsj.com/articles/tens-of-thousands-march-in-baghdad-against-u-s-troops-in-iraq-11579860644.

Cumhuriyet. 2013. 'Erdoğan'ı kefen giyerek karşıladılar,' December 22. https://www.cumhuriyet.com.tr/haber/erdogani-kefen-giyerek-karsiladilar-21491.

Curtius, Mary, and Marjorie Miller. 2000. 'Hamas Threatens New Bombings in Israel—Los Angeles Times,' October 8. https://www.latimes.com/archives/la-xpm-2000-oct-08-mn-33290-story.html.

Diktepe, Bülent. 2018. 'Afrin şehidi Astsubay Ömer Bilal Akpınar'ın ağlatan vasiyeti,' February 11. https://www.hurriyet.com.tr/gundem/afrin-sehidi-astsubay-omer-bilal-akpinarin-aglatan-vasiyeti-40738235.

Erturk, Omer. 2022a. The Myth of Turkish Islam: The Influence of Naqshbandi-Gümüşhanevi Thought in Turkish Islamic Orthodoxy. *British Journal of Middle Eastern Studies* 49 (2): 223–247. https://doi.org/10.1080/13530194.2020.1782727.

Erturk, Omer. 2022b. 'Anatomy of Political Islam in Republican Turkey: The Milli Görüş Movement as a Legacy of Naqshbandism.' *Contemporary Islam* 16 (2–3): 295–320. https://doi.org/10.1007/s11562-022-00500-x.

Fischer, Michael M. J. 1980. Iran: From Religious Dispute to Revolution. Madison: University of Wisconsin Press.

Fox, Kara. 2017. In Ankara, Celebrations for Erdogan Mask a Turkish Schism, *CNN*, 17 April. https://edition.cnn.com/2017/04/17/europe/turkish-referendum-result-reveals-fractured-society/index.html.

Haber7. 2014. 'Başbakan Erdoğan'a Kefenli Destek Yürüyüşü - Partiler Haberleri,' March 9. https://www.haber7.com/partiler/haber/1135505-basbakan-erdogana-kefenli-destek-yuruyusu.

Habertürk. 2016. 'Cumhurbaşkanı'nı Ağlattı Mektup: Benim Ömrümden al Ona Ver,' March 7. https://www.haberturk.com/gundem/haber/1206124-kadin-iscinin-mektubu-cumhurbaskanini-aglatti.

Mbembe, Achille, 'Necropolitics,' trans. 2003. 'Libby Meintjes.' *Public Culture* 15 (1, Winter); 11–40.

Milliyet. 2016. 'Şehit kaymakam Muhammed Fatih Safitürk son yolculuğuna uğurlandı.' *Milliyet*, Nowember 2016. https://www.milliyet.com.tr/gundem/sehit-kaymakam-muhammed-fatih-safiturk-son-yolculuguna-ugurlandi-2343866.

Oliver, Anne Marie, and Paul F. Steinberg. 2005. *The Road to Martyrs' Square a Journey into The World of The Suicide Bomber*. Oxford: Oxford University Press. https://doi.org/10.1093/acprof:oso/9780195305593.001.0001.

9 NECROPOLITICS AND TURKISH SOCIETY   193

Popan, Adrian Teodor. 2015. 'The ABC of Sycophancy. Structural Conditions for the Emergence of Dictators' Cults of Personality.' Ph. D, Austin: The University of Texas. https://repositories.lib.utexas.edu/handle/2152/46763.

Sky News. 2021. 'Taliban Fighters March through Kandahar in Uniform on Afghanistan's Independence Day | World News | Sky News,' August 20. https://news.sky.com/video/taliban-fighters-march-through-kandahar-in-uniform-on-afghanistans-independence-day-12385857.

TRT Avaz. 2016. Cumhurbaşkanı Erdoğan'ı Ağlatan Görüntüler - 15 Temmuz Şehitleri -. https://www.youtube.com/watch?v=xOYxl5mkcS4.

———. 2017. Şehit İkizlerin Babası Ali Oruç - 15 Temmuz Şehit Yakınları ve Gaziler Programı -. https://www.youtube.com/watch?v=frXdEPFjIcI.

Yarar, Ahmet. 2013. 'Ak Parti'nin toplantısına kefenle geldi.' December 29. http://www.kocaelimeydan.com/gundem/ak-partinin-toplantisina-kefenle-geldi-h14305.html.

Yeni Şafak. 2017. 'Oğlum Cihat Ederken Şehit Oldu, Şeref Duyuyorum,' November 4. https://www.yenisafak.com/video-galeri/gundem/sehit-babasi-oglum-cihat-ederken-sehit-oldu-seref-duyuyorum-2158917.

———. 2018. 'Tabuta Sığmayan Şehit: Selçuk Paker,' January 30. https://www.yenisafak.com/video-galeri/hayat/tabuta-sigmayan-sehit-selcuk-paker-2168704.

Yilmaz, Ihsan. 2021. *Creating the Desired Citizens: State, Islam and Ideology in Turkey*. Cambridge and New York: Cambridge University Press.

Yilmaz, Ihsan, and Galib Bashirov. 2018. The AKP after 15 Years: Emergence of Erdoganism in Turkey. *Third World Quarterly* 39 (9): 1812–1830. https://doi.org/10.1080/01436597.2018.1447371.

Yilmaz, Ihsan and Omer Erturk. 2021. 'Populism, Violence and Authoritarian Stability: Necropolitics in Turkey.' *Third World Quarterly* 42 (7): 1524–1543. https://doi.org/10.1080/01436597.2021.1896965.

Yilmaz, Ihsan, Erdoan Shipoli, and Mustafa Demir. 2021. 'Authoritarian Resilience through Securitisation: An Islamist Populist Party's Co-optation of a Secularist Far-Right Party.' *Democratization*. Published on-line. https://doi.org/10.1080/13510347.2021.1891412.

CHAPTER 10

The Authoritarian Role of Necropolitics and Martyrdom in Turkey Under AKP Rule

Necropolitics has played an important role in Turkish politics since the establishment of the Republic in 1923. The project of building the Turkish nation was deeply influenced by the trauma Turkish people experienced during the end stage of the First World War, in which the Ottoman Empire was dismembered by its enemies. This experience influenced the leadership of the new Republic, which remained deeply suspicious of Western intentions towards Turkey, even as it sought to imitate Western political and legal systems (Yilmaz 2016; Yilmaz 2021). The new secular regime was fearful that Western powers would attempt to further dismember Turkey and perhaps even return the Turks to Central Asia. This mentality led to many Turkish people coming to believe that Westerners and others coveted Turkey's territories, and that it was the duty of the Turkish people to defend their homeland from foreign incursions, and if need be die in order to protect the 'fatherland' from external threats (Yanık and Hisarlıoğlu 2019, 57; See also Bircan 2014; Yilmaz and Erturk 2021a; 2021b; Yilmaz and Erturk 2022).

In this atmosphere of fear and suspicion of foreign powers, and in which Mustafa Kemal was attempting to establish a secular Republic, secular nationalist martyr-icons such as Kubilay were hailed by the regime and held to be heroes worthy of imitation by the Turkish public. The Kemalists sought to encourage Turkish people to be willing to sacrifice their lives for the secular nationalist regime. Although they were not

© The Author(s), under exclusive license to Springer Nature   195
Singapore Pte Ltd. 2023
I. Yilmaz and O. Erturk, *Populism, Authoritarianism and Necropolitics*,
https://doi.org/10.1007/978-981-19-8292-7_10

above cynically instrumentalizing Islam, their necropolitical martyrdom narrative was largely absent of Islamic terminology such as references to jihad and rewards in the afterlife. Instead, religious Muslims, especially the Islamists, who were demanding the restoration of caliphate and Shari'a, were demonized by the Kemalist regime, and therefore the necropolitical language was primarily nationalist, and revolved around the notion that the Turkish fatherland required protection, and it was the duty of the Turks to sacrifice their lives for their homeland and the Kemalist principles when required.

Throughout their decades of rule, the Kemalists used necropolitical narratives to maintain power (Yilmaz and Erturk 2022). The use of necropolitical martyrdom narratives helped to militarize Turkish society, normalize death in service of the regime, and has led to notions of 'the fatherland', martyrdom, and blood becoming common throughout Turkish society (Bircan 2014). Not only did the ruling elite perpetuate the nationalist necropolitical narrative, but popular poets such as Mithat Cemal Kuntay wrote verses claiming, 'what makes a flag a flag is the blood on it; earth can only become a fatherland (*vatan*) when there are those willing to die for it.'

The rise to power of the AKP did not immediately initiate a new form of necropolitics in Turkey. The AKP, having won government in 2002, governed as Muslim democrats (Yilmaz 2009) throughout most of their first decade in power, and sought to integrate Turkey within the European Union and adopt its laws and values to get rid of the secularist Kemalist tutelage led by the military and judiciary. However, as the AKP gradually dismantled the Kemalist tutelage and thus moved away from its initial Muslim democrat and pro-European period, it began to add an Islamist (Yilmaz and Bashirov 2018) civilizational populist metanarrative into Turkey's established necropolitical narrative, by returning back to its founders' old ideology of radical 'Turkish Islamism' (see in detail now, Erturk 2022a; 2022b). The Kemalists' secular nationalist martyr-icons were replaced by the AKP's alternative Islamist martyr-icons, and a new narrative was constructed that drew on Islamic texts, and merged Islamism and Turkish nationalism. Of course, secular nationalism can demand martyrs, yet it cannot offer the promise of a reward in the afterlife, but only recognition after death on Earth. Islam, however, has its own independent martyrdom narrative and promises rewards in the afterlife for martyrs, and therefore its instrumentalization by authoritarian regimes in Muslim majority nations has potential to prove highly effective. In other words, much more than its secular predecessor and in an astonishingly unprecedented intensity, the AKP fetishized dying on behalf of the nation, its people, Muslim World, religion and the leader of the Ummah (Erdoğan), and 'valorized and championed martyrdom' (Carney 2018, 94, 101). The AKP added, the Islamist civilizational populist element to its call for martyrs gradually and accelerated it after the mysterious coup attempt in 2016, making its necropolitics especially effective and persuasive in majority Muslim Turkey.

As Turkey became increasingly Islamist civilizational populist and authoritarian in the second half of the 2010s under AKP rule in the face of economic and political challenges, the regime began to rely more on a necropolitical narrative which encouraged martyrdom—defined in Islamic terms—to maintain its rule and perpetuate its Islamist civilizational populist ideology. Thus, while the use of necropolitics remained after the election of the AKP in 2002, and indeed appears to have grown in importance in subsequent years, the character of the necropolitical narratives has substantially changed in the last decade, taking an Islamist civilizational populist, radical and jihadist turn

The key turning point was the 15 July 2016 failed coup. The mysterious failed coup presented Erdoğan and his party with a golden opportunity ('gift of God,' in Erdoğan's words) to destroy their enemies (dissidents, undesired minorities, human rights advocates and remaining independent media), and reshape Turkish identity and society in a new Islamist civilizationalist and neo-Ottoman shape of their own choosing. One of their chief means of reshaping Turkish society was through a new necropolitical martyrdom narrative based around the events of the failed coup. As the coup was taking place, Erdoğan and his allies mobilized supporters to defend the regime, resulting in clashes between pro-AKP civilians and soldiers associated with the coup, and the deaths of 251 anti-coup protesters and around 30 Turkish soldiers, who were claimed to be coupists by the government. Following the defeat of the coupists, Erdoğan framed the events as the result of Crusader Christian foreign interference (chiefly the USA) in Turkish internal affairs and portrayed those who died as martyrs protecting not only the fatherland but also Islam and the Muslim World, from foreign powers and their traitorous internal Turkish allies, i.e. the dissident groups and opposition parties. The events of the evening of 15 July 2016 and the 'martyrs' who died defending the 'fatherland' and religion thus became cornerstones of the New Turkey Erdoğan was creating. Since then, Erdoğan and the AKP have sought to create a collective memory of the failed coup, and to mythologize the events, amplifying their importance and treating them as the foundation of a new nation that is destined to lead the Muslim World into its emancipation from the Western oppression. Thus, Erdoğan and the AKP have added Islamist elements into Turkey's necropolitical narratives, strengthening its power by harnessing Islam's discourses on martyrdom and jihad and merging them with Turkish nationalist discourse. Following the coup attempt, this newly Islamized civilizational populist necropolitical narrative based on martyrdom became a consistent and powerful theme in Turkish political discourse. The emergence of the coup attempt, according to Erdoğan, was 'God's gift' (Champion 2016), and the civilians who were fearless of death and willing to die for their nation and faith were heroes that saved Turkey from an existential assault (Erdoğan 2016). This framing allowed Erdoğan to further promulgate the notion that without willing martyrs, Turkey and thus the Muslim World would fall to its Western and Zionist enemies, who had allies within Turkey (dissidents, minorities, human rights advocates and journalists) working against the nation and the Muslim World. To protect the country, Ummah and Islam, Erdoğan supposedly required more people who would willingly sacrifice their lives for the nation and its culture and religion. Equally, the coup attempt provided Erdoğan with the grounds to begin a purge of the state, in which tens of thousands of suspected and real opponents of the regime were fired and sometimes imprisoned.

Erdoğan's increasing control over Diyanet, the media and Turkey's education system allowed him to re-imagine Turkey as an Islamist civilizational populist martyr nation, in which public declarations of a desire to kill and die on behalf of the nation have become prominent and frequent in the public sphere. In this new necropolitics, Islamist language became increasingly merged with secular nationalist calls for death in defence of the fatherland. Martyrs were encouraged to die for the homeland with promises of a reward in heaven for the deaths. At the same time, and supporting this new narrative, Islam and the nation were merged as concepts, with Erdoğan increasingly portraying himself as the leader & saviour of the Sunni Islamic world, and Turkey as the prime defender of Muslim peoples across the globe.

The AKP regime's instrumentalization of Islam is greatly assisted by its close association with the Diyanet, with which it has developed a patron–client relationship. While the Diyanet has long been a politicized organization, its expansion and turn toward pro-AKP Islamism under AKP rule is unprecedented. Indeed, the Diyanet previously promoted a 'moderate' Islam designed to convince the Turkish population to accept secular authoritarianism of the state. Today the Diyanet operates at times as a radical Islamist and jihadist arm of the AKP, and the body almost consistently issues sermons and produces literature that supports the party's political narratives.

The Diyanet supports the AKP in three major ways: by promoting militarism, jihadism, and Islamist glorification of martyrdom in Friday sermons. While the Kemalists attempted to militarize Turkish society, the AKP did not initially follow their example but instead sought to initiate a peace process with the Kurds, and moreover sought to integrate Turkey within the European Union. During this period, the Diyanet supported the AKP's peace initiatives, and their sermons rejected a securitized approach to the Kurdish issue. However, following the 2010 constitutional referendum and rejection by the European Union, the failure of the Kurdish peace process, and especially the Gezi Park protests in 2013, the AKP began to assert greater control over Turkey's military. Diyanet sermons soon began to reflect this change, particularly in the years 2015 and 2016, when the AKP began to turn toward authoritarian Islamism. While pre-2015 Diyanet sermons often included pro-martyrdom rhetoric, this language was essentially secular nationalist, and celebrated Turkish nationalist martyrs. After 2015, under the direction of the AKP regime, Diyanet began to use Islamist language in sermons discussing the Turkish military. In the second half of the 2010s, Diyanet sermons began to switch from describing the Turkish military merely as defenders of the Turkish homeland, and instead began to describe them as defenders of the entire *ummah* (Yilmaz 2021; Yilmaz and Albayrak 2022). Thus, the fight against Kurdish militias in Syria was increasingly described in sermons as a religious battle, in which Islam was threatened and had to be vigorously defended. Kurds, Gülenists, secularists, Zionists, and the West were increasingly framed by sermons as the enemies of Muslims and portrayed as waging a war against the Turkish people, Islam and the Muslim World.

In this civilizational populist narrative, as a response to the alleged existential crisis brought about by non-Muslim enemies of Islam, the AKP appears to have encouraged Diyanet leaders to promote *jihad*. Breaking from the largely spiritual and personal Sufistic Turkish tradition of defining *jihad* as self-disciplining the AKP and Diyanet began to use *jihad* in an aggressive, militaristic, and emancipatory sense. At the same time, sermons began to speak more of unity among the *ummah* rather than national unity based on shared citizenship. In 2011, the AKP appointed pro-AKP Islamist Mehmet Görmez as leader of the Diyanet, cementing the change in the institution towards radical Islamism. As leader, Görmez claimed that the 'hero ancestors' of today's Turks 'sacrificed their blood and their lives for God and Islam' (Diyanet Friday sermon, 18 March 2016). In the same year, Diyanet began to speak of *jihad* as an armed struggle, and to describe Turkish military operations as *jihad*. Turkey itself was described in sermons as the hope of the oppressed peoples of the world and protector of Muslims, and not merely another secular state among many others. It's military, then, was said to have a special purpose: to protect Islam and Muslims the world over. Thus, this new emphasis on *jihad* was used by Diyanet to support the AKP's militarist and expansionist foreign policy, which became more aggressive in the 2010s, and to justify it on religious grounds.

Diyanet sermons also supported the AKP regime by promoting martyrdom. Martyrdom was downplayed during the early years of AKP rule in Diyanet sermons, especially during the period in which the AKP was attempting to make peace with the Kurds and convince the European Union to permit Turkey's inclusion. Following the failure of these initiatives, however, the language of martyrdom returned to Diyanet sermons, though this time in an Islamist context. Thus, martyrdom moved from a praiseworthy action albeit one which ought to be avoided, to the ultimate honour a Muslim person must actively pursue. Martyrdom was increasingly glorified in Diyanet sermons in the second half of the 2010s, where it was spoken of as something that patriotic and religious citizens should desire. For the AKP, the glorification of martyrdom served its wider necropolitical narrative, and not merely glorified sacrifice but demonized opposition forces and alleged enemies of Turkish people and Muslims (Yilmaz 2021; Yilmaz and Erturk 2021a; 2021b).

Martyrdom was increasingly propagated in sermons as something both desirable, and a cost that Turkey must bear if it wishes to defend the homeland and Islam from internal and external enemies. Sermons claimed that martyrs were rewarded in the afterlife as well as in the collective memory of Muslim Turks (Diyanet sermon, 16 March 2018). Moreover, martyrdom was described as *sherbet*, or as a sweet drink, which one should wish to taste in ten sermons between 2010 and 2020. Self-sacrifice and martyrdom have become commonplace in sermons and integrated into the wider AKP siege mentality, which posits that Turkey and Islam are locked in battle with hostile infidels, and that martyrs must rise and defend the homeland and Islam.

Much as it has instrumentalized Islam through Diyanet to perpetuate its own ideology and legitimize its rule, the AKP has asserted control over almost the entire Turkish media and television and used its power to produce and fund television series which promote the regime's ideology and civilizational populist necropolitical martyrdom narrative. Television has proven very important to the regime, which has produced numerous programmes that provide the public with political propaganda more than entertainment yet has proven relatively successful at promoting the government's narratives and justifying its autocratic style.

TV series such as Diriliş: Ertuğrul (Resurrection: Ertuğrul, 2014, TRT), Payitaht: Abdulhamid (TRT, 2017), İsimsizler (The Nameless, 2017, Kanal D), and Mehmetçik Kutül-Amare (TRT, 2018) are some of the media and popular culture instruments with which the AKP tries to indoctrinate the public—through their political technology—into their cult of death and martyrdom. These series propagate a siege mentality in which the Turkish people, their nation and religion, are under attack from internal and external enemies, who wish to destroy the country by removing Erdoğan from power (Sinanoğlu 2017). Equally the series posit that infidels are working hard to topple Erdoğan and take possession of Turkish lands, and moreover that it is only the brave martyrs and Erdoğan himself who are protecting Turkey from its enemies. The series does this by focusing on historical conflicts in which Turkey was threatened by external forces and drawing a comparison between them and present conflicts, to show how even today Turkey is threatened by 'dark forces' which wish to destroy the country. Equally, Islam and the Ottoman Empire are shown in a positive light throughout the series, while the secular Turkish Republic is Islamized, to portray a continuity between past and present, and to present the AKP as the embodiment of Turkishness and Islam.

Education has the power to shape the minds of each new generation, and thus the AKP is focused on Islamizing the education system in Turkey, to produce a generation of pious Muslims loyal to the AKP. In reaction to, or perhaps merely capitalizing on the failed coup in 2016, the AKP sought to indoctrinate Turkey's children into its cult of death and martyrdom, sometimes enlisting the help of the Diyanet. The new national curriculum teaches literature promoting martyrdom and jihad, though in ways that diverge from traditional understandings of these notions, and instead seek to teach children to die for the regime and its particular Islamist neo-Ottoman agenda. Children are taught to be pious Sunni Muslims, Islamists and Turkish nationalists, to be willing to kill the regime's enemies, love Erdoğan, and if need be, die in the service of his regime. The regime appears to hope these teachings will create a loyal generation of AKP voters and soldiers, or at the very least that young Turks will accept the regime's framing of military and civilian deaths as 'normal' martyrdom events, and the dead as people who ought to be praised, admired, and imitated. This is a dangerous policy, however, and it may be that the young—who are essentially brainwashed by the regime into accepting martyrdom and death as normal—may be psychologically pre-disposed to these activities. Moreover, they may eventually come to believe that the regime is insufficiently Islamist and aggressive and may themselves turn to violence unsanctioned by the regime.

Thus, after 2016 the Turkish public discourse became dominated by the AKP, and its Islamist civilizational populist necropolitical martyrdom narrative. This necropolitical martyrdom narrative, as we have shown, served several important purposes. For example, the regime uses the necropolitical martyrdom narrative also to deflect blame and responsibility for accidents and disasters, some of which may otherwise be directly attributed to the AKP and/or Erdoğan. This tight control is vital to the regime, because without it the public may begin to question and ultimately hold the government responsible for deaths associated with its foreign and domestic policies. The necropolitics practiced by the AKP regime in Turkey is characterized by a tight control of political narratives, in which the deaths of Turkish soldiers and citizens are framed as martyrdom events, rather than as tragic accidents or examples of government failure. The regime uses presentational strategies, we find, to manipulate public opinion by reshaping events to suit its preferred narrative, and attempting to turn events that may cause the public to turn against the regime into positive events which create support for the regime. For example, the regime successfully distracted the public from the failure of a pro-AKP religious community, which failed to prevent the deaths of eleven female students and a teacher in a fire, by framing it as an act of fate, a tactic it had used during an earlier mining disasters (Shafak 2016).

The party plays a carrot and stick game with the families of the people it designates martyrs, promising them rewards if they comply with the narrative, and punishing them when they attempt to hold the government responsible for the loved one's death. Perhaps the most profound aspect of the AKP's narrative control involves its attempt to turn blame into credit. The AKP's necropolitical martyrdom narrative is especially useful in completing this task, insofar as it has immense power to frame deaths which occur due to government negligence or failure into martyrdom events. When 15-year-old Eren Bülbül was killed by PKK fighters while assisting Turkish military forces, Erdoğan turned military incompetence into a martyrdom event, praising the boy and promising his mother that she, her son, and her other thirteen children will be rewarded in heaven for her boy's willing sacrifice (Beyazgazete 2017). In doing so he skilfully used the necropolitical martyrdom narrative to turn a potentially disastrous situation, in which Bülbül's mother was blaming the government for her son's death, into a positive event which buttressed the government's narrative and anti-Kurdish policies.

AKP's civilizational populist necropolitical narrative is also used to legitimize its authoritarian regime and justify its repression of opposition politicians, dissidents, activists, journalists, human rights advocates, undesired minorities and academics. To do this the July 16 martyrs are sacralized and turned into myth and heroic history. School textbooks describe these martyrs and their actions that saved the Turkish homeland on 15 July 2016. Buildings, public places and spaces are renamed after the martyrs. Billboards are put up showing their names and faces. In doing these things the regime creates necropolitical spaces in which the dead are displayed, and the memory of them and their deeds is kept alive. Moreover, keeping this memory alive, and making it the cornerstone of the 'new' Turkey, serves the regime by enabling it with the ability to associate itself with the sacred memory of the dead and their righteous cause. The ubiquitous public presence of the martyrs also serves to demonize opposition forces who are alleged to have supported the coup or provided insufficient support for Erdoğan during the coup attempt. By all these, the AKP aims that the actions of the regime in repressing opposition forces are perceived by the public as legitimate, and necessary to protect by the people and national of Turkey, but also to protect and honour the memory of the martyrs and ensure they did not die for a lost cause.

Co-optation is also a vital element of the AKP's ruling strategy, and this too is assisted by the martyrdom narrative. As we have shown, the AKP's turn against the Kurds and the Kurdish peace process gave the party space to co-opt the previously hostile MHP, Turkey's decades old far right party The far right ultra-nationalists in the MHP were attracted by the AKP's newfound nationalism and anti-Kurdish policies, as well as the AKP's decision to allow the MHP to fill the bureaucracy with its members. Yet the MHP, because of their alliance, also appears to have bought into the AKP's new foundational narrative based on the July 16 failed coup and the martyrs who 'saved' Turkey from an uncertain fate. Equally, the AKP is able to maintain its alliance with the MHP by ensuring that its members are able to attend the funerals of martyrs, while the members of opposition parties are prevented from attending. Thus, by co-opting the MHP the AKP has strengthened its necropolitical narrative, which now enjoys the support of the nationalist far right MHP.

What is the result of the AKP's civilizational populist necropolitical narrative, instrumentalization of education, the media, the directorate of religious affairs, and through them their promotion of this narrative and authoritarian policies? The AKP's necropolitics has been received well by the party's supporters and voters, who perpetuate the message through different strata of Turkish society. This is not surprising, as the party is able to reach its supporters and the wider public through a variety of means. Under the AKP rule, the Turkish people live in an environment in which they are surrounded by 'post-truth' news from pro-AKP media, conspiracy theories, and in which they are encouraged to believe that Turkey is under siege and in the process of being attacked by foreign 'infidels' and internal enemies such as the Gülenists, journalists and human rights advocates In this environment, in which Turkish people are told by their leaders to feel fearful of foreign nations and non-Muslims, the AKP encourages citizens to seek to overcome the nation's enemies by seeking martyrdom. Thus, the party uses all the tools available to it to convince citizens that it is sweet and fitting to die for their country, religion, and for Erdoğan himself.

The AKP is also able to coerce the public, through a reward and punishment approach, into echoing its core martyrdom narrative. Thus, the political success of the AKP is the result of both the propagation of its core narrative throughout Turkish society, as well as the system of privileges and punishments the party has established. The government's supporters are rewarded with positions in the bureaucracy and government contracts, while its enemies are purged, marginalized, jailed and sometimes tortured. This dynamic plays out when the AKP is forced to deal with the families of soldiers and civilians who were—as the party puts it—martyred in the fight against the nation's enemies. The party requires the families of the dead to accept their loved one's designation as a martyr. To attain this acceptance, the AKP publicly praises the family in extravagant and may promise them material rewards or implies that they will receive monetary compensation or other privileges. Yet when families refuse to accept the martyrdom status of their loved ones the AKP punishes and denigrates them.

At the same time, President Erdoğan, like other authoritarian leaders, frequently glorifies sacrifice, martyrdom, and violence against enemies. In response, his followers echo his language, and at times compete with one another to prove their loyalty and readiness to fulfil Erdoğan's demands. For example, when Erdoğan speaks at AKP rallies his supporters will at times interrupt him by chanting 'Tell us to kill, we will kill! Tell us to die, we will die; Erdoğan, Erdoğan, Erdoğan!' to publicly demonstrate their support for their leader (Fox 2017). This suggests that—in a manner like the old communist regimes of Europe and the secular dictatorships of the Middle East—the AKP probably enjoys the support of genuine believers but probably many of them are mere sycophants who support the party and Erdoğan to gain material rewards. It is difficult to decipher how many people buy into the propaganda and how many simply support the party to gain material rewards. Either way, the AKP's narratives create an ugly and violent environment in Turkey, in which death and dying for the nation is normalized, and enemies (i.e. dissidents, undesired minorities, journalists, and human rights defenders) can be hated, purged, and imprisoned.

Adding an Islamist element into Turkey's secular nationalist martyrdom narrative has only helped Erdoğan and the AKP to increase the potency of its message. The AKP's Islamist necropolitical martyrdom narrative has energized the AKP's supporters, who have brought to Turkey religio-political traditions hitherto unknown, such as marching through the streets wearing white shrouds. Equally, the introduction of Islamic aspects into the martyrdom narrative has allowed the AKP to draw support from religious Muslims in Turkey, who may genuinely believe that the party is defending Islam from non-Muslim (or false Muslim) enemies. With the help of the Diyanet (Yilmaz and Albayrak 2022), the AKP is able to instrumentalize Islam, and present itself as the defender of Islam and Muslims worldwide, and as the arbiter of what is good and holy in Turkish society.

The merging of Turkish blood and soil nationalism with Islamism is a key part of the AKP's authoritarian necropolitics. For instance, at the funeral of an AKP martyr, Muhammet Fatih Safitürk, Erdoğan praised martyrdom and claimed that martyrs ranked only below the prophets in Islam, before claiming that Turkish soil is special and capable of producing an especially high number of martyrs (Hurriyet 2016). These martyrs, he claimed, will continue to rise and through their actions, Turkey will defeat its enemies—which Erdoğan does not name—and reach the victory that God has already determined (Hurriyet 2016). By combining Islamism and Turkish nationalism Erdoğan is thus able to buttress his party's martyrdom narrative, and to both frame the death of Safitürk as ordained by God and encourage more Turkish people to martyr themselves to attain the victory promised by God.

Islam also plays a role in the personality cult centred on Erdoğan. In the AKP propaganda, Erdoğan is himself portrayed by the party as the modern-day equivalent of an Ottoman Sultan, who defends Islam and protects weak and oppressed Muslims across the world. Not only does this instrumentalization of Islam serve to legitimize Erdoğan's rule and actions as leader but encourages the growth of his personality cult. This cult of personality, which resembles the cults around communist leaders in Europe and Asia, is a vital part of the AKP's populist rule. Moreover, the cult of personality around Erdoğan is also a site from which the necropolitical martyrdom narrative is propagated. The cult's necropolitical power is displayed when, for example, the families of the AKP's supposed martyrs do not merely offer up more of their sons and daughters to die on behalf of the nation, but rather specifically claim they wish for them to die for Erdoğan. Or when crowds of AKP supporters at rallies will shout that they are willing to kill and die for their leader, Erdoğan, but do not always mention the nation itself as an object worth dying for.

In sum, the electoral and political success of the AKP and Erdoğan are a symbol of the power of necropolitics. The AKP's co-opting of its rivals, the destruction of its Gülenist and secularist enemies, silencing of the media, repression of human rights advocates and its ability to tightly control narratives around death in Turkey, have been greatly assisted by its martyrdom narrative (Yilmaz and Erturk 2021a). The necropolitical martyrdom narrative of the AKP, also helps the party shield itself from blame when Turkish civilians or soldiers die due to party domestic or foreign policies and allows it to securitize all opposition forces and thus perpetuate its domination of Turkish politics and public life. The party's martyrdom narrative, while not entirely new, has a potent new element: Islamism. Through the party's manipulative use of Islamist informal law

10 THE AUTHORITARIAN ROLE OF NECROPOLITICS ... 207

(Yilmaz 2022) and concepts such as *jihad*, the AKP is able to present its martyrs as Islamic heroes, to be admired and imitated, and the party's enemies (i.e. critics and dissidents) as anti-Muslim. In a largely religious society, this framing is particularly powerful and has helped the AKP win the support of many Muslims who feel afraid of losing their culture and religion. To increase this anxiety, the AKP has frequently reminded the masses the Kemalist exclusion of religion from the public sphere, threatening that their privileges would be in danger in the AKP's absence.

Despite possessing diametrically opposed imaginings of Turkish identity, Kemalists and Erdoğanists both embraced necropolitics and a martyrdom narrative to realize their political and social goals. The flexibility of necropolitics and martyrdom narratives is a key to their strength, and a reason why Turkey still suffers under a necropolitical regime almost one hundred years after the founding of the Republic. The secularist and Islamist rulers of Turkey have both well understood the tremendous power of necropolitics and martyrdom, and have used this power to mobilize support, create new martyrs, and collect memories, and ultimately to perpetuate their authoritarian rule over the nation.

References

Beyazgazete. 2017. 'Erdoğan, Eren Bülbül'ün annesiyle yaptığı görüşmeyi açıkladı | Şehit, Cumhurbaşkanı, Recep Tayyip Erdoğan, Antalya.' *Beyazgazete*, August 13. https://beyazgazete.com/video/webtv/siyaset-3/Erdoğan-eren-bulbul-un-annesiyle-yaptigi-gorusmeyi-acikladi-463172.html.

Bircan, Düzcan. 2014. 'Çanakkale İçinde Kurdular Beni: Şehitlik İmgesi Üzerinden Toplumsal Bedenin İnşası'. In *'Öl Dediler Öldüm' Türkiye'de Şehitlik Mitleri*, edited by Serdar Değirmencioğlu. Istanbul: İletişim Yayınları.

Carney, Josh. 2018. 'Resur(e)Recting a Spectacular Hero: Diriliş Ertuğrul, Necropolitics, and Popular Culture in Turkey.' *Review of Middle East Studies* 52 (1): 93–114. https://doi.org/10.1017/rms.2018.6.

Champion, Mark. 2016. 'Coup Was "Gift From God" for Erdoğan Planning a New Turkey'. *Bloomberg*, 18 July 2016. https://www.bloomberg.com/news/articles/2016-07-17/coup-was-a-gift-from-god-says-Erdoğan-who-plans-a-new-turkey.

Erdoğan, R. Tayyip. 2016. '"Ölümden Korkmayan Bir Milleti Durduracak Hiçbir Güç Yoktur"'. *T.C. Cumhurbaşkanlığı*. 22 November 2016. https://www.tccb.gov.tr/haberler/410/61088/olumden-korkmayan-bir-milleti-durduracak-hicbir-guc-yoktur.html.

Erturk, Omer. 2022a. 'The Myth of Turkish Islam: the influence of Naqshbandi-Gümüşhanevi thought in Turkish Islamic orthodoxy.' *British Journal of Middle Eastern Studies*, 49 (2), 223–247. https://doi.org/10.1080/135 30194.2020.1782727

Erturk, Omer. 2022b. 'Anatomy of political Islam in Republican Turkey: the Milli Görüş Movement as a legacy of Naqshbandism.' *Contemporary Islam* 16 (2-3), 295–320. https://doi.org/10.1007/s11562-022-00500-x

Fox, Kara. 2017. 'In Ankara, Celebrations for Erdoğan Mask a Turkish Schism.' *CNN*. https://edition.cnn.com/2017/04/17/europe/turkish-referendum-result-reveals-fractured-society/index.html.

Hurriyet. 2016. Erdoğan şehit kaymakamın tabutu başında konuştu, *Hurriyet*, 12 November 2016, https://www.hurriyet.com.tr/gundem/erdogan-sehit-kaymakamin-tabutu-basinda-konustu-40276051.

Shafak, Elif. 2016. 'After Turkey's Failed Coup, a Sense of Fatalism Has Set In.' *The Guardian*, December 21. sec. World news.

Sinanoğlu, Semuhi. 2017. 'Parti Ebed Müddet: Bir Siyaset Teknolojisi Olarak Yeni Osmanlıcı TRT Dizileri - Semuhi Sinanoğlu'. *Birikim*, 30 March 2017. https://birikimdergisi.com/guncel/8236/parti-ebed-muddet-bir-siyaset-teknolojisi-olarak-yeni-osmanlici-trt-dizileri.

Yanık, Lerna K., and Fulya Hisarlıoğlu. 2019. '"They Wrote History with Their Bodies": Necrogeopolitics, Necropolitical Spaces and the Everyday Spatial Politics of Death in Turkey.' In *Turkey's Necropolitical Laboratory: Democracy, Violence and Resistance*, edited by Banu Bargu, 46–70. Edinburgh University Press.

Yilmaz, Ihsan, and Galib Bashirov. 2018. 'The AKP After 15 Years: Emergence of Erdoğanism in Turkey.' *Third World Quarterly* 39 (9): 1812–1830. https://doi.org/10.1080/01436597.2018.1447371.

Yilmaz, Ihsan. 2009. 'Muslim Democrats in Turkey and Egypt: Participatory Politics as a Catalyst.' *Insight Turkey*, 11 (2), Apr. 2009, pp. 93–112.

Yilmaz, Ihsan. 2016. *Muslim Laws, Politics and Society in Modern Nation States: Dynamic Legal Pluralisms in England, Turkey and Pakistan*. Reprint. London and New York: Routledge.

Yilmaz, Ihsan. 2021. *Creating the Desired Citizens: State, Islam and Ideology in Turkey*. Cambridge and New York: Cambridge University Press.

Yilmaz, Ihsan and Omer Erturk. 2021a. 'Populism, Violence and Authoritarian Stability: Necropolitics in Turkey.' *Third World Quarterly* 42 (7), 1524–1543. https://doi.org/10.1080/01436597.2021.1896965.

Yilmaz, Ihsan and Omer Erturk. 2021b. 'Pro-Violence Sermons of a Secular State: Turkey's Diyanet on Islamist Militarism Jihadism and Glorification of Martyrdom.' *Religions* 12 (8) 659. 10.3390/rel12080659.

Yilmaz, Ihsan. and Ismail Albayrak. 2022. *Populist and Pro-Violence State Religion: The Diyanet's Construction of Erdoğanist Islam in Turkey*. Singapore: Palgrave Macmillan.

Yilmaz, Ihsan and Omer Erturk. 2022. 'Authoritarianism and Necropolitical Creation of Martyr Icons by the Kemalists and Erdoganists in Turkey.' *Turkish Studies*, 23 (2), 243–260, DOI: https://doi.org/10.1080/14683849.2021.1943662

Yilmaz. Ihsan. 2022. *Authoritarianism, Informal Law, and Legal Hybridity: The Islamisation of the State in Turkey*. Singapore: Palgrave Macmillan.

Index

A

Abdulhamid II, 35, 53, 92–95,
100–102, 107, 108
academics, 203
accountability, 141
activists, 203
adhan, 188
Afghanistan, 182
Africa, 32
Afrin, 118
Afrin Military Operation, 76
Akar, Hulusi, 146
Alevis, 4, 10, 123, 183
Aliyev, Ilham, 103
Allies, 32
Alparslan, 93, 102
al-Qaida, 189
Anatolia, 33, 34
ancestors, 72, 75, 80, 86
ancient, 10
Ankara, 33
anniversary, 16, 17
antagonistic, 6, 115
anti-Semitic, 75

anti-Western(ist), 94, 114
anxiety(ies), 32–34, 117, 131
Armenia, 33
Armenian(s), 113, 116
Armistice of Mundros, 33
army, 71, 73, 74, 76–79, 86, 87
Atatürk, 14, 34, 36–39, 53, 57
atheists, 123
August 30 Victory, 14
authoritarianism, 3–5, 8, 12, 41, 50,
72
authoritarian stability, 5, 6, 21, 168,
175, 181
autocratization, 70, 79
Azerbaijan, 75, 103
Azzam, Abdallah, 189

B

Bahai, 123
Balkans, 32
barracks, 96
Battle of Dumlupınar, 37
Battle of Gallipoli, 37
Battle of Manzikert, 37, 57, 119

© The Editor(s) (if applicable) and The Author(s), under exclusive
license to Springer Nature Singapore Pte Ltd. 2023
I. Yilmaz and O. Erturk, *Populism, Authoritarianism and Necropolitics*,
https://doi.org/10.1007/978-981-19-8292-7

212 INDEX

bayonet(s), 51, 96, 97
behead, 168
beheaded enemies, 107
beverage of shahada, 106
billboards, 15, 16
biopolitics, 12
BJP, 8
blame avoidance, 17, 20, 21,
    141–143, 145, 147, 151–153,
    158
blame management, 153, 158, 181
blood, 10–13, 55, 56, 62, 125–127,
    167, 168, 170, 171, 182, 186,
    189, 190, 196, 200, 205
body corpse, 118
Bosphorus Bridge, 14, 59, 151, 157
British, 33, 101
Bülbül, Eren, 148, 153, 159
bureaucrats, 181
burials, 9
business, 6
Byzantine, 105

C
Caesars, 10
Caliph, 35
Caliphate, 17, 33, 37, 55, 95, 100,
    105
call to prayer, 115
camouflage, 13
Çanakkale, 72, 77, 81
cancer, 169
Carney, Josh, 2, 9, 15
Caucasus, 32
Çavuşoğlu, Mevlüt, 184
cemetery, 9, 11
Central Asia, 12, 34, 195
championing of death, 15
children, 17, 20
chosen trauma, 32, 56
Christian(s), 7, 10, 58, 103, 104,
    106–108

CIA, 51, 54, 55
citizenship, 113, 116, 123
civil death, 59
civilization, 34, 39, 197
civilizational populism, 3–6, 8, 12, 13,
    18, 59, 114, 122, 123
clientelism, 6
coffin, 148, 155, 156
collective memory, 9–12, 15, 49, 50,
    61, 63, 198, 200
collective myths, 40
commemoration(s), 14, 16, 38, 40
commemorative projects, 15
conquest, 95, 103
conquest of Istanbul, 14, 37
conspiracies, 6, 55, 56
conspiracy theories, 185, 204
conspiratorial, 18, 92, 93
conspiratorial rhetoric, 53
conspirators, 168
Constantinople, 102
Constitutional Court, 51
co-optation, 5, 6, 168, 172–174, 203
corrupt elite(s), 7, 19, 92–94
corruption, 6
coup, 197, 198, 201, 203, 204
coup attempt, 11, 14–17, 70, 72, 74,
    83
coupists, 63
Crusader(s), 8, 58, 101, 103, 188
cult, 201, 206
cult of martyrdom, 16, 20
cult of personality, 189, 191, 206
cultural heritage, 94

D
dangerous others, 7
da'wa, 182, 185, 186, 190
Day of Democracy and Martyrs, 14
death, 35, 39, 40, 49, 54, 59–63, 70,
    76, 78, 85–87, 141, 142,
    145–151, 157–160, 167, 168,

INDEX 213

170, 171, 174, 196–198,
201–203, 205, 206
death-in-life, 9
death on behalf of the nation, 2, 9
death penalty, 187
decapitate, 168
Demirtaş, Selahaddin, 170
democracy martyrs, 169, 171, 172
depoliticization of death, 145
desired citizens, 32
die, 183, 184, 186, 187, 190
Directorate of Religious Affairs, 2, 4,
18, 32, 34, 115. *See also* Diyanet
disasters, 141, 142, 145, 150, 153,
158
discourse, 3, 6, 8, 15, 19, 22
discursive hegemony, 9, 64
disinformation, 53
dissident(s), 4, 9, 18, 19, 203
Diyanet, 2, 18, 20, 22, 23, 32, 34,
36, 69–72, 74–80, 83–87, 115,
120, 121, 128–130, 149,
198–201, 205
Diyanet Çocuk Dergisi, 128, 129
Diyanet Islam, 36, 37, 50
dramas, 183
dying, 167
dying for the homeland, 117, 127
dying for the nation, 2
dying for the regime, 126

E
education, 2, 4, 17, 20, 23, 31, 32,
35
education system, 198, 201
Egypt, 10, 182
Elvan, Lütfi, 153
emotions, 12, 32
encouragement to die, 11
enemy(ies), 33, 50, 54, 56, 58, 59,
61, 63, 94, 95, 98, 100, 101,

103, 104, 106, 107, 109, 116,
117, 121, 123, 127, 167, 169,
172–175, 195, 197–202,
204–207
enmity, 1
Ensar Foundation, 121
Erbakan, Necmettin, 50–52, 54
Erbaş, Ali, 69, 75–78
Erdogan, Emine, 119
Erdoğanism, 14, 15, 31, 50, 75, 167,
175
ethnic cleansing, 32
ethnocentrism, 113, 116
Europe, 32
European, 34
European Union (EU), 52, 113, 196,
199, 200
everydayness, 15
evolution theory, 115
Evren, Kenan, 35, 36
excommunicative, 18
existential anxiety, 32
existential threats, 32, 36, 37, 167
extrajudicial acts, 169

F
far-left, 3
far-right, 172
fatherland, 12, 13, 16, 195–198
fear(s), 3, 4, 6, 12, 17, 19, 22, 31,
32, 55, 56, 195
Felicity Party, 52
fetish, 2, 9, 15, 197
First World War, 3, 33, 195
flag, 13, 78, 81, 84, 115, 117,
124–127, 129, 183, 186, 188,
196
foreign plots, 94, 101
foreign powers, 56
foundational myth, 50, 63
Freemasons, 101

214 INDEX

Free Republican Party, 38
French Revolution, 10
Friday sermons, 36, 70–72, 74, 79,
 80, 83, 86, 199
funeral, 147, 148, 155, 156, 185–187
funeral Chopin, 99
Furkanists, 183

G
Gallipoli, 57, 58, 77, 85, 119, 122
Gazi, 34
general will, 6
Gezi Park Protests, 14, 52, 53, 199
ghazi, 118
gift from God, 53, 59
gift of God, 15, 168
glorification of martyrdom, 10, 11,
 35, 117, 126, 128, 199, 200
glorious history, 119
glue-sniffers, 123
God, 2, 4, 13, 18, 22
God's gift, 198
Goebbels, Joseph, 151
Görmez, Mehmet, 69, 200
grave, 129
Great Powers, 33
Greece, 10, 32
Greek, 113, 116
grief, 9
grudge, 126
Gülenist(s), 4, 52, 60, 183, 199, 204
Gülen Movement, 55, 108, 109, 124

H
Halisdemir, Ömer, 18, 49, 60–63,
 188
HAMAS, 107, 183
hatim chain, 122
HDP, 79, 170, 172, 173, 182, 183
heaven, 128, 131
hegemonic struggle, 91

hegemony, 92
Hellenistic period, 10
hell fire, 118, 129
helmets, 96
hero ancestors, 200
heroes, 96, 101, 104
heroism, 113, 116, 117, 122, 126,
 127, 130
Hindu, 8
Hindutva, 8
holy struggle, 51
homeland, 2, 4, 5, 11, 22, 70, 72–76,
 78, 81, 82, 84–87, 187–190
Homo Diyanetus, 37
homogenous, 6
hush money, 153
hypocrites, 123

I
icon-heroes, 11
iconography, 34
ideational narratives, 12
ideology, 2, 4, 6–8, 14, 15
idolatries, 188
imaginaries, 15
Imam Hatip, 121, 124
immigrants, 7
immortalization, 16
imperialism, 55
independence, 72, 76, 80, 81, 83
India, 8
indoctrination, 99
Infants school, 120
infidel(s), 8, 19, 59, 95, 105, 108,
 122, 123, 201, 204
interest lobby, 54
internal enemies, 3, 19, 23
invention of tradition, 15
Iran Islamic revolution, 183
Iraq, 5, 182
ISIS, 107, 109, 146–148, 155

INDEX   215

Islam/Islamism/Islamist, 2, 3, 22,
33–36, 39, 40, 49–53, 55, 57,
61, 70, 93, 95, 102, 105, 106,
108, 183, 184, 189, 196, 199,
205, 206
İslam, Ayşenur, 151
Islamist populism, 8
Islamo-nationalist, 13
Israel, 183
Israeli offspring, 150
Istanbul, 33
İzmir, 17, 31, 37

J
Jews, 10, 101
jihad, 4, 18, 39, 51, 70, 74–79,
85–87, 93, 95, 102, 107, 108,
117, 119, 130, 196, 198–201,
207
jihadism, 10, 18, 70, 74, 86, 93, 95,
97, 103, 106, 107, 109, 120,
147, 199
journalists, 181, 203
Judeo-Christian, 7
July 15 coup attempt, 14

K
Kabul, 182
Kandahar, 182
Karakoç, Sezai, 105
Karaman, Hayrettin, 121
Kayi tribe, 105
Kemalism/Kemalist, 4, 13, 17, 18,
21, 31–37, 39–41, 49–52,
55–57, 59, 63, 69–71, 73–75,
83, 86, 92, 93, 97, 104, 106,
107, 109, 110, 115, 117, 126,
130, 167, 174, 175, 183, 196
Kemalist regime, 2, 3, 18
Kemal, Mustafa, 33, 34, 36, 38, 106
Khomeini, 182, 184

Kılıçdaroğlu, Kemal, 146
killing, 100, 106, 108, 183, 185
Kısakürek, Necip Fazıl, 38, 39
Kotku, Zahid, 51
Kubilay, 17, 18, 31, 37–41, 49, 58,
60
Kuntay, Mithat Cemal, 13
Kurdish movement, 187
Kurdish nationalist(s), 3, 147
Kurdish problem, 72
Kurds, 4, 170, 172–175, 199, 200,
203
Kut'ül Amare, 96, 120

L
law, 7, 12
Lebanon, 182
leftists, 4, 92
legitimation, 2, 6, 12, 21, 167, 168,
171, 172, 175
liberalism, 3, 7
liberals, 4
Libya, 147, 148
living dead, 9
love of the homeland, 36, 117, 125
lover of God, 54
lynch, 19

M
magazines, 115, 128
management of death, 145
martyr, 3–5, 10, 11, 13, 15, 16,
20–23, 36–41, 49, 50, 58–63
martyrdom, 31, 36–41, 50, 58, 61–64
Martyrdom of democracy, 125
Martyr Icons/martyr-icons, 17, 18,
31, 37, 49, 58, 61
martyr nation, 168
Martyrs' Day, 72, 80, 81
martyrs' hill, 148
Masjid al-Aqsa, 75

216 INDEX

Masons, 101
Mbembe, Achille, 1, 2, 9, 80, 82, 186
Mecca, 101
media, 12, 15, 32, 37, 38, 204
Mehmed II, 37
mehmetçik, 71, 73, 76, 78, 79, 86
Mehmet, Derviş, 37, 39, 40
memorial, 14, 15
Menemen, 17, 31, 37–41, 49, 58, 59
Menzil, 60
Mesopotamia, 10
MHP, 3, 127, 172–175, 203, 204
MI6, 55
Middle East, 32
Middle Eastern, 182, 183
militarism/militarist, 12, 13, 17, 18,
    31, 35–37, 52, 70, 86, 117, 126,
    199
military, 6, 14, 20, 92, 96–99, 105,
    108, 169, 199, 200, 202, 203
military coup, 6
military junta, 2
military nation, 35, 58
military operation, 118, 121, 189
mine disaster, 145, 150, 151, 154
minorities, 3, 4, 7
misogynistic, 128
mobilization, 9, 12, 21, 167, 172,
    175
model citizens, 11
Modi, Narendra, 8
Mongols, 103, 105
monuments, 11, 16
Mossad, 55
mujahid, 51
murder, 93
Muslim Brotherhood, 183
Muslim democrats, 1, 2, 196
Muslims, 32, 34, 36
Muslim world, 50, 55, 58, 95, 103
Myth, 49, 57, 58, 60, 61, 63
myth making, 11

myth of origin, 113

N
Naqshbandi, 51, 60, 62
nation, 188–190
national anthem, 13
national curriculum, 12, 20, 114–116,
    119, 123, 124, 129, 130, 201
nationalism, 3, 4, 7, 10, 20, 22, 35,
    36, 172, 173, 183, 196, 204–206
national psyche, 32
national unity, 36
national will, 16, 53, 169, 172
nationhood, 113
native and national, 56
necrogeopoliticization, 13
necropolitical images, 93, 109
necropolitical spaces, 11, 15
necropolitical tool, 183, 184
necropolitics, 31, 40, 70, 79, 80, 82,
    87
neo-Ottoman, 93, 197, 202
neo-Ottomanism, 8
neo-patrimonial, 6
New Turkey, 5, 8, 14, 15, 54
noble nation, 81
non-Muslim, 4, 113, 116, 117, 123,
    127
normalization of death, 145
Nursi, Said, 40

O
obedience, 34, 36
official Islam, 71
Olçok, Abdullah Tayyip, 18
Olçok, Erol, 18, 61, 157
Olçok, Nihal, 157
ontological insecurity, 32
opposition, 3, 6, 18, 19, 21, 55, 59,
    63, 115, 125, 200, 203, 204,
    206

INDEX 217

Ottoman army, 96
Ottoman Empire, 3, 14, 32–34, 53,
    55, 93–96, 100, 101, 103, 104,
    116, 195, 201
Our Pledge, 35
Özhaseki, Mehmet, 170

P
Palestine, 107
paradise, 13
Patronage, 6
pawn(s), 3, 8, 18, 19, 55, 168
Peker, Sedat, 151
Pericles, 10
personality cult, 15, 22, 34, 53, 54
Pharaohs, 10
phobia, 131
pious generation, 115
PKK, 3, 55, 61, 79, 124, 148, 150,
    155, 156, 172
plots, 94, 99, 101, 105
polarization, 7
political culture, 2, 13, 17, 31
political technology, 95
politicians, 181, 187
politicization of death, 9
politics of victimhood, 1
pop culture, 33
popular culture, 12, 32
populism, 1, 6–8, 33, 34
populists in power, 1
post-mortem, 9
post truth news, 185
prepolitical, 15
pride, 17
propaganda, 16, 17, 19, 20, 76, 79,
    83, 85, 114, 115, 119, 130, 131,
    188–191
propagation of death, 181
Prophet Muhammad, 123, 128
protector, 18

pro-Western, 14
public education, 34
public opinion, 77, 78
puppet, 16
pure people, 6

Q
Quds, 75
Qur'an, 118, 121, 128, 186
Qur'anic school, 146

R
Radio and Television Supreme
    Council, 91
rally around the flag, 55
Referendum, 171
religion, 5, 7, 10, 17, 23, 31, 32,
    34–36
religio-nationalist, 31
religious, 31, 32, 34, 36–38, 40, 41
religious duty, 36, 37
religious institutions, 12
repression, 5, 6, 21, 167, 168, 171
Republican People's Party (CHP), 72,
    82, 146, 156, 170, 183
resentful, 52, 56
responsibility, 142, 149, 150, 152,
    156
restorative nostalgia, 94
revenge, 190
right to kill, 10, 11
rituals, 10, 11
Roman, 10
ruling elite, 6, 13

S
sacrifice, 2, 3, 10, 12, 13, 19, 20, 32,
    36, 37, 50, 55, 56, 62, 72, 73,
    78, 80–84, 122, 125, 127, 130
sacrificing lives, 35

218 INDEX

Safitürk, Muhammed, 18, 49, 61, 62, 98, 117, 118, 148, 156, 157, 185–187, 189
Salafist, 51
Şanlıurfa, 184
saviour, 7, 18, 23
scapegoat, 143
school textbooks, 181
secular/secularism/secularist, 8, 12, 14, 17, 18, 31, 33, 35, 37, 39–41, 49, 92, 102, 183, 199
secular elite, 98, 99
securitization, 168
Selçuk, Zehra Zümrüt, 152
self-devotion, 119, 129
self-sacrifice, 35, 119, 127, 130, 183, 185, 189, 200
Seljuk Empire, 14, 57
Sèvres Syndrome, 12, 13
Shari'a, 37, 186
shedding blood, 117, 126
sherbet, 200
sherbet of martyrdom, 82, 83
Shi'a, 10, 123
shroud, 126, 182–184
siege mentality, 1, 19, 55, 56, 117, 185
sites of violence, 9
socialism, 7
social media, 183, 187
soil, 205, 206
soldiers, 2, 4, 14, 21, 22, 51, 59, 60, 96, 97, 101, 106–109, 197, 202, 204, 206
Soldier's Pray, 96
solidarity, 10, 36
Soma, 145, 146, 150, 153, 154
sorrow, 17
sovereignty, 7, 80
sovereign violence, 12
Soylu, Süleyman, 146
speech acts, 71

Stalinist, 34
State of Emergency, 114, 124
statues, 15
struggle, 118
Suleiman Shah, 106, 108
Sultan, 33
Sunni Islam, 4, 10, 34, 114, 123
Sunnism, 34
suspicion, 195
sweet drink, 4
sword, 106, 107
Sykes–Picot, 33
symbols, 11, 14, 15
Syria, 5, 22, 75–78, 82, 85, 86, 118, 121, 122, 128, 147, 182, 188, 199
Syrian Arab, 78
Syrian civil war, 72

T
takfir, 51
Taliban, 182
Tanzimat, 93
tawhid, 95, 122
Tayyar, Şamil, 147, 155
Templers' Castle, 106–108
terrorist attacks, 131
textbooks, 33–35, 38
traitor(s), 117, 122, 127, 168, 189, 190
trauma, 17, 31, 32
Treaty of Karlowitz, 32
Treaty of Kuchuk-Kainarji, 32
Treaty of Lausanne, 33
trolls, 183
troops, 105, 108
True Path Party, 51
Turan, 97
Turkey, 1–5, 8, 11–13, 15, 17–19, 21, 22
Turkish–Islamic Synthesis, 114, 116

Turkish Anti-Terror Law, 150
Turkish Army, 147, 149
Turkish flag, 13
Turkish Islam, 34, 36
Turkish Judiciary, 150
Turkish media, 198
Turkish nationalist, 3
Turkish national psyche, 33
Turkishness, 35, 37, 201
Turkish Republic, 31, 33, 34, 113, 116
Turkish War of Independence, 33, 37, 117, 125, 127
TV series, 181, 183
Twitter, 54, 183

U
Ülkücü, 3
Ulusalcıs, 3
ummah, 53, 56, 70, 73, 75, 78, 95, 104, 186, 188, 190, 199, 200
unbelief, 13
United States President, 33
USA, 51, 183

V
veteran, 77, 81–84, 190
victim, 142, 148–150, 152–156, 158–160
victim families, 142, 150, 152–155, 159, 160
victimhood, 1, 33, 55, 56
Victory Day, 72, 80
Victory of Manzikert, 14

villains, 98, 101
violence, 1, 8, 9, 19, 39, 63, 76, 86, 93, 109, 167, 174, 181–183, 189, 202, 205
violent rebellion, 6
violent rhetoric, 168
Virtue Party, 50–52
virus, 169

W
wahdat, 122
War of Independence, 33, 37, 53, 58, 117, 119
West, 50, 55, 71, 199
Western, 19, 33, 94, 99, 101, 116, 120, 125, 168, 172, 195, 198
Westernism, 57
Western powers, 3, 16
WHITE MEN, 120
White Turks, 56
Wilson, Woodrow, 33
World War I, 33, 146

Y
Yıldız, Taner, 155
Yazidi, 123
Yilmaz, Ismet, 120
Young Turks, 33, 35, 36
youth, 115, 117–119, 123–126, 131

Z
Zionism, 8, 50, 54, 188, 198, 199